The Canadian Shields

THE
CANADIAN SHIELDS

Stories and Essays

by Carol Shields

EDITED BY NORA FOSTER STOVEL

UNIVERSITY OF MANITOBA PRESS

The Canadian Shields: Stories and Essays
© Estate of Carol Shields 2024
Introduction and Conclusion © Nora Foster Stovel 2024

28 27 26 25 24   1 2 3 4 5

University of Manitoba Press
Winnipeg, Manitoba, Canada
Treaty 1 Territory
uofmpress.ca

Cataloguing data available from Library and Archives Canada
ISBN 978-177284-082-7 (PAPER)
ISBN 978-177284-084-1 (PDF)
ISBN 978-177284-085-8 (EPUB)
ISBN 978-177284-083-4 (BOUND)

Cover photograph courtesy of Donald Shields, c. 1970s.
Cover design by David Drummond
Interior design by Karen Armstrong

The University of Manitoba Press acknowledges the financial support for
its publication program provided by the Government of Canada through
the Canada Book Fund, the Canada Council for the Arts, the Manitoba
Department of Sport, Culture, and Heritage, the Manitoba Arts Council,
and the Manitoba Book Publishing Tax Credit.

Funded by the Government of Canada | Canadä

For Carol Shields's Readers

How wonderful to be a woman
living and writing in Canada.

—Carol Shields, "The Short Story (and Women Writers),"
in *Startle and Illuminate* (107)

BOOKS BY CAROL SHIELDS

Novels

Small Ceremonies
The Box Garden
Happenstance
A Fairly Conventional Woman
Swann: A Mystery
A Celibate Season (with Blanche Howard)
The Republic of Love
The Stone Diaries
Larry's Party
Unless

Short Stories

Various Miracles
The Orange Fish
Dressing Up for the Carnival
Collected Stories

Poems

Others
Intersect
Coming to Canada
Carol Shields's Collected Poetry

Plays

Departures and Arrivals
Thirteen Hands
Fashion Power Guilt and the Charity of Families (with Catherine Shields)
Anniversary: A Comedy (with Dave Williamson)
Women Waiting
Unless (with Sara Cassidy)

Larry's Party—The Musical (adapted by Richard Ouzounian
   with music by Marek Norman)
Thirteen Hands and Other Plays

Criticism

Susanna Moodie: Voice and Vision

Biography

Jane Austen: A Life

Anthologies

Dropped Threads: What We Aren't Told (edited with Marjorie Anderson)
Dropped Threads 2: More of What We Aren't Told
   (edited with Marjorie Anderson)

Essays

Startle and Illuminate: Carol Shields on Writing

CONTENTS

PART 2: Carol Shields's Previously Published but
Uncollected Essays

"'A Soap Bubble Hovering over the Void': A Tribute to Carol Shields"[1]

by Margaret Atwood

Carol Shields began publishing in the 1970s, and her first break-through was *The Republic of Love*. But her glory book was *The Stone Diaries*, short-listed for the Booker Prize and winner of the Canadian Governor General's Award and, in 1995, the Pulitzer Prize. Carol wore her newfound prominence with generosity. Her final novel, *Unless*, was a hymn to the beauty and fragility of day-to-day life. Her voice—astute, compassionate, observant, and deeply human—will continue to speak to her many readers everywhere.

I began reading Carol Shields's books many years ago, with *The Box Garden*. In that novel there's a passage that made me laugh so hard I thought I would do myself an injury. It's the chapter describing a mother with scant taste but a lot of energy, who spends her time like a down-market and rather crazed Martha Stewart, relentlessly decorating her modest house—papering and re-papering its walls, hand-painting its lampshades, dyeing its scatter rugs—much to the alarm of her adolescent daughter, who never knows what new, ferocious colour the house will be when she gets home from school.

This, I thought, was not only terrific satire, but fine comedy as well. Yet when I recently read the passage again, it no longer struck me as all that funny. Now, years later, and with several demented decorating episodes of my own behind me, I find it poignant, even faintly tragic. The mother is defeated by her house, in the end. She abandons her doomed attempts to make it into a work of art. She recognizes the futility of her efforts. Time claims her. She sinks down. She gives up.

This ability to strike two such different chords at once is not only high art, it's also the essence of Carol Shields's writing—the iridescent, often hilarious surfaces of things, but also their ominous depths. The shimmering pleasure boat, all sails set, skimming giddily across the River Styx.

Carol Shields died on July 16, 2003, at her home in Victoria, British Columbia, after a long battle with cancer. She was sixty-eight. The enormous media coverage given to her and the sadness expressed by her many readers paid tribute to the high esteem in which she was held in her own country, but her death made the news all around the world.

Conscious as she was of the vagaries of fame and the element of chance in any fortune, she would have viewed that with a certain irony, but she would also have found it deeply pleasing. She knew about the darkness, but, both as an author and as a person, she held on to the light.

Earlier in her writing career, some critics mistook this quality of light in her for lightness, light-mindedness, on the general principle that comedy—a form that turns on misunderstanding and confusion but ends in reconciliation, of however tenuous a kind—is less serious than tragedy and that the personal life is of lesser importance than the public one. Carol Shields knew better. Human life is a mass of statistics only for statisticians: the rest of us live in a world of individuals, and most of them are not prominent. Their joys, however, are fully joyful, and their griefs are real. It was the extraordinariness of ordinary people that was Shields's forte. She gave her material the full benefit of her large intelligence, her powers of observation, her humane wit, and her wide reading. Her books are delightful, in the original sense of the word: they are full of delights.

She understood the life of the obscure and the overlooked partly because she had lived it: her work reveals a deep sympathy with the plight of the woman novelist toiling incognito, appreciated only by an immediate circle but longing for her due. Born in 1935 in the United States, Shields was at the tail end of the postwar generation of North American college-educated women who were convinced by the mores of their time that their destiny was to get married and have five children. This Carol did; she remained a devoted mother and a constant wife throughout her life. Her husband Don was a civil engineer; they moved to Canada, beginning with Toronto in the '60s, a time of poetic ferment in that city. Carol, who was already writing then, and attended some readings, said of that time, "I knew no writers." Undoubtedly, she felt relegated to that nebulous category, "just a housewife," like Daisy in *The Stone Diaries* and like Mary Swann, the eponymous poet who is murdered by her husband when her talent begins to show.

After obtaining an M.A. at the University of Ottawa, Shields taught for years at the University of Manitoba, in Winnipeg, where she began publishing in the '70s. But this was the decade of rampant feminism, in the arts at least. Her early books, including *Others*, *Intersect*, *Small Ceremonies*, and *The Box Garden*, which examined the vagaries of domestic life without torpedoing it, did not make a large stir, although some of their early readers found them both highly accomplished and hilarious. She had her first literary break-through—not in terms of quality of writing, but in terms of audience size—in Britain rather than in North America, with her 1992 novel *The Republic of Love*.

The Stone Diaries was short-listed for the Booker Prize and won the Canadian Governor General's Award and then, in 1995, the Pulitzer Prize, a feat her dual citizenship made possible. Her next novel, *Larry's Party*, won the Orange Prize in 1998. To say that she was not thrilled by success would be to do her an injustice. She knew what it was worth. She'd waited a long time for it. She wore her newfound prominence with graciousness and used it with largesse.

Unless, her last novel, was written in the small space of time she spent in England and France, after beating cancer the first time and before it came back.[2] It's a hymn to the provisional: the sense of happiness and security as temporary and fragile is stronger than ever. Those who had heard Carol Shields interviewed earlier were probably surprised by a frankly feminist strain in the novel—particularly the angry letters her protagonist, writer Reta Winters, addressed to male pundits dismissive of woman writers—because in conversation she was discreet and allusive. The little frown, the shake of the head, said it all. Possibly feminism was something she worked into, as she published more widely and came up against more commentators who thought excellent pastry was a facile creation compared with raw meat on skewers, and who in any case could not recognize the thread of blood in her work, though it was always there.

xiv The Canadian Shields

The problem of the luminous is that its very luminosity obscures the shadows it depends on for its brilliance.

Unless was published in 2002; although it was short-listed for just about every major English-language prize, after a certain number of prizes you are shot into the stratosphere, where you circulate in radiant mists, far beyond the ken of juries.

I last saw Carol Shields at the end of April 2003. Her new house was spacious, filled with light; outside the windows, the tulips in her much-loved garden were in bloom. Typically for her, she claimed she couldn't quite believe she deserved to live in such a big and beautiful house. She felt so lucky, she said.

Although she was very ill, she didn't seem it. She was as alert, as interested in books of all kinds, and as curious as ever. She'd recently been reading nonfiction works on biology, she told me: something new for her, a new source of amazement and wonder. We did not speak of her illness. She preferred to be treated as a person who was living, not one who was dying.

And live she did, and live she does; for, as John Keats remarked, every writer has two souls, an earthly one and one that lives on in the world of writing as a voice in the writing itself. It's this voice—astute, compassionate, observant, and deeply human—that will continue to speak to her readers everywhere. For who is better at delineating happiness, especially the sudden, unlooked-for, unearned kind of happiness, than Carol Shields? It's easier to kill than to give birth, easier to destroy than to create, and easier for a writer to describe gloom than to evoke joy. Carol Shields can do both supremely well, but it's her descriptions of joy that leave you open-mouthed. The world may be "a soap bubble hovering over the void," but look, what astonishing colours it has, and isn't it amazing that such a thing exists at all?

Such a world—various, ordinary, shimmering, evanescent but miraculous—is a gift; and it's the vision of this gift that Carol Shields has presented us with in her extraordinary books. We give thanks for it—and for her.

ACKNOWLEDGEMENTS

After devoting many hours, days, and weeks to sifting through more than two hundred boxes of files over a period of several years in the Carol Shields Fonds in the National Library in Ottawa, I had gleaned more than two dozen previously unpublished stories and essays and over two dozen essays that had been published in journals and magazines, but never collected, and hence difficult to access. My aim, as always, is to make the writings of a writer I admire more easily accessible to readers. Several individuals proved an invaluable help in realizing this goal.

I wish to acknowledge, first and foremost, Carol Shields's family, especially Don Shields, Anne and Nicholas Giardini, and Sara Cassidy, as well as Karen McDiarmaid, the Carol Shields Estate, and the Carol Shields Literary Trust. I wish to thank the Canada Council for the Social Sciences and Humanities Council of Canada Strategic Grant and the Insight Grant that enabled me to research the Shields Archives at the National Library and the University of Alberta Faculty of Arts for the McCalla Professorships that allowed me to edit this collection of Carol Shields's previously unpublished and previously uncollected stories and essays, as well as her complete poetry in *The Collected Poetry of Carol Shields* (2021). I want to thank Catherine Hobbs and the archivists of the National Library for their assistance in locating previously unpublished writings by Shields. I wish to thank Lauren Corcoran, who helped digitize this material and footnote references. I want to thank my dream team at the University of Manitoba Press, beginning with senior editor Jill McConkey, whose professionalism and proficiency were so impressive, the managing editor Barbara Romanik, whose patience accommodated my revisions and whose meticulous care prevented errors, and Sarah Ens and Allyn Lyons, who tactfully and patiently oversaw the cover copy and arranged interviews and book launches, as well as my copy editor Dallas Harrison, who treated my manuscript with respect, while correcting any errors and providing valuable information.

I especially wish to thank Margaret Atwood for permission to reprint her splendid tribute to Carol Shields and Lorna Crozier for permission to reprint the moving passage excerpted from her memoir *Through the Garden: A Love Story (with Cats)* (201–3).

Shields's texts have been reproduced as exactly as possible. Where necessary, typographical and other errors have been corrected, but such errors in Shields's writings are very rare indeed. Many typescripts include numerous holographic insertions, which have all been included in the texts, while her excisions and those of the Carol Shields Literary Trust have been honoured. Because some of Shields's essays were published in Canadian journals and others in American magazines, they employ either Canadian or American spelling. In the interest of consistency, Canadian spelling has been employed throughout.

At the time that this book went to press, the news of the crimes committed by Alice Munro's second husband against her daughter Andrea, and of Munro's failures to protect Andrea, had just broken. This book does not address these revelations. It is clear in some of the writing collected here that Shields was among the many who admired Munro's work. We have elected to maintain the historical integrity of Shields's texts and retain these few references to Munro. Written before 2003, they do not reckon with what we now know, thanks to the courage of Andrea Skinner, as future readers and scholars surely will.

ABBREVIATIONS

CP	*The Collected Poetry of Carol Shields*
CS	*Carol Shields: The Collected Stories*
DT	*Dropped Threads*
FCW	*A Fairly Conventional Woman*
LP	*Larry's Party*
MF	*A Memoir of Friendship*
RI	*Random Illuminations*
RL	*The Republic of Love*
SC	*Small Ceremonies*
SD	*The Stone Diaries*
SI	*Startle and Illuminate: Carol Shields on Writing*

The Canadian Shields, or How an American Writer Became an Award-Winning Canadian Author

Imagine the rejoicing that would ensue if another novel by Jane Austen were discovered. So it is when previously unpublished writing by any beloved author is released. *The Canadian Shields: Stories and Essays* includes fifty short writings by Carol Shields, including three previously unpublished stories and two dozen previously unpublished essays, as well as two dozen essays previously published in magazines and journals but never before collected.

American-born Carol Ann Warner (1935–2003), together with her young Canadian husband, Donald Hugh Shields, entered Canada with her ironing board in the back of their old blue six-cylinder Ford, on a Sunday afternoon in July 1957, as she recalls in "Writing from the Edge" (*SI* 131–40). The ironing board and their wedding presents became transformed into "Settler's Effects" and Carol into a "Landed Immigrant" at the Bellingham, Washington, border crossing.[1] Serendipitously, 1957 was the year of the founding of the Canada Council, of which Shields eventually became a valued member.

Emigrating from the United States to Canada as a young bride, Carol Shields was puzzled by many questions, such as the difference between a prime minister and a premier, kilometres and centimetres, Fahrenheit and Celsius. What lay behind the mysterious abbreviations CBC, NRC, NFB, and PNE? She acknowledges in her essay "The Feminine Line" (contained herein): "I find, as an immigrant, a woman fiction writer in mid-life, that I have more questions than I have answers." For example, she was puzzled by the joke "Why did the Canadian cross the road?" and the answer "To get to the middle."[2]

In a previously unpublished account titled "Coming to Canada" (included herein), Shields recalls people asking her, "Wasn't it a terrible wrench? To leave the country of your birth?" But she was too much in love to care. "Years later I understood what it means to cross a border," she reports: "Moving to a new country was like falling down a dark hole, but for a long while I was too busy to notice." In her afterword to Moodie's *Life in the Clearings Versus the Bush*, contained herein, Shields claims that, in Moodie's "adopted culture" of Canada, her "consciousness was stretched across two cultures, two continents, and two political philosophies" (262, this volume). The same could be said of Carol Shields.

In a 1997 talk, titled "The Unity of Our Country," included in this collection, she acknowledges, "This is, perhaps, one of the easiest immigrations in the world," but adds, "Nevertheless—and I think you who have undergone the transplantation experience will understand this—nevertheless, it took me years to understand how things worked in my adopted country: the political system, the intricacies and pressures of geography, the Canadian character." She believes the epithet "'Friendly Neighbour to the North' is so enshrined that it has prevailed over tariff tangles or occasional rumbles at the border." She interprets Robertson Davies's dictum "we in Canada are the attic of North America" as "suggesting that there's plenty of room in that dark and empty attic to shout" (*SI* 131).

Margaret Atwood recalled, in a 2020 CBC TV interview, a contest in which contestants were challenged to invent a Canadian simile parallel to "as American as apple pie," such as, perhaps, "as Canadian as cranberry sauce." The winning comparison was "as Canadian as possible under the circumstances," a slogan that Atwood considered captured the essence of the national psyche.

How did Shields get from there to here? How did American-born-and-raised Carol Ann Warner become Carol Shields, a quintessential Canadian writer? How did the denizen of Oak Park, Illinois, the birthplace of Ernest Hemingway,[3] become an award-winning Canadian author? Her daughter Anne Giardini comments in "Reading My Mother," "Like Furlong [Eberhart, the draft-dodging, plagiarizing novelist of Shields's first novel, *Small Ceremonies* (1976)], she is a completely Canadian writer (whatever that means) who was born and raised in the US (although, unlike Furlong, she does not try to keep this a secret)" (9). How did this transformation occur?

Shields made the first step toward becoming a Canadian writer by crossing the 49th parallel, the first of many border crossings for the budding writer and for her subsequent protagonists. In "Benign Neglect," in a special issue of *Maclean's* on "The Vanishing Border" of 20 December 1999, Andrew Philips recalled that "Margaret Atwood once noted that the 49th parallel is less the world's longest undefended border than its biggest one-way mirror" (25). Shields, however, demonstrates that it is a two-way street, as her protagonists Daisy Goodwill Flett of *The Stone Diaries* (1993) and Larry Weller of *Larry's Party* (1997), like Shields herself, prove to be border crossers, criss-crossing the 49th parallel.[4]

Thirteen years after her immigration, Carol Shields applied for and received Canadian citizenship. She became truly Canadian after living in several major Canadian cities, plus twenty years in Winnipeg, where she taught creative writing and English literature at the University of Manitoba and later served as chancellor of the University of Winnipeg, from 1996 to 2000. Canadian author Guy Vanderhaeghe recalls a visit in the 1990s to a Canadian literature class at Middlebury College in Vermont, where students had read The Republic of Love (1987), set in Winnipeg. Some women students told him that they wanted to move to Winnipeg because, they explained, "It is such a romantic city: it's the city of love."[5] No wonder Winnipeggers revere Shields for what she did for their city.

Winnipeg took her to its heart: in 2009, Winnipeg established a formal hedge maze in her honour, inspired by Larry Weller's hedge mazes in Shields's 1997 novel *Larry's Party*, and erected a bronze bust of Shields on the University of Manitoba's Innovation Plaza.[6] It also established the Carol Shields Winnipeg Book Award in 1999, inaugurated an annual Carol Shields Festival in 2009, and even instituted the Carol Shields Manitoba Self-Directed Drive and Stroll Tour, the Carol Shields Festival of New Works at the Prairie Theatre Exchange, and the Carol Shields Auditorium in Winnipeg's Millennium Library, with "Larry Weller's bench" ensconced at the University of Winnipeg. Awards were established in her name, including the Carol Shields student award at Red River Community College by the Manitoba Writers' Guild, the Carol Shields Writer-in-Residence award at the University of Winnipeg, and the Carol Shields Winnipeg Book Award. She was also awarded the Order of Manitoba in 2001.

In "Carol Shields and Winnipeg: Finding Home," William Neville claims Shields and Winnipeg enjoyed a mutual love affair: "Winnipeg laid claim to Carol Shields" (37), while she was "the epitome of 'the good citizen' in Winnipeg" (34). She was elected to the Winnipeg Citizens' Hall of Fame and named "Winnipeg Citizen of the Year" in 2001. Neville records an emblematic story explaining why Carol and Don Shields took Winnipeg to their hearts: after they ran out of gas on Pembina Highway one cold winter night, a city bus pulled up, and the driver ordered all able-bodied men to push their car to a gas station (32). Shields affirmed, "we soon realized that everything was there that we needed or wanted . . . we had our daily rituals and a huge network of friends . . . it provided the most complete sense of community that I had known since growing up in the American Midwest" (Neville 31).

Ironically, in "A Note," Shields records that the CBC, in their desire to "universalize or 'Toronto-ize'" her early radio play *Women Waiting*, which won the CBC's Annual Literary Contest and was broadcast on CBC in 1983, changed the names of certain Winnipeg locations, including "Wellington Crescent," where Carol and Don Shields lived, in what she terms a "form of colonization." She recalls that Morley Callaghan's early books were published in "split editions," American and Canadian, with the American version set in Chicago and the Canadian version set in Toronto. Her Canadian publisher wanted her to relocate *A Fairly Conventional Woman* (1982) from Chicago to Toronto, but she refused. She mentions that novelist Peter Carey told her that the same thing used to occur with Australian and New Zealand writers. She claims, "Writers living at the edge of the world felt obliged to switch settings and, in fact, whole sets of vocabulary and punctuation standards so that those readers in the UK and in the United States would not feel shaken or disoriented by the exoticism of unfamiliar locales" (18). She adds that, by the time she wrote *The Republic of Love* (1992), it seemed natural to set her novel in her adopted city.

Shields lived in Canada for forty-six years, or over two-thirds of her life, twice as long as she had lived in the United States. She resided in several cities across the country, beginning in Toronto and Ottawa for a decade, continuing for two years in Vancouver, then two decades in Winnipeg, and finally her last three years in Victoria. The Shields family were also citizens of the world, as they lived in Manchester from 1960 to 1963 and spent sabbaticals in France, Berkeley, and London. Nevertheless, it was many years after immigrating to Canada that Shields wrote these words in her poem "Coming to Canada—Age Twenty-Two":

> It took years to happen:
>
> . . .
>
> and years before COME
>
> BACK SOON changed to
>
> here and now and home the place I came to
>
> the place I was from (*CC* 27; *CP* 150).

Shields had travelled a great distance from coming *to* Canada to coming *from* Canada. Her five children, however, were all Canadian from the outset.

The transition from American to Canadian, however, was a time-consuming process. In "Coming to Canada," Shields recalls, "It took me a dozen years to decide to become a Canadian citizen, but I knew my perspective had shifted when I returned to Chicago for a visit and heard myself bragging to my American relations about our winter weather—exaggerating the height of the Canadian snow drifts, lingering over our wicked sub-zero temperatures, and providing anyone who would listen with the fascinating details of our most recent fuel bill." She adds, "And now, after living for periods of time in Vancouver, Toronto, and Ottawa, I find myself settled in Winnipeg, where there is no need to inflate the meteorological facts. Winnipeg really is the coldest city in the world, colder than the most northerly point of Maine, colder than Moscow. Some days it's colder than it is at the North Pole. Now that's something to be proud of, something to warm the heart. And it offers an opportunity to join Canada's favourite sport, which is complaining about the weather." She confirms this view in her essay "At Home in Winnipeg," contained in this collection. She adds, "The summers, of course, are glorious, as Canadians are eager to tell you. During the warmer months, the 49th parallel seems to soften in the sun." Perhaps that is why she, along with some of her protagonists, frequently criss-crossed that parallel.

By taking pride in her ability to survive Winnipeg winters, perhaps echoing Atwood's 1972 study of Canadian literature, *Survival*, Shields thought she was becoming genuinely Canadian, although she did not embrace patriotism, which seemed to her almost *un-Canadian*. In her essay "Coming to Canada," she observes, "Canadians are quietly moderate about their country's virtues. I've heard Canadians say they're proud of their history and content to be citizens of a decent country, but I've never heard the word *patriotism* voiced. Even the concept is somehow embarrassing."[7] In a 2021 CBC documentary, Atwood remarked that the country you claim as your own is not the one of which you are most proud but the one about which you are the least embarrassed.

Shields was proud, however, of the Canada Council. In "The Visual Arts," a previously unpublished speech about Canadian culture on the fortieth anniversary of the council in 1997, also the fortieth anniversary of her immigration to Canada, she defines the force that holds a diverse society together as not only leadership or a railway or a postal service or a health program but "this body of aesthetic expression that becomes our definition and shared experience." She believes "The arts are vital to Canada's economic and social and cultural health, as art, and the transcendent experience that art provides, can save us from despair." The need for the arts is greater than ever now in the shadow of the pandemic. Shields celebrates Canadian culture, both literature and other arts, in numerous essays, such as "A View from the Edge of the Edge," "The Short Story (and Women Writers)," and "The Visual Arts," the last item being contained in this volume.

Shields was born and raised in Hemingway's hometown, Oak Park, Illinois, but four of her five children were born in Canada, and all of them were raised in Canada.[8] A sabbatical year in France in 1976, plus vacations at their family home in France, added to their experience of living abroad. "Blood critics," as she called her children when they critiqued her writing, she took their advice to heart. In a 9 December 1996 email to Blanche Howard, she recalled that her daughter Meg said of her draft of *Larry's Party*, "Oh, Mum, you've made a cultural boob. You have to say 'heavy metal,' not 'hard metal'" (*MF* 341).

Her claim to being a Canadian writer, however, is based less on the number of years that she resided in Canada or even on her achieving Canadian citizenship in 1971 than on her reading and writing. As Shields affirms in her essay "Writers Are Readers First," "I've never been able to separate my reading and my writing life" (*SI* 1). The first books she read were her parents' books borrowed from the bookcase in her home, including the Horatio Alger and Bobbsey Twins books. One novel that especially delighted her in childhood was Canadian, her mother's copy of *Anne of Green Gables* by L.M. Montgomery, which particularly resonated with Shields. She recalls, "My mother loved *Anne of Green Gables* because Anne was a model to millions of girls who weren't ever able to act out the kind of battles that she had" ("Interview" 32). Shields reflects in "Writers Are Readers First,"

> It's easy to see what she found in Anne of Green Gables. She found what millions of others have found, a consciousness attuned to nature, a female model of courage, goodness, and candour, and possessed of an emotional capacity that triumphs and converts. Unlike Tom Sawyer, who capitulates to society, Anne transforms her community with her exuberant vision. She enters the story disentitled and emerges as a beloved daughter, loving friend, with a future ahead of her, and she has done it all without help: captured Gilbert Blythe, sealed her happiness, and reshuffled the values of society by a primary act of re-imagination. (*SI* 3)[9]

Shields applies that "primary act of re-imagination" to her own writing, eventually earning the title "The Canadian Shields."

When asked to describe the literary character she would most like to be for a "Saturday Books" section feature, Shields responded, "Anne Shirley pops straight to mind, finer and more heroic in every way than Tom Sawyer. Not only did she become 'a good girl' [recalling Norah Winters in Shields's final novel, *Unless* (2002)], but she transformed her society to a vision of goodness and won the heart of Gilbert Blythe" (*SI* 3). In "Carol's Kindness," writer Martin Levin, a former student of Shields, comments, "Much of this might serve as epitaph for Carol herself, except that she won a great many more hearts" (133).

Thus, Shields became a Canadian writer partly by reading Canadian literature. Her work was recognized by the Marian Engel Award for lifetime achievement, which had been initiated to honour Canadian author Marian Engle,[10] who was a founding member of the Writers' Union of Canada and a recipient of the Order of Canada, and who died mid-career. It was previously won by Audrey Thomas, Edna Alford, and Merna Summers and subsequently by a list of writers who could stand as a who's who of Canadian novelists, including Jane Urquhart, Katherine Govier, and Elizabeth Hay, to name but a few.

Shields opened her acceptance speech for the award by saying, "I have been given about three minutes to express my gratitude and invoke a few names. First Virginia Woolf who invoked in me the impulse to be serious. And then Margaret Laurence who said through her writing, 'serious, yes, but watch out for earnestness.'"[11] Thus, she cited women writers as educating her.[12]

In her speech she affirms, "I came to Canada as a young bride in 1957."[13] She did not read a contemporary novel by a Canadian writer, however, until 1970, the same year that she finally applied for Canadian citizenship. The first contemporary Canadian novel she read, serendipitously, was *The Honeyman Festival* by Marian Engel. In fact, Shields stayed up all night reading the novel, which, coincidentally, is set during one night. She wondered why she loved the novel and affirmed in "Writing from the Edge," "This was a woman I recognized" (*SI* 139).[14] She resolved to write the kind of novel that she wanted to read.

Shields also read Laurence's *The Stone Angel*—arguably the great Canadian novel—and the next year she found herself registering as an MA student at the University of Ottawa and studying Canadian literature—"'*Canadian* literature!' my friends and family exclaimed."[15]

In *Random Illuminations*, she explains, "When we went to Ottawa and my husband joined the University of Ottawa, I realized that I had this free tuition. Being very thrifty about these things, I decided I'd better take advantage of it" (38). She notes, "I signed up for an MA in Canadian literature. I was reading Canadians." Despite later pursuing a thesis on this nineteenth-century Canadian woman pioneer, she adds ironically, "I'd never heard of Susanna Moodie" (Wachtel, 1989, 23).

Shields received an excellent introduction to Canadian literature at the University of Ottawa. She records, "the University of Ottawa was involved in Canadian lit. I went to hear Al Purdy, Northrop Frye, I went to hear everybody." She asserts, "I was involved in it" (Wachtel, 1989, 25). In "Carol Shields and the University of Ottawa," Lorraine McMullen, the supervisor of Carol Shields's master's thesis on Moodie, recalls, "The period of Carol's tenure as a graduate student coincided with the great surge of enthusiasm for Canadian studies in the late 1960s and early 1970s" (39). Shields took courses with McMullen on the Canadian short story and new directions in Canadian poetry, plus a course on the Canadian novel with Glenn Clever. During her five years as a master's student, she also composed papers and talks on Sara Jeannette Duncan and Susanna Moodie, both contained herein, and on F.P. Grove and on Sheila Watson's *Double Hook*.[16] She also met Canadian writers, including Pat Lowther, who was writer-in-residence in the English Department in 1974 while Carol Shields was a graduate student, and the two women became friends.[17] While teaching creative writing at the University of Ottawa in 1976, Shields became friends with Joy Kogawa, who was composing *Obasan* as writer-in-residence while Shields was writing *Happenstance*. She also attended an InterAmerican Women Writers conference in 1978 that included Margaret Atwood.

McMullen recalls, "Carol enjoyed CanLit symposia," and quotes Shields's statement, "I remember being thrilled by it all, especially the rather emotional final session in which Irving Layton castigated the ghost of Klein for abdicating his role as a poet and selling out to commerce" (40). McMullen also remembers Shields finding the Lampman and Crawford symposia exhilarating. However, Carol told her that, when she heard someone's analysis of "'a log jam as a metaphor for gang rape,'" she said, "a certain skepticism about literary scholarship was born in my head that day" (40).

After completing her MA thesis in 1975, titled "A Critical Study of Three Major Themes Occurring in the Novels and the Nonfiction Books of Susanna Moodie," Shields published it as *Susanna Moodie: Voice and Vision* in 1977. She even made her first female protagonist-narrator, Judith Gill, heroine of her first published novel, *Small Ceremonies* (1976), occupied with composing a biography of Moodie. Elizabeth Waterston claims, "Judith echoes Moodie in self-mockery, [in] insecurity, and in the shrewd wry tone of her acceptance of reality" (59). Waterston adds, "A more serious kind of [Canadian] nationalism appears in [Shields's] focus on Susanna Moodie" (58), as "Shields, like Moodie, was a mid-life immigrant" (59).

After submitting her thesis, and just before turning forty and flying to France with her husband for a sabbatical year, Shields learned that *Small Ceremonies* had been accepted for publication by McGraw-Hill Ryerson after McClelland and Stewart, Macmillan, and Oberon had rejected it. She had arrived as a writer. "I thought, I'm going to be a novelist all my life," she recalled (*RI* 42).

Shields returned from her year in France having completed her second novel, *The Box Garden* (1977). She entered the doctoral program at the University of Ottawa, planning to pursue a dissertation on nineteenth-century female Canadian authors, as her graduate term papers on Susanna Moodie and Sara Jeannette Duncan, included here, demonstrate.[18] After a heart-to-heart discussion with a fellow writer, Sandy Duncan,[19] Shields decided to devote her time to writing rather than completing her doctoral studies. Nevertheless, she went on to have a successful academic career as a professor of English at the University of Manitoba and as chancellor at the University of Winnipeg.

Shields returned to the University of Ottawa, twenty years after completing her master's thesis on Susanna Moodie (the first in Canada), on the occasion of being awarded an honorary degree, the first of fifteen. As David Staines recalls in his introduction to *The Worlds of Carol Shields*, she was praised in these words: "Carol Shields is a wise and articulate chronicler of contemporary men and women as they search for meaning in this life, as they search for meaning in their own lives. Whether her focus is urban marriage or a self-absorbed academic world, she holds up a compassionate mirror to the pains and joys, frustrations and misunderstandings, that characterize and give meaning to the human condition" (3).

Shields's interest in Canadian literature persisted. In her essay "Writing from the Edge," a retitling of "The View from the Edge of the Edge," she observes, "We may not yet have in Canada such a universally shared cultural reference [as the American fictional hero Tom Sawyer or the British fictional hero David Copperfield], though the name Hagar Shipley from Margaret Laurence's *The Stone Angel* goes a long way in that direction" (*SI* 137).[20] She declares, "We can, speaking roughly and without stepping on too many toes, take the year 1960 as the real beginning of our literature. That was the year—just to peg it for you—when there were five Canadian novels published in English in Canada. Five!" (*SI* 136).

Waterston observes, "She became officially Canadian as a crucial era in Canadian literary history opened. She was experiencing a unique Canadian spring, like so many of us. In 1972 Margaret Atwood published both *Survival* and *Surfacing*. The next year my own *Survey: A Short History of Canadian Literature* was accepted as a text across the country in the new high school CanLit courses suddenly popping up on the curriculum" (58).

Carol Shields became a champion of Canadian literature. In "Writing from the Edge," Shields proudly celebrates the success of Canadian literature, claiming, "Canadian writing . . . is in a state of exuberant good health" (*SI* 131), especially writing by Canadian women. In "Open Every Question, Every Possibility" (*SI* 115–30), she observes, "Looking at writing in Canada, the storyboard does seem to be growing here rather than shrinking. Voices formerly at the margin are now being heard, bringing with them their different rhythms, and their alternate expectations. More is permitted; more can be said" (*SI* 129). Noting that the Canada Council was founded the same year that she immigrated to Canada, she asserts, "Canada, this country on the edge, could afford its own culture" (*SI* 138). "*Vive le* Canada," she wrote to Howard on 2 November 1995, following the Quebec Referendum (*MF* 329).[21] Shields refers in "A View from the Edge" to "national identity," "cultural cohesiveness," and "Canadian identity" (17–18).

In "A View from the Edge of the Edge," she addresses the literary canon and marginalized social sectors and political subjects, including, ironically, the middle class and the Midwest. Shields celebrates the recent success of "marginal" writing, since Canadians, women, western-ers, and Indigenous people write from that edge, "the exotic margins of the planet" (18), sending "reports from the frontier" of fiction, offering "fresh news from another country" (*SI* 135).[22] She affirms, "It seems we are almost all at the edge, and that edge embraces aboriginal writing, gay writing, immigrant writing, and women's writing" (*SI* 135). Speaking of recent Canadian texts that address its complicated, multicultural reality, Shields states, "They are in an almost literal sense reports from the frontier, and the frontier has been shifting in recent years—in terms of geography, demography, gender, and certainly lit-erary form" (*SI* 135). Finally, she believes Canadian fiction has gone beyond "The 'Maps and Chaps' recording of history" (*SI* 35).

Marta Dvořák argues in "'Controlled Chaos' and Carol Shields's 'A View from the Edge of the Edge'" that Shields's essay "shows how hard it is to locate the edge. Many have posited, like Shields, that a British reading public long perceived Canadian literature as coming 'from the exotic margins of the planet, the far edge.'" She adds, "Others have held that, like a poor cousin, CanLit is not exotic enough. In her introduction to the Clarendon Lectures she gave at Oxford University, Margaret Atwood suggested that the British find Canadian literature too boringly similar, 'lacking the exoticism of Africa, the strange fauna of Australia, or the romance of India'" (100). Dvořák situates Shields's view of the centre versus the edge in her personal situation:

> Centre and edge in Shields's essay repeatedly melt like Dali's clocks. Winnipeg, where the writer was living at the time, is smack in the middle of the country (and continent) but is "certainly not the literary centre of Canada" ("A View" 19). Shields states she was born "in the centre of the United States," but then points out that "Midwesterners were, culturally, at the edge" (19). She helps readers tick off a check list. First, Shields's home town Chicago, one of the largest cities in the United States, but not even the capital of Illinois, wields little political power. Secondly, Shields comes from the middle class, also "at the edge"—"the middle being nowhere near the centre." (100)

Dvořák concludes that Shields grew up in a "leafy green *suburb*, of a relatively happy family," which doubly places her "at life's margin," at least in "romantic literary terms" (100).

Shields, a resident first of the United States and then of Canada, is in a unique position to compare Canadian literature with American literature—"Can.Lit." and "Am.Lit.," as she puts it in *Small Ceremonies* (*SC* 94). In "Writing from the Edge" she explains, "It may be the noisy and varied writing coming out of Canada today that makes it difficult to compare that literature with that of the United States, but I don't think such a comparison has ever been easy" (*SI* 136–37). She reflects, "Canadians, these days, are directing serious attention to that very seething, smoking, chaotic multicultural muddle that is, in fact, our reality. This is risky; one almost wants to whisper: un-Canadian" (*SI* 135). Dvořák argues that Shields finds "the shape and force of a national literature" valid only if it is fluid and does not cement literature "belly-to-belly to the national destiny," because Shields considers that "People are bonded and nourished by a common literature, but only if it has flourished naturally, unproved by politicians and flag-wavers and the prescriptive notions of the Academy" (101).

As a literary critic, Shields becomes something of a feminist, as well as a nationalist, as she claims, "We have wonderful women writers here in Canada" (*RI* 175), noting that journalists in London wondered why so many books by Canadian women were appearing. In "The Short Story," she affirms the value to her of the models provided by recent Canadian women writers: "Mavis Gallant shows how it is possible to be intelligent on the page without being pedantic. Margaret Atwood, who is, I suppose, Canada's first international star, is just plain brave—she'll tackle any orthodoxy and almost always with wit" (*SI* 105). In her essay "Is There a Feminine Voice in Literature?" she writes, "Almost from the start in this country women have chosen to write about the relationships between people and particularly between men and women" (85).[23] Shields herself became one of those esteemed Canadian women writers. Staines asserts that Shields "carved out her special place in Canadian letters . . . among the most honoured of Canadian writers" (2).

Bearing out her claim regarding the inextricable connection between her reading and her writing, Shields reviewed many novels by British, American, and Canadian women writers. As Alex Ramon notes in "'Little Shocks of Recognition': Carol Shields's Book Reviews," "Published between the late 1970s and the early 2000s, these critiques were initially written for specialist academic journals and then, later, commissioned for national and international publications, such as *The Globe and Mail*, *The New York Times Book Review* and *The Times Literary Supplement*, as Shields's own literary celebrity increased" (219–20). He elaborates: "While Shields's private judgements on literary texts could be both acerbic and unorthodox—letters find her briskly dismissing *The Double Hook* [by Sheila Watson] as 'dreadful imitation Faulkner' (*MF* 10), [and] *The English Patient* [by Michael Ondaatje] as 'awfully studied, terribly solemn, taking itself incredibly seriously' (*MF* 274)—her published reviews generally lack such sharpness of tone, indulging in few outright 'pans' or 'sweeping dismissals'" (220). When Howard calls Shields's review of Erica Jong's *Fear of Fifty: A Midlife Memoir* "acerbic but restrained, and subtle" (*MF* 304), Shields acknowledges, "I seem to lack the courage for demolishment, knowing how it feels, I suppose" (qtd. in Howard 19). She calls brutal reviews "cruelies" (*MF* 4), such as Robert Lecker's review of her first novel, *Small Ceremonies*, "All Plot, Little Thought," or Barbara Amiel's review of her second novel, *The Box Garden*, "Look Back in Stupor." In "The Writing Life" (contained herein), she explains the writer's vulnerability to harsh reviews and declines to reveal what she terms "a glint of the fang" in her reviews of other writers' books.

Soon after becoming a Canadian citizen, Shields categorized herself as a Canadian writer, referring in "Writers Are Readers First" to "we Canadians" and to the centennial celebrations of Confederation in 1967 as "our centenary" (*SI* 4). When she talks about "The Unity of Our Country," she is referring to Canada. In that speech, she emphasizes the importance of the arts in defining a community and the importance of the Canada Council as a unifying force. She recalls the value of Canada Council grants to artists, especially women writers who were also mothers—including Margaret Laurence, Marian Engel, and herself. The grants enabled the authors to find time for writing through labour-saving devices, such as washing machines in Engel's case, or, as was true for Shields herself, electric typewriters and, eventually, computers, although Laurence, who was uncomfortable with technology, gave away the computer that her publisher, Jack McClelland of McClelland and Stewart, presented to his authors. In "The Unity of Our Country," Shields writes, "money does provide permission as well as *real* support. I used my first grant of $600—this was in 1973 when I had five small children—to hire household help, to send my husband's shirts to the laundry, and to order the odd pizza dinner for the family. In a year I had a book" (134, this volume). Shields concludes her acceptance speech for the Marian Engel Award by exclaiming, "how wonderful to be a woman living and writing in Canada in the year 1990," reaffirming the sentiment by repeating it verbatim in a talk to the Manitoba Writers' Guild, titled "The Short Story (and Women Writers)" (*SI* 107).

Canada welcomed the American-born Carol Shields with open arms, awarding her numerous prizes. She was appointed an Officer of the Order of Canada in 1998 and a Fellow of the Royal Society of Canada in 1998, as well as a *Chevalier dans l'ordres des Arts et des Lettres* by France in 2000. She was also named one of *MacLean's Magazine*'s Acclaimed Persons of the Year in 2001. She was made a Companion of the Order of Canada in 2002 and received the Queen Elizabeth Golden Jubilee Medal in 2002. She was also named Libris Author of the Year by the Canadian Booksellers Association in 2003.

As a writer who lived for decades in both the United States and Canada, Shields offers distinct insights into the differences between

Canadian and American fiction. In "Writing from the Edge," she acknowledges that it is "difficult to compare [Canadian] literature with that of the United States [because] Canadian writing, reflecting the immigration patterns of the country, is more community centred, while American writing focuses on the individual, the Canadian *who are we* rather than the American *who am I*" (*SI* 135–36). Shields shared that communal perspective, being revered by her fellow writers for her generosity.

In her work, Carol Shields crosses borders figuratively as well as literally by crossing gender boundaries. Impatient at being dismissed as a "woman writer," she composed two novels featuring male protagonists—historian Jack Bowman in *Happenstance* (1980) and maze maker Larry Weller in *Larry's Party* (1997). Shields writes about gender in her essays, including "Writers' Gender Swapping" (contained herein).

Shields was an inveterate border crosser not only in geographical but also in literary terms, for she frequently moved from one genre to another, blurring the boundaries between them, as she argues in her 1990 paper "Crossing Over," included in the essay "To Write Is to Raid" (*SI* 31–36). There is considerable slippage between Shields's fiction and non-fiction, especially between her stories and essays. As Christl Verduyn comments in "(Es)saying It Her Way: Carol Shields as Essayist," "Her essays move fluidly into the realm of fiction, and she makes ready use of the tools and techniques of fiction writing, including characters, dilemmas, metaphor, the narrative pause, exaggeration, word-work or language, and imagination. There is no irreconcilable difference between fact and fiction, between the observable and the speculative in Shields's essays" (74). Verduyn explains, "Shields moved easily between the Montaigne and Bacon forms of essaying—indeed, combining or synthesizing the two traditions" (68).[24] As Giardini affirms in her foreword to *Relating Carol Shields's Essays and Fiction: Crossing Borders*, "The explorations collected here are essays in the best sense, worthy descendants of the 'attempts'—'essay' coming from the French '*essai*,' meaning 'an attempt'" (xix).

Giardini addresses in her foreword the similarities and differences between her mother's stories and essays, in which Shields often breaks the "'fourth wall' between the imaginative and the actual" (xix). She enjoyed collaborating, perhaps as a result of her experience in theatre, and she collaborated with friends and family members on stories, essays, plays, and even novels, in the case of *A Celibate Season* (1991), co-authored with Blanche Howard. Giardini is well positioned to draw such a comparison between the short story and essay genres in her mother's writerly practice since she collaborated with her mother on the short story "A Wood," included in the 1985 collection *Various Miracles*, and on the essay "Martians in Jane Austen," which they presented dialogically at the Jane Austen Society of North America Annual General Meeting in 1996 and published in *Persuasions* (the Jane Austen Society of North America journal).

Shields argued that contemporary women's writing was breaking down the old rigidities of genre. In "The New New New Fiction," she addresses the future of fiction: she believes it is alive and well and in the process of transforming from traditional realism and recent postmodernism into new forms that convey the subjective consciousness—what cannot be conveyed on the film or television screen. In "Boxcars, Coat Hangers and Other Devices" (*SI* 23–30), Shields claims, "Diurnal surfaces could be observed by a fiction writer with a kind of deliberate squint that distorts but also sharpens beyond ordinary vision, bringing forward what might be called the subjunctive mode of one's self or others, a world of dreams, possibilities, and parallel realities" (*SI* 29). Her stories and essays demonstrate the "squint that distorts but also sharpens beyond ordinary vision," and the numerous previously unpublished works of fiction and non-fiction in this collection convey that "world of dreams, possibilities, and parallel realities."

Shields moved back and forth from fiction to non-fiction with ease, showing that, like Canada and America, the genres have similarities as well as differences. This collection reveals valuable connections between Shields's fiction and non-fiction, since her essays illuminate her fiction and offer good advice to nascent novelists. It complements the Giardini edition of *Startle and Illuminate: Carol Shields on Writing* (2016), which includes fourteen of her essays that focus on writing, and it will further enable the type of research demonstrated in *Relating Carol Shields's Essays and Fiction: Crossing Borders* (2023), which contains essays by fourteen scholars who read her fiction through the lens of her essays.

By comparing her stories and essays, we can better understand Shields's protean gifts. *The Canadian Shields* helps to define and distinguish her brilliance in both fiction and non-fiction. Although she remained an inveterate border crosser, as her daughter Anne Giardini confirms, Shields "is a completely Canadian writer" ("Reading My Mother" 9). By writing about her adopted country and its writers, she earned the title "The Canadian Shields."

PART 1

Carol Shields's Previously Unpublished Stories and Essays

"Protein Dust" opens this section, although it might have been the last of the stories composed by Carol Shields that are included here. The original title of the typescript is "Pain," but "protein dust" is a phrase that reverberates throughout the story, having particular relevance now to the COVID-19 pandemic. It also suggests the phrase "ashes to ashes, dust to dust" in the service for the dead. This seems to be relevant to the story's sixty-year-old narrator Irene's awareness of her aging self as Irene flies across Canada to tend to her niece, who is dying of cancer. Shields, who travelled extensively between Canada and the United States, as well as globally,[1] became not only a woman with dual citizenship but also a true citizen of the world. She even attended the conference convened in her honour at the University of the Sorbonne in Paris in 2003 by Manina Jones and Marta Dvořák, by which time Shields was quite unwell. She often portrays characters aboard airplanes, flying across Canada or across the Atlantic between North America and Europe. When her daughter Anne Giardini, director of the Carol Shields Literary Trust, was asked whether she approved of the revised title, she responded in the affirmative, adding that the original title just made her think of French bread.

Other stories in this section include "A Message from Beyond," dramatizing a rapprochement between a mother and daughter, and "The Golden Boy, or Some Things Only Happen Once," chronicling a family drive across Canada to the prairie city of Winnipeg, where the Shields family lived for two decades.[2] These stories reflect Shields's ongoing interest in the relationship between mothers and daughters, so central to her final novel, *Unless* (2002), as we see in her essay "I've Always Meant to Tell You: A Letter to My Mother," as well as her interest in travelling and her love of Winnipeg, where Shields lived for longer than she lived anywhere else, as we see in her essay "At Home in Winnipeg."

This section also includes two dozen previously unpublished essays, from autobiographical memories of Christmas in "Gifts" and "Christmas Interruptus" to memories of emigrating from the United States to Canada in "Coming to Canada," with all the challenges of learning about her new country and comparing it with the country of her birth. "Did Anything Much Happen to You in the Fifties?" reflects on social progress from the 1950s to the 1960s and introduces the emergence of famous Canadian women writers. It also includes essays on the interrelationship of reading and writing, always so important to Shields, including "Writers Are Readers First" and "The Reader-Writer Arc," in which she discusses poetry and drama, followed by "Books that Meant," which focuses on her formative childhood reading.

In "The Writer's Second Self," Shields addresses the tendency of reviewers and critics to mistake an author's fiction for autobiography. In "The Writing Life," she acknowledges a writer's anxiety about reviews and the reactions of friends and family to one's books: "How fragile we writers are," she admits (*MF* 81). She mentions the excuses that men offer for not reading her books, claiming that they are buying them for their wives. At one book launch, she was so tired of hearing this excuse that, when a man explained "I'm buying this for my wife," adding "She's the reader in the family," Shields, according to her daughter Anne Giardini, responded, "Oh, but you know, there are programs for people like you."

In "Making Words/Finding Stories," Shields focuses on narrative and, by reviewing several of her own novels and short stories, explains how she attempted to write the kinds of books that she wanted to read. "My Back Pages" features writers writing about writing, for Shields excels at metafictional and meta-autobiographical elements. Sarah Maloney's assertion in *Swann*—"Pick up a pen and a second self squirms out" (22)—echoes Shields's essay "What You Use and What You Protect," in which Shields reveals her reaction to seeing her face on the cover of her book: "She's my shadow self, my subjunctive self, a distant cousin who is only on nodding acquaintance with the person in the room with the shut door" (*SI 65*).

Several of Shields's essays focus on women's writing, including "Women's Voices in Literature," in which Shields acknowledges the emergence of women writers, particularly in Canada; "Women and the Short Story," in which she discusses the special success of women writers in the short story genre; and "The Feminine Line," in which she traces a line of descent in Canadian women's writing from the nineteenth century to the twentieth century, from Susanna Moodie to Smaro Kamboureli. Shields's discussions of literature—especially fiction, as Shields challenges the notion of the death of the novel—inform "The New Canadian Fiction." She affirms, "I see evidence of fresh news from another country, which satisfies by its modesty a microscopic enlargement of my own comprehended sense of the world." She adds, "I wouldn't dream of asking for more."

Her preoccupation with women's writing inevitably leads to an interest in gender and the relationship between genders as expressed in fiction. In "Crossing Over," Shields discusses "the experience-plus-imagination recipe that makes fiction possible." In "Writers' Gender Swapping," she discusses authors who focus their novels on a character of the opposite sex from their own, producing some of the greatest novels, and heroes and heroines, ever written, from Gustave Flaubert's *Madame Bovary* to Thomas Hardy's *Tess of the D'Urbervilles* and Leo Tolstoy's *Anna Karenina*.[3] Shields explores the particular problems facing women writers, including male critics' opposition to women's composition of narratives featuring male protagonists. In some of her essays, beginning with "Women's Voices in Literature" and continuing with "Women and the Short Story" and "The Feminine Line," her discussion of writing becomes more explicitly feminist.

Three of Shields's numerous convocation addresses, each previously unpublished, are included here: her "Address to University of Winnipeg Graduands" in 1996, "University of Winnipeg Luncheon Address," and her "University Leadership and Social Change: Change and Preservation—Culture, Values, and Society" at the University of Ottawa, her alma mater, in 1998. In the first address, Shields announces, "instead of advice, instead of wisdom, I offer, against the tidal wave of the electronic era, a few thoughts about the reading of books" because, she argues, "attentive readers of serious fiction cannot help but be compassionate and ethical citizens." She believes that "reading shortens the distance we must travel to discover that our most private perceptions are, in fact, universally felt." She wrote in a notebook, "When I meet someone who says I read cookbooks as if they were novels, I want to say, maybe you'd be a more interesting person if you read novels," adding, "And not so fat."[4] In "University Leadership and Social Change," Shields, with her characteristic love of literature, especially fiction, frames her address as a series of five stories or emblematic narratives.

This section includes two of Shields's term papers from her years as a graduate student studying Canadian literature at the University of Ottawa. "Idealism and Pragmatism in Two Novels of Sara Jeannette Duncan" focuses on *The Imperialist* (1904) and *Cousin Cinderella (1908)*. "The Two Susanna Moodies" refers to the actual author Moodie—as reflected in her writings, including *Life in the Clearings* and *Roughing It in the Bush*—and the fictional Moodie as portrayed in Margaret Atwood's poetic sequence *The Journals of Susanna Moodie* (1970). Shields claims that the actual Moodie "bears little resemblance to Atwood's dour introspective Susanna" and concludes, "it is to be hoped that someday someone will write a narrative poem about the real Susanna Moodie, whose spirit not only survived but overcame." These two term papers should give heart to graduate students because they demonstrate how a student can become an award-winning author who deserves to be dubbed "the Canadian Shields."

"The Healing Journey," in which Shields reflects on her life, might be her most autobiographical and metafictional essay in this collection. One of the last pieces that she composed, it acts as a retrospective on her writing career as she reviews the various periods of her life, comparing them to the chapters of a novel.

By making her previously unpublished and uncollected stories and essays available to readers, I hope that this volume can illuminate the chapters of Carol Shields's writing life for her admirers.

STORIES

Protein Dust[5]

Irene at sixty wears her tinted hair in a soft, straight cut. She's kept her figure, more or less, and people often comment on her exemplary posture, head erect, those nicely shaped shoulders of hers, her straight back.

It gives her a kind of ironic pleasure to announce that she has been gently brought up, meaning that as a child she had been taught certain behaviours were acceptable in society, and others were not. She would never, for instance, apply lipstick while seated at a restaurant table, as many women do these days, whipping out their compacts, smoothing and pursing their lips, smacking their mouths, so that anyone, friends or strangers, bear witness to this private act—which is only a notch, in Irene's opinion, above the public picking of teeth or the scratching of elbows.

And certainly, she knows better than to file her nails in a public place. But something happened, an emergency of sorts. The middle nail of her left hand broke off crudely as she was removing a glove, and so she pulled an emery board from her bag and tried to smooth away the damage.

She was on an airplane when this occurred, flying over Quebec, on her way to Halifax to spend a few days with her niece, Caroline, who was dying of a rare form of spinal cancer. Caroline is thirty-three years old and has a husband and two small daughters.

The young man seated beside Irene, the aisle seat, started when he saw her nail file working away. Or rather, he strained abruptly against his seat belt. "Do you realize," he said in a loud voice, "that you're scattering your protein dust on those who don't necessarily want it?"[6]

Other passengers seated nearby turned briefly at the sound of his accusation, or at least it seemed to Irene they did.

"I interpret your tone as being offensive," Irene said after a minute, and then they sat rigid in their seats, the two of them, Irene finding it difficult to draw in breath normally. She should have basked, she told herself, in the priestly stillness of a debt, which, for the moment, seemed settled. At the least, she had replied. But this young man's petty irritation at her trimming a single fingernail, when placed against the broadside tragedy she was about to encounter, stung like an electric shock. In fact, she found herself shaking all over.

The flight attendant—who was not beautiful as they once used to be and not even particularly charming—offered drinks from the trolley. Irene's seat mate ordered a beer—wouldn't you know it—which he sipped at sullenly, and Irene chose tomato juice with lemon. It tasted of metal. She should've stuck with her usual mineral water.

Protein dust, protein dust. That's what Irene is now, a compaction of dust, even though sixty is not really old, not an age when one is prepared to surrender and revert to primordial matter. Protein dust. The phrase rang in syncopation with her beating heart. How to dismiss its diminishing echo, shut it off? She must distract herself, but how? Dust clouds. Dust balls. Dust to dust.

Twenty years were added suddenly to her body, which tingled now, burning, freezing, protesting, cramped against itself. This leaky, needy, self-disclosing body. She drew a magazine from her bag and pretended to read. Would this officious young man beside her look up from his beer and newspaper and observe that she had brought for reading matter not some cheap escapist fiction which is believed to be the regular fare for Irene's age group but the most recent issue of *The Circle*, a respected literary quarterly which he can't possibly be acquainted with? Irene is, in fact, the editor and founder of *The Circle*, but to this crudely barbered person she is only an elderly woman who files her nails in public. Who has no place aboard a public aircraft. An irritant to others, an outrage.

The Circle's winter issue is dedicated to the question of poetry in the twenty-first century. Not what poetry will become but whether it will continue to exist at all in the future. Irene's good friend Aaron Jaffe has contributed a remarkable piece, but then everything that comes out of that man's pen is perceptive and elegant. Grete Jarr Hanson, writing on the subject of the prose poem, its failures, its tediousness, has brought a much-needed counterargument to the pages. Poetry is doomed by its own elitism, Hanson contends, and has overstayed its welcome. Irene's own modest introduction rides a middle ground between the two.

She busies herself with these thoughts. She is proud of her thoughts, proud of their detachment and range.

It happens that her peripheral vision is excellent—a driving instructor once commented on the fact; this would have been forty years ago—and now, from the corner of her eye, she can see an idea working across her seat mate's face. His eyelids stretched involuntarily, and then his lip muscles twitched, rather unattractively. It was not difficult to imagine his throat dealing with a series of hard, careful swallows.

She could tell he was framing a secondary attack on her person. For example: Her perfume overwhelms and disgusts him. Her elderly arms with their bumps and veins are an affront and the backs of her hands. Her apparent sexlessness threatens all that his sprung, muscular body embraces. What right does this woman have, he is thinking, contaminating the space of others and infringing on their (his) liberties, never mind that she is a serious person on a serious errand, hastening to the bedside of a beloved niece.

Irene waits for the explosion to come. She turns the pages of the winter issue. There is a typo on page seven. Another on page twelve. She couldn't care less. But what does she care about? She's left that place behind, the world where people are standing on their hind legs and saying, "Ah" or "Magnificent."

Concentration is impossible now. All she can think is dust, dust, my dust. My body, my brain. Filling up the healthy world with its powdery inconsequence.

She's noticed in her relatively long life how sudden disappearances of feeling or illusion can occur. Pain enters people's lives like a hot needle, or else it drops a rock on their heads or comes at them like an advancing wall of earth. Which is more injurious?—these major assaults or small accidents of spite? And how is such pain to be measured?

One minute Irene's arrangements seem as simple as sand or glass; an instant later she is gasping for air and for some indication that she is worthy and deserving of a place on the planet. The shadow comes from nowhere. She should be conditioned to it, able to say here it comes again! But it is always a surprise. She had boarded the plane this morning feeling she might offer comfort and diversion to Caroline and her family, but now she sees what reality is.

Oh, she sees it clearly. She is a troublesome, needy relative who will only be in the way. Who asked her to come, anyway?—someone may actually voice this consciousless question. What to do with her? The eccentric aunt with her literary pretensions, her circle of intellectual friends, who have nothing better to think about than the death of poetry—this in the face of real death, a young woman, her body devoured and discoloured by bruises while the undeserved health of others brings only rebuke.

She has assigned herself a foolish errand. If she had the power to turn the plane around, to go home, to forget this mission, she would.

Once, years ago, a man said to her, "I love you, but I wonder if I could express just one quibble."

"What?" she asked, thinking he was about to say something playful, something sensual.

"It's the way you're always digging around in your handbag."

"What?" she said again, not quite understanding.

"It gets on my nerves. I know it's a little thing, but when you do it, when you *rummage* like that, I look at you, and I'm sorry but—I can't stand it."

She hated him. Hated him for possessing such a quibble, for articulating it, and for opening his silly mouth and speaking of it. Instantly, the flash of hatred became a solid force, and she immediately cut off all contact with him. Being labelled *a purse rummager* inflicted much greater pain than the generalized sexual deceit she'd known from other men and was more destructive by far than the rejection she sometimes encountered in the literary world. She remembers that she went to bed for three weeks after the purse rummaging accusation. Her friends worried about her or at least pretended to worry. She lost twenty pounds. Other people recover from such slights, but it seems Irene doesn't have that ability. Even after all these years, her body remembers the bruising and holds onto it.

But this man seated next to her had provoked an even greater ire. It tormented her that he should know that she once had lovely arms and for that reason favoured sleeveless dresses—there was one in particular, in deep pink linen, beautifully cut. He had no idea about her three weeks in bed, a casualty of a casual remark, or her confusion following last week's meeting of *The Circle* board, the suggestion that it might be time for her to step down as editor, that a more aggressive and contemporary policy was called for. And certainly, he knew nothing about her approaching grief for a niece who is really more of a daughter to her.

For this man, Irene was a bundle of protein dust, shedding it carelessly, littering the earth, spoiling the world.

And now, just as the plane was beginning its descent, he finished his beer. An audible gulp, Irene was sorry to notice. He wore a disgusting wetness about his lips. He turned to her and said something which she didn't really hear or want to hear, but her old courtesy, her instincts, compelled her to lean in his direction.

"Forgive my earlier rudeness," he said. "Please."

Forgiveness. An old-fashioned word not often heard these days. Perhaps he learned it from strict parents or from some Jesuit boarding school he'd been sent to and made aware of the healing arc of confession and absolution. To forgive. A poetic verb with a poem's rounded allusiveness. But it's too much to ask, isn't it?—the dispensing of easy consolation. Some injuries will not repair themselves or allow themselves to be buried. Besides, the day may soon come when Irene's injuries are all that is available to her.

She heard her seat mate gather up his breath into a sort of sob, and that odd strangled human noise almost, but not quite, undid her. "I cannot afford to forgive you," she told him, speaking the truth. "I regret to say that I cannot."

A Message from Beyond[7]

As a colour, I like purple. Also certain shades of violet. Mauve I can take or leave. Dusty rose—well, it depends; I once had a dusty rose dressing gown, voluminous and furry, a present from Arthur. But pink I detest. Always have. Almost every year it seems I pick up a fashion magazine down at the hairdressers and read that shrill message: "Pink Is Back." There'll be a model with a wide-open mouth and a banner angled across her skinny hips saying, "Paint the Town Pink" or "Get into the Pink of Things." I always sit back and shake my wet head and mutter, not me, not me.

And now, suddenly, Arthur and I have a grown-up daughter, age twenty-eight, who's moved back in with us, and her name is Pinky.

It used to be Arlene, after Arthur's Aunt Arlene in Brampton. Auntie Arlene once took me aside—this was back in 1954, the day before Arthur and I got married—and she said, "You are embarking on a grand adventure." I remember looking at her small fruity eyes and dented chin and thinking, what would Auntie Arlene know about marriage? She'd never married herself, never even moved out of her two-storey house in Brampton, Ontario, a house with a grey painted porch and the smell of mothballs within; she'd never done anything; she had a scratchy voice which sounded like she'd swallowed a cardful of hairpins. Nevertheless, she was whispering into my ear and promising me a grand adventure—which was more than I'd been led to expect. It did turn out to be an adventure—I think I knew this in the first week of our marriage—and out of gratitude we named our baby daughter Arlene—though Arthur would've preferred the name Astrid.

Now she's twenty-eight, divorced, and working as a pediatrician at the Calgary General. And when the phone rings these days, the person most often asked for is Pinky. Is Pinky there? May I please speak to Pinky? Only a week ago someone even said in a deep growl, is this Pinky's place? As a matter of fact, he phoned again today. "Yes," I said with a spot of vinegar on my tongue, "yes, this is Pinky's place. And this is Pinky's mother." Would he care to leave a message?

"A message?" He said this as though it were a word in a foreign language. Then he said, "Could you tell Pinky that Robert phoned. She's got my number."

Oh, she does, does she?

You might wonder how anyone could go, almost overnight, from Arlene to Pinky. What happened was that she married a rather quiet and polite man called Andrew Rose, and before we knew it she was calling herself Pinky Rose. A friend of hers started it, a kind of joke, and it stuck. Then she left Andrew; they wanted different things, she said. What things?—we felt we had a right to ask. Just things, she said in that maddening way she has. She dropped the Rose but kept the Pinky. "I've always wanted a nickname," she tells me. "And as a matter of fact, I've always hated my name."

She says this in a bent, bitter voice in which I can hear more than a portion of blame. Clearly, I am the guilty one, the one who had given her a name that was blatantly unacceptable and which did not lend itself to a nickname. It is, she hints, a kind of deprivation.

"Your father wanted Astrid," I tell her in a sly move to shift the blame.

"Astrid's just as bad," she says. "You can't get a nickname out of Astrid. At least not a decent nickname."

"Lots of people don't like nicknames," I tell her. "They think they're silly. They think they're demeaning."

"When I was in junior high," Arlene says, "I would have given any-thing, *anything*, to be a Molly or a Polly or a Missy or a—"

I tell her about an old school friend of mine named Stephanie Lester. "We called her Stuffy. Imagine that! How would you like to go through your whole life being called something like Stuffy?"

"I love being called Pinky," she says. "It makes me feel like a different person. It makes me feel thinner and prettier. And more cheerful. I wish you and Dad could get used to—"

"We're trying," I say. "Just give us time."

It's six o'clock in the evening. Arlene has just got home from the hospital, and we're having this discussion in the kitchen, where I am standing, with a knife in my hand, deboning chicken breasts. As it happens, it's one of the few things I do extremely well. All it takes is confidence—so said Madame Margot Gulcher of the Cordon Bleu, with whom I studied French cooking one winter when we lived in Halifax. You've got to bear down on that translucent ridge of bone, you've got to maintain pressure, and the knife must be very sharp. You need an excellent overhead light. Plus a steady hand.

"You should make soup out of those bones," says Pinky/Arlene.

"Hmmmmm," I say.

"Makes a terrific soup base," she says. "Better than that powdered stuff."

"I suppose." I want to be agreeable.

"And the nutritional value—"

I am melting butter in a cast iron frying pan, hoping she won't notice how much. This is tricky territory.

"And the broccoli," she says, lifting the lid of my saucepan. "All those stems you throw away. They're great in soup too."

What kind of mother am I? I have neglected to provide my daughter with a nickname, not to mention a sibling. I have failed to produce hearty homemade soups. And what else? Oh, yes, the worst thing of all. All the moving around we've done over the years.

We started out in Toronto, Arthur and I. Then there were three years in Thunder Bay—only it wasn't called Thunder Bay then. Then the Ottawa stretch—Arthur couldn't very well say no to a chance like that—and then the two years in Halifax, then back to Ottawa, and then, finally, out here to Walnut Hills, a grassy green suburban chunk on the west side of Calgary. We've been here six years now, and the way the economy is going it looks as though we may be here forever.

I should explain that there is only one walnut tree in Walnut Hills, a black walnut stuck between two garages on Second Avenue. If you go down the back lane and peer over the high cedar fence, you can get a good look at it. It seems that in 1923 a man and his wife came here from Minnesota determined to grow black walnuts as a cash crop. But the climate here was wrong for the species, and all the trees died except for this one, which seems to have been especially hearty or fortuitously sheltered. I discovered all this—though not what happened to the couple from Minnesota—when I was helping out with the local history project for the Walnut Hills Library.

"It's ironic," Arlene says. "I mean, finally, when I grow up and get married and move away, then finally the two of you decide it's time to settle down."

I try to defend myself. And Arthur too. "It's the company that decides, not us."

"The company!" She gives a snort. She has a round clever face like her father's. The roundness frightens her. Every morning I hear her weighing herself, and quite often I wake to the thump-thump-thump which is Arlene in the room next to ours, landing hard on her exercise mat. Her room has a hectic temporary air with a carton or two in the corner still unpacked. She keeps her jewellery, her earrings and beads, in a pottery bowl I made when I was in my pottery phase. That was in Ottawa, our first time there.

I still hear from Doris Hart, who was in the pottery group. Also Louise Symington and Cathy Ford. At Christmas, I get cards from all these people, with scrawled messages—field dispatches as it were. "Children all in university" or "We're off to Mexico" or "I'm back at university, imagine that!" I also hear from people in Thunder Bay, Halifax, and Toronto. Sometimes there are messages about deaths or divorces or terrible operations. Sometimes there are messages which say "Not much news," and in a way these are the worst of all. Sometimes there are appalling newsletters, jokey duplicated sheets, some in rhymed couplets, which tell us who in the family has taken up the French horn and who has got his Senior Swimming Award and so on. Nevertheless, I read every word, grateful and always a little surprised to be connected to this intense and random network.

Instead of counting sheep at night, I do a mental slideshow of all our houses, starting at the duplex in Willowdale, four rooms and a bath. I go over it slowly like a prospective buyer, taking my time, opening closet doors, looking out the windows, knocking on the tops of radiators, running a hand over the yellow wallpaper we put in the baby's rooms, yellow stripes with grey kittens tumbling over each other. Then moving to Port Arthur, a complete break, a split level, brand new with attached garage, raised fireplace—smoky though—and then, before we knew it, we were in Ottawa refinishing floors in a tall tippy house in Sandy Hill and installing a new light fixture in the kitchen, and then—but by then I'm usually sound asleep.

Something used to happen to Arthur when a transfer was in the air, a new look of liveliness, a shine in the eye. We'd get out the atlas, carry books home from the library, and send away for newspapers. There was a heady countdown to the final day, and we could feel ourselves growing lighter and lighter. The air seemed almost too thin to breathe, and the two of us would lie in bed hanging on to each other and taking a perverse pleasure in the emptying house and the thought of a new house, a new neighbourhood, and new green trees leafing out in seasons that would be subtly different. Bending over carboard cartons filled with bedsheets and kitchen plastic, we felt ourselves to be young and braver than we were, the sort of people who were willing to take on anything.

And our daughter Arlene? How did she take these moves?

Ah, but here is where I don't entirely trust my memory. Six different schools, she says to me in aggrieved tones. Six schools in twelve years!

It would be hard on anyone; new friends, new teachers, new rules to memorize. Why then do I see in my mind's blue eye a little girl dancing with excitement, rushing through bare rooms, flinging open windows, shrieking with discovery. Or, in another mood, her small face, sober and thoughtful, making measured comparisons: Mrs. Whetstone was prettier than Miss Purse, the buses were more modern than the old buses, there were more kids in the new neighbourhood, the school was closer, the crossing guard not so bossy. She always mailed postcards back to the old friends, and one friend, Sue Grumchuk from Grade Five, still writes occasionally and even sent a wedding gift when Arlene married Andrew.

"I suppose Dad will want a martini when he gets home," Pinky/ Arlene says, opening a cupboard and getting out three glasses.

"Yes," I say in a voice which I hope sounds offhand and speculative. "He probably will."

"You should try to get him to switch to spritzers instead," she says.

"Oh?" My question-mark voice, bright and zestful.

"Less alcohol," she tells me bluntly. "And fewer calories." At the word *calories*, her eyes travel to my hips.

"I'll have a club soda," I say quickly. "With a slice of lemon."

"And Dad?"

"His usual, I guess."

"You don't think he'd at least like to try a spritzer tonight?"

"I don't think so."

"I think, if he tried one, he'd like it. He'd probably—"

"I don't think so," I say more firmly. The chicken is turning golden in the pan. Using my Belle Cuisine tongs, I turn each piece with care. There is a rising scent of fresh ginger. "And by the way, someone called Robert called."

"Robert? Really?"

"Really. He wants you to phone him."

"Did he leave a number?"

"He said you had it."

"I do, yes."

"Who's Robert?" Normally, I lack the courage to pry, but something about the way Arlene is staring into her spritzer makes me brave.

"Robert? Oh, he's just someone I've met. At the hospital."

"Nice?" What a question. What does nice mean anyway?

"Nice enough."

It's time to transfer the tender pieces of chicken to a heated casserole and make the orange-cognac sauce.

"Well," Arlene says socially, "how did your day go?"

"Fine. Fine." I set the casserole gently in the oven.

"Get any painting done?"

"Not today, I'm afraid. I—"

"I thought you were going to work on that still life. The cream jug with the pear sitting next to it."

"Just couldn't find a minute all day."

"I thought you were going to start taking your painting more seriously."

"I am. I really am."

"I thought you were going to give it *priority*."

"Well, I am, but today was a Chestnut day."

"Oh, them!" Pinky/Arlene moans.

I used to belong to a book discussion group called The New Nuts, new because we were all people who had recently moved to Walnut Hills, but a year ago we decided we'd come of age and were now a bunch of old chestnuts—so now we're The Chestnut Reading Club.

"We had an interesting discussion," I tell Arlene.

"Oh?" She looks interested. Mildly interested.

"About the impermanence of life."

"Such as?"

"Such as we are living in a throw-away world. Think of the ballpoint pen. We just throw them away, admit it. People used to get a fountain pen for graduation and keep them the whole of their lives."

"What if you got tired of it?"

"And books. A book used to be a prized possession. You'd hand it down from father to son."

"Or mother to daughter," Arlene says. A subtle correction.

"And now we toss them out or leave them on buses. And people used to save letters. Tie them up with ribbons. Now we just telephone. You can't save a telephone call."

"Speaking of telephones, I'd better call Robert back."

I'm just warming up. "And pictures. People used to have pictures that they valued and kept forever. Now they just have posters, and when they get a bit ragged around the edges you just throw them out and get more."

"Not everyone," Arlene says. "*You* don't."

"That's true," I say, pleased with myself and pleased with Arlene for noticing.

Arthur and I treasure our pictures, and whenever we've moved I've worried that one of them would be damaged. But the moving companies are surprisingly careful. They have special cartons of rigid cardboard for pictures, and each one is separately packed. Once, though, one of the boxes must have got jiggled too much, and when we opened it we saw that the picture, a watercolour of pansies in a blue bowl, had come unglued from the mat and was hanging crooked behind the glass. This was when we moved to Ottawa, the second time. Arlene, who was in high school at the time, offered to fix it. I remember that she sat down at the kitchen table and removed all the little nails at the back of the picture with a pair of pliers. (She had always been good with her hands.) And there, between the picture and the brown paper backing was a little strip of paper with something written on it. A message.

Today I remind her about the picture and ask her if she remembers the message.

"Vaguely," she says. Her forehead puckers prettily.

"It was written, or rather printed, on a little scrap of paper," I tell her. "And it said, 'Peace be with you, now and forever.'"

"Is that what it said? I thought it said, '*Love* be with you, now and forever.'"

"Maybe you're right. Yes, I think you're right. It was love."

"It was so neatly printed. I remember now just how it looked."

"And we tried to figure out how it had got there."

"A true mystery."

"It had to be someone or other at the framers. One of the people who worked there."

"Why would anyone do that? I wonder."

"Well, this was a few years ago," I remind her. "There was lots of peace and love and brotherhood going around in those days. A regular epidemic."

"But just imagine," Arlene says dreamily. "Imagine someone sending us a message like that. Out of the blue."

"The really amazing thing is that it was there all those years. I can't even remember where it was I had it framed."

"We should have saved it," Arlene says.

"Yes, we should have."

She's smiling across the kitchen. "It's really marvellous getting a message like that."

Marvellous, she'd said. And it was. It had seemed remarkable at the time, but somehow even more remarkable seen from this distance. "It was like getting a message in a bottle," I said.

"From a total stranger too."

"Who could be anyone at all in this world."

"Maybe someone who's famous now." Her voice trails off.

"Maybe someone who's dead now."

"Dead as a doornail," Arlene says.

An interesting expression that, dead as a doornail. I read something about it not long ago. The theory is that it refers to a certain type of decorative brass nail that was used on oak doors in the Elizabethan times. Dead meant the nail was driven in straight, dead straight. I explain this to Arlene, but she doesn't seem to be listening.

"Mother," she says.

"Yes?"

"About the man who phoned today."

"Robert?"

"Yes."

"What about him?"

"He's—"

"He's what?"

"He's really quite an interesting man."

I fluff the rice with a fork and say, "Uhuh." It doesn't seem politic to say more than this.

"What I mean is he's intelligent, he's got a kind of vitality about him that, well, that Andrew never seemed to have."

"I see."

"For instance, he's done a lot of travelling. He's been everywhere. Europe. The west coast of Africa. Everywhere."

"Wonderful."

"He sails. And plays soccer like a pro."

"Really? That's wonderful."

"No, it isn't," she says. "It isn't." Her voice has become suddenly ragged, and I busy myself by checking the sauce, giving it a stir.

"He's married," she says. And then she says it again. "Married."

"Oh," is all I can manage.

"With three children. A boy and two girls."

"Oh." Such eloquence.

"One of the little girls is three, and the other is five."

There is a short silence. I don't move. Then Pinky/Arlene says, "I'm not going to phone him back. I was going to, but I'm not. It's just too . . . too damn untidy. Don't you think so?" The word *untidy*, a strange fussy word, hangs in the air along with the ginger fumes and the smell of orange peel. It's a word I seldom use. My mother used it. Women like Auntie Arlene used it.

I have an urge to reach out and stroke my daughter's hair. It is an overwhelming urge, and I *do* reach out and stroke her hair, my baby, my little girl, my Pinky. Pinky. I say it out loud, and she looks up smiling.

"You said it," she says.

I have said it. Heaven knows why. Not to cajole her or reward her or give her comfort or to send her a message. Suddenly, for no reason at all, it seems to be her proper name.

The Golden Boy,
or Some Things Only Happen Once[8]

Every summer, as soon as school's out, we get into the car and drive to Saskatchewan, where my grandmother lives. From Toronto, this takes exactly four days. Not exactly a ride around the block—as my mother likes to say. At night, we camp out in this old blue tent we have, which is the part I used to hate before this thing happened last year.

When we drive to Saskatchewan, we have a countdown. Day One is getting out of the city, and then you're into farms and lots of little towns. "What do you suppose they do *here* on a Saturday night?" my father says when we go through some of those little towns. Day One goes fast because my brother and I read comics in the back seat, and we always stop at Wawa to have our picture taken sitting on this big goose statue they have there.

Days Two and Three are bush. This is the part my father really hates. When you've seen one mile of jack pine, he says, you've seen it all. You just drive along the highway, and all you see is this curving road cutting through trees. Boring boring boring. Once in a while there might be a lake, and if you're lucky you might get to see a moose poking his head out of the trees, being nosy. Which has happened to us four times. Gophers we don't even count. There are millions of gophers.

Day Four is prairie. What a relief, my mother always says, and for a while it is. There are grain elevators you can see fifteen miles off and towns with hilarious names, but it's a long way just the same to Alsask, where my grandmother lives. My mother says this must be the only country in the world where you can drive two thousand miles and not see one single city. "What about Winnipeg?" my father asks, but my mother would rather bypass Winnipeg, and so that's what we always used to do.

Grandma lives in a yellow wood house with a woodstove in the kitchen and potbelly stove in the front room. My parents sleep in my father's old bedroom that smells like mildew, and my brother and I set up the tent in the backyard, and that's where the two of us sleep.

Grandma is a bit balmy. She gets lost just going to the store for a loaf of bread. She gets our ages and even our names all mixed up, and lots of times she calls me Colin, which is my dad's name. "You need a haircut, Colin," she said to me last summer. "You need to have your ears set out." Most of the time Grandma hardly knows we're there. She just sits there dunking her toast in her tea and watching TV. One funny thing is that her favourite program is *Loveboat*. It spooks me when I think of Grandma sitting in her kitchen watching *Loveboat* the same as we do in Toronto.

Sometimes she knits mittens in front of the TV, but they're always miles too small for us. We have a whole drawerful of these too-small mittens at home, and every time my father looks at them he shakes his head and says, "Well, it's sad." "Poor old Gran," he says, just as though she was his grandmother instead of his mother.

Grandma never says to us kids, "Here's a quarter to spend" or "Come give Grandma a big kiss." She just sort of lets us do what we want. We can pick raspberries any time we want, even in the middle of the night if we get a hunger attack. We can make hideouts in her bushes and stay up half the night reading Dad's old Hardy Boys books,[9] which are still there, all lined up on a shelf in his old bedroom. After a week of this, though, we're bored out of our skulls and can't wait to start off for home. Another four days on the road. This has been going on for years.

There's a radio in the car, but it never works right except for a little while around Winnipeg and maybe when you get close to Thunder Bay. I read comics in the car, but my brother, Gary, gets carsick after a while. Sometimes we play "Twenty Questions" or this animal game we made up where you get one point if you see a chicken or a cow, twenty points for a white horse, fifty points for a sheep, and a thousand for a camel or an elephant. We also have this card we can spin, and it asks you skill questions like what is the capital of Prince Edward Island? or what is the provincial flower of Newfoundland? The answers are Charlottetown and the pitcher plant. We know them backwards and forwards.

It seems like it's twice as far going back. Just to break the monotony, we always ask if we can stop at Winnipeg,[10] where my mother grew up, but until last year we never did. There's a bypass right around it, and we always took that. My mother says it makes her feel too sad to go back to Winnipeg. There aren't any relatives left there, and she's lost track of her old friends from school, and the worst thing is that the house where she used to live got torn down. It's just not worth it, she says, putting herself through an emotional wringer.

"What's a wringer?" Gary asks.

"Honestly," my mother says, "you modern kids!" And then she tells us what a wringer is, which is part of an old-fashioned washing machine.

It gets hot in the car, and there are always about a hundred flies buzzing away or maybe even a wasp. My mother sleeps when my father drives, and he sleeps when she takes over. Gary sleeps most of the time. I never sleep, and that's my problem. I can't sleep in the car, and I can't sleep at night when we get to the campsite. Travelling gives me insomnia.

"You don't get insomnia when you're eleven years old," my dad says.

"Well, he certainly *seems* to have it." My mother says this as though I'm in the next room instead of right next to her at the campsite pumping up my air mattress.

"Maybe he puts too much air in that thing," my father says. "You've got to leave it a little bit of slack."

"Maybe you're cold," my mother says, which is hilarious because we've got these down-filled sleeping bags.

"He could be allergic to something." My father has a lot of theories about allergies.

"Maybe he's scared of bears," my brother, Gary, says.

My parents stop and look hard at me. Last summer there was a bear nosing around the tent one night, looking for food. But I know a bear wouldn't get in where we are. We keep the food locked up in the trunk of the car, and besides he's more scared of us than we are of him. That's what it says in our *See Canada* guidebook.

The truth is I don't know why I have insomnia. It just seems there are always so many things to be thinking about. I start in thinking, and then I just can't get settled down to sleep. So I lie there half the night, just turning over and over and listening to the sounds outside, the owls hooting and the wind blowing and, inside, to Gary snoring and my mother and father breathing away. They all sleep like logs. When the birds start singing and the sky starts getting light—that's when I finally get to sleep. That's when my father comes along and says, "Come on, kiddo, we want to get an early start today."

One night last summer, when we were lying there in the tent with the light off, we got to talking about different ways to fall asleep. Gary says he shuts his eyes and starts to recite the capitals of all the countries in Asia and Europe. Then he starts on South America, and halfway through, wham, he's asleep. Not bad for nine years old. That's how he does it, just lying there thinking of that long list. My father, yawning, says it must be a form of self-hypnosis.[11]

There's a little silence, and then my mother says, "I think of throwing freethrows."

"What do you mean, freethrows?" my father says.

"Like in basketball," she says. "Back in junior high, I used to play basketball."

You could tell my father was surprised to hear this. They've been married for eighteen years, and he never knew this, that my mother had played basketball. "You never told me that," he says.

"You never asked," she says back.

"Were you a star?" I can't help asking.

"Well," she says, shifting in her sleeping bag and trying to sound modest, "I guess you could say I was. At least in the freethrow department."

"But why?" My father was sort of laughing, and I could tell he was trying to picture my mother standing in a gym and throwing a freethrow.

"I don't know exactly," she says. "We had this basketball hoop on the back of our garage, and I used to practise all the time. I remember I used to go out in the morning even before school had started. Then at lunchtime I'd be out there again squeezing in half an hour's practice. And after school we'd shoot baskets until suppertime and then, after supper, the same thing."

"What about the snow?" I ask. "I thought it was supposed to be cold and snowy in Winnipeg."

"Not in the summer," my mother says. "And there was fall and spring and—"

"But why freethrows?" my father asks. "I mean, why not a real game?"

My mother has to stop and think. "It must have been because there weren't always enough kids around for a game. With freethrows, you could be on your own."

"You were a real expert then?" My father still can't believe all this.

"Well," she says, trying to sound nonchalant, "well, in a way. I mean, anyone *would* be, spending all that time practising. I could do fifty out of fifty, I remember that. But I could never do a hundred out of a hundred. That was my ambition, to sink a hundred out of a hundred."

"Fifty out of fifty! That's amazing," Gary says. "Do you think you could still do it?"

"I'm sure I couldn't. I couldn't do one out of ten now. But I could then."

"I wish I'd seen you," Gary says slowly.

My mother goes on talking. "I used to dream about freethrows," she says. "For about a year, maybe two years. It was the most important thing in my life. I thought of freethrows the first thing in the morning and the last thing at night. And what I liked best were the ones that went straight through the hoop without banking on the board. They just sank through clean and sort of swished through the net. I used to dream about those shots at night."

"Sounds sort of Freudian," my father says.

"What?" Gary says.

"And," my mother is saying, "sometimes when I'm trying to go to sleep, even now, I think of the ball leaving my hands and going up into the air and then swishing through the net. It's like magic. Like a sleeping pill. In two minutes, I'm sound asleep, even on this awful old air mattress, even thinking about bears nosing around—"

"You don't have to worry about bears," I tell her. "They're more afraid of you than—"

"I have a sort of trick too," my father was saying from his side of the tent.

"What kind of trick?" my mother asks. Her voice sounds excited and young, like she'd like to go on talking about throwing freethrows.

"A trick for falling asleep," my father says. "What I do is shut my eyes and think about a black tulip."

"A black tulip?" my mother says. "You mean like a flower?"

"Exactly. A black tulip. They grow in Holland. I read about it, maybe four or five years ago, an article in the paper or in a magazine or something. They've been trying for years and years to develop a black tulip, and they finally did it."

"Who'd want a black tulip?" my mother says.

"I don't know, but people do. They'd been able to produce these very dark purple ones for years, but they could never get one that was truly black."

"It sounds awful," my mother says. "I can't imagine it."

"They're very much in demand. Something like orchids. And very expensive."

"Just imagine," my mother says, "if someone brought you a black orchid. What would you think?"

"Well," my father says, giving a giant-sized yawn, "that's what I think of when I want to go to sleep. I just shut my eyes and try to picture this tulip with its big waxy-looking petals, black as ebony."

"Are the leaves black too?" Gary asks.

"I don't think so," my father says. "Anyway, I only think about the flower itself. And, before you can say 'Jack Robinson,' I'm sound asleep. It works like a charm."

"Speaking of going to sleep," my mother says, "maybe we should."

"If we want to hit the road early," my father says.

In a few minutes, they are all asleep, and there I am tossing and turning as usual. I try to picture the list with all the capitals of Europe and Asia, but I get stuck at Hungary. Then I try to think of my mother sinking freethrows, and I even try to picture a big black tulip just sitting there on the end of a stem, but nothing seems to work. It was sad. I was the only one who didn't have a cure. It didn't seem fair.

When we finally got to Alsask last year, things had changed. My grandmother was moving out of her old yellow house and into a room at the retirement centre on the edge of town. We all helped carry over her things for her, her pictures and her dishes and her favourite chair. There was a lounge at the centre with a colour TV that Grandma really went for. She seemed a little less balmy after a couple days and even remembered our names and asked us how we liked the mittens she'd sent us. Instead of staying at the yellow house, we stayed in a motel, and after four or five days my father said to my mother, "Well, what do you think? Should we hit the road?"

"We could be home by the weekend," my mother said, sounding happy, and in an hour we were packed up and on our way. We didn't even go to have egg-foo-yung at the Chinese restaurant in Alsask, which is something we always do, like taking our picture in Wawa every summer sitting on the goose.

"Why don't we drive straight through tonight," my mother said when we were halfway across Manitoba.

"Well," my father said, "I suppose we could this once." You could tell he liked the idea.

"Can we go through Winnipeg?" Gary asked. He always asks this same question. "I've never seen Winnipeg."

"Well," my mother said, still sounding happy, "maybe just this once."

And that was how we happened to be in the middle of Winnipeg at two o'clock in the morning. I must have fallen asleep for a few minutes because all I remember is that my dad had stopped the car and was shaking me and saying, "Well, kiddo, there it is."

It seemed like part of my dream. Here all of a sudden, just jumping up out of the darkness, was this gigantic lighted-up building with a dome and a statue on the top.

"It's the parliament building," my father said.

"The legislative building," my mother said. "That's what they call it here." Gary was rubbing his eyes and trying to wake up. "And on top," my mother said, sounding like a schoolteacher, "is the Golden Boy. Can you see him, kids?"

I rolled down the window so I could see better. There was this golden statue, a kid, balancing up there on one foot. It looked all alone up there, like he was the only one who lived here in Winnipeg. At first, it didn't seem real, and then, after I looked at him for a minute, he seemed almost more real than real.

And this was the funny part. It started to feel like the Golden Boy wasn't just a statue anymore, just something I was looking at in the middle of the night. It was like that statue up there was *me*. I was the one up there balancing on one foot and glowing all over in the light. I could feel what golden skin felt like, cool and smooth with a breeze blowing and the black air all around.

My father said, "I'll give a dollar to whoever can guess how big he is."

"He's not very big," Gary said.

"Bigger than you think," my father said. "I looked it up in the guidebook."

"I really should know," my mother said slowly. "I was the one who grew up in Winnipeg."

"Take a stab."

"Twenty feet," she said at last.

"It's not that big," Gary said. "I'll guess four feet and six inches. Including his arm."

"Well," my dad said, waiting for me to guess, "well, what do you guess?"

"Thirteen feet," I said straight out.

"Sounds like a wild guess to me," my father said. "You sure you don't want to change your mind?"

I was wide awake then. "No," I said. "I'll stick with thirteen feet." I don't know why I said that. It was just something that came to me.

"Then you're exactly right," my father said. "Right on the mark. Thirteen feet exactly."

He had to put on the little overhead light to find a dollar bill in his wallet. I folded it in a special way I have and put it in my jeans pocket.

"Pretty good guess," my mother said. "You sure you didn't sneak a look in the guidebook today?"

"No," I said.

"I'll bet he did," Gary said.

"No," I said again. I hate to be accused of something I didn't do. "I swear on a stack of Bibles."

I don't know whether they believed me or not. It was even hard for me to believe. It was like something had whispered the answer to me, because when I opened up my mouth and said thirteen feet I knew I was going to be right.

My father started the car, and we drove down some dark streets and over a bridge, and before you knew it we were out on the highway again with dark wheat fields running past us on each side, and we seemed to be sailing along in the car, just as smooth as a boat out on the ocean.

In the morning when I woke up, my father was asleep, and my mother was driving. We'd left the prairie behind. There was a lake with jack pine around it and the road curving ahead through the trees.

I felt in my pocket for the dollar. There it was. I pulled it out and took a good look at it. Not that a dollar is such a big deal. As my mother says, what can you buy with a dollar these days? I decided not to spend it. I decided to keep it to remind me of what happened the night before.

I'm still not sure what happened. But I think that sometimes, if you're lucky, something happens to you, and whatever it is it has the same shape as the inside of your head. It all just fits. Like putting a dime in a slot and hearing it go clink. No, it's more like a clunk. But you're the only one who can hear it, that's the funny part.

We may not drive out to Saskatchewan next summer. My mother and father were thinking of flying out there instead, and Gary and I can go to Y camp. I'd like to go back to Winnipeg someday, but it probably wouldn't happen again anyway. Some things happen over and over again, but some things only happen once. When I think about that, I get sort of sad, almost like I'm going to start crying or something. Pretty weird.

But at least I don't get insomnia anymore. I'm cured. I just shut my eyes and think about the Golden Boy up there. He's always just about to step into space with his skin all glowing and not afraid of a single thing. It works like a charm. Before you can blink, wham, I'm sound asleep.

ESSAYS

Gifts[12]

It was Christmas morning, and my brother and sister and I were awake early, sick with excitement, frantic to go downstairs and see what treasures had been heaped under the tree. I was eleven; my brother and sister, twins, were thirteen; it had been years since we'd believed in Santa Claus, but we knew our parents had been up half the night, whispering, wrapping, arranging, preparing for the tableau of Christmas excess, Christmas enchantment.

Our father descended first to make a pot of perked coffee and plug in the tree lights and tune in the radio to Christmas music. Then came my mother in her chenille bathrobe, her coffee cup in hand, positioning herself in the middle of the blue sofa, from which perspective she would be able to see our expressions as we plunged down the stairs with a wild whoop and fell on our presents. Other families, we knew, opened their gifts one at a time, solemnly stretching out the ceremonies, but we were allowed on this one day to plunge and whoop like barbarians.

I was too old for dolls. The Christmas before there had been a slender little wristwatch for me under the tree, subtly disappointing at first but redeemed by its grey cushioned box and the wonderful golden shine of its little hands. And this year there was—but could that possibly be for me? That old blue and white bicycle with rust spots on the back fender and chipped chrome handlebars? "It's second hand," my father explained, "but it's good and solid. I had a run on it myself last night."

I suppose I must have reached out and touched the cold frame.

"I'll adjust the seat for you after breakfast," my father said.

"And tighten that chain guard," my mother added brightly.

There must have been other gifts to open, board games, slippers, but I have no memory of anything but a choking sorrow and a curious muffled humming in my ears. My brother and sister seemed to be moving past me in a different layer of reality, breathing another, richer, variety of oxygen. We must have sat down to my mother's Christmas waffles before we put on our new Christmas mittens and scarves and went out to play. I smiled hard, miming joy, then got on that rattling, rusting bicycle and rode around the neighbourhood, numb with misery. Later I locked myself in the bathroom and wept, with a towel stuffed in my mouth so no one would hear me.

This was the Christmas of 1946, and in these postwar days new bicycles were hard to come by. I knew that perfectly well. My parents had done well to find a second-hand model. Yet the bitter grief of that Christmas lingers and a certain amount of shame too—what kind of ungrateful child was I?—I who grew up to love old things, scarred pine furniture, musty books, antique jewellery. What was it about that bicycle?

Probably only the realization that enchantment could fail, that it could not be guaranteed. And that even in disappointment I was under an obligation to go on smiling and pretending. For there stood my mother and father, beaming, proud, so confident in their expectations. Almost like children themselves. I was going to have to protect them in whatever way I could. It was not going to be easy.

Christmas Interruptus[13]

A few weeks before Christmas my mother took from the highest shelf in her cupboard a large silver-plated tray. She always shook her head when she looked at this tray, the way it had blackened since the previous Christmas. Then, quickly, she busied herself with a tin of silver polish and a linen cloth, taking a concentrated, anticipatory pleasure in the task. When restored to its traditional lustre, this tray was centred on our walnut coffee table, ready to receive the annual onslaught of Christmas cards.

These came slowly at first, then soon became a toppling pile. My mother saved them all, even those sent from our insurance company or from the gas and light utility thanking her for her patronage. Cards, often with photos enclosed, arrived from her old college friends, now married and scattered: Joe and Helen Shoe, Bernard and Isabel Sprafka, Grace and Gladys Betcheler (who never found themselves husbands, the poor things), and Wally and Hap Hartley (she was called Hap at school, my mother explained, because of her happy disposition, though by forty she'd become chronically depressed—but never too depressed to discontinue the exchange of cards).

A card would come one day from my mother's sister in California, covered with tiny, indecipherable writing and containing a five-dollar bill to "help out." This "helping out" gesture never failed to send my mother into a snit, but it was Christmas time—she was soon cheerful again.

The most eagerly awaited card, really a mimeographed letter, came from a man called Alvah Swain. My mother had met Alvah Swain—a journalist, a politician, a friend of Will Rogers —on a train trip she took when she was twenty, and it flattered her to think such an important person remembered the brief connection and honoured it each Christmas season with a detailed account of his busy year. She opened his letters breathlessly and read them aloud to the family, always, of course, setting Mr. Swain into historical context.

My mother's Christmas cards made me see her differently. Her life was wider, more vivid, more thrilling than it appeared. Furthermore— and this seemed close to impossible to believe—she had had a real life before she met my father, before her children were born. Before me.

She might, perhaps, have arranged her Christmas cards on the mantel, as most other people did in those days, or strung them on red yarn in swags up and down the banister. But, no, *this* was her tradition, the silver tray centred on the coffee table, where anyone might sit comfortably on the sofa and take pleasure going through the separate greetings, registering their separate warmth. I never doubted but that she took pride in her act of elegance and originality.

I, too, arrange my cards every year on a silver tray. On the coffee table. I can't imagine doing anything else.

It was years later before it occurred to me that my mother's friend Alvah Swain might have been more than a casual acquaintance.

My mother had rescued the wreath from the attic, unwrapped it from its layers of newspaper, and hung it on the front door. She'd lace the stair rails with ribbon and pinecones, which she'd dipped in a dish of green and silver glitter. Now it was time to make a centrepiece for the dining room table.

These were the great days of centrepieces, the '40s, the '50s. From simple objects, a candle, a fabric remnant, paper towel tubes, tin foil, cotton swabs, pipe cleaners, china figurines, anything at hand, she concocted her seasonal table ornaments. (Our household also boasted centrepieces with Easter and Thanksgiving and Halloween themes, but Christmas received special attention.) She sought ideas from women's magazines and from her friend, Eileen Vogel, who was the local queen of centrepieces. Eileen Vogel once constructed on her dining room table an entire Santa Claus village from twisted crepe paper and burnt-out light bulbs which she'd spray-painted gold and silver.

It's easy to laugh at such arrangements today, but these enterprising women with their resourcefulness and creativity were fuelled by the notion of making something out of nothing—and they did. They yearned to bring a flurry of colour to their tables and to their (our) lives. They glued and cut, wired, stapled, stitched; then they stood back, looking at what they'd accomplished, and said, "Well, well!"

We always had two Christmas trees.

There was the main tree, a balsam usually, since Scotch pines were only for the wealthy. The whole family, my parents, my brother and sister and I, piled into the car on an early dark December night for the annual purchase of the tree, which took place at a neighbourhood lot. After much discussion—height, evenness, health of needles—a tree was chosen and tied by ropes to the car roof. My father later carried the tree into the house and screwed it into the iron stand where it was allowed to "relax" for a day before he put up the eight strings of lights. (Yes, eight! Other families made do with two or three strings, but for some reason our family were rich in Christmas lights.) This setting up of the tree, as far as I remember, was my father's only contribution to our Christmas festivities.

One of my women friends believes that, if Christmas rituals were handed over to men, we would rapidly lose all sense of holiday celebration. What man would select and write and mail a hundred Christmas cards to old school friends? What husband would remember where the Christmas wreath was stored or who wanted a basketball hoop or a nylon backpack for a gift? Why, in fact, would anyone bother? The energy that went into decorating a house with holly and seeking out new ways to decorate sugar cookies belonged to our mothers. They persevered. They did it year after year and with what appeared to be undiminished joy.

Our second tree was a small artificial one with cunning limbs that could be folded out when the Christmas season approached. This tree sat on a table in the front hall of our house, and its only decorations were two dozen or so wishbones. My mother collected these wishbones from our Sunday chickens, dried them carefully, and painted them with brilliant pink nail polish, then hooked them over the tiny branches. According to my mother, everyone "raved" about this tree and especially about the originality of its ornaments. She might have gleaned the idea from *Better Homes and Gardens*, or perhaps she invented it herself during one of her sleepless nights.

What became of that collection of bright and brittle bones? I have no idea. Nor have I replicated the concept, having ambiguous feelings about animal parts. Nevertheless, I glimpse something important about my mother through this memory. She was daring, original, bold, adaptive. She was, in fact, an artist, though she would have laughed out loud at the thought.

Other families had turkey for Christmas dinner, or perhaps a goose, but we had a large roast beef and for dessert something called Plum Duff. This meal could not possibly have come from my mother's Swedish heritage but more likely from the ever-reliable *Better Homes and Gardens*. Our Christmas menu was English. It was different. My mother liked to mention to people the fact that we had an "English" Christmas dinner.

Besides the immediate family, we would be joined at the table—Spode china in the Basket-of-Flowers pattern on a deep brown linen cloth that set it off beautifully—by my mother's bachelor brother, Lloyd, and by my father's sister, our Aunt Marjorie, who was divorced. Aunt Marjorie had once been married to Uncle Fred, but it turned out Uncle Fred was "a rolling stone" and hadn't been heard of in some years. We children were asked not to mention Aunt Marjorie's predicament to those outside the family.

I married, moved to Canada, and acquired an Icelandic mother-in-law whose idea of Christmas dinner closure was something called Carrot Pudding. It sounded outrageous—a dessert made of a common root vegetable. But I was wrong. It was delicious. My own children fell, somehow, into the pattern of making this pudding on a Sunday afternoon in November, with everyone required to give it one stir, for luck, before it was steamed and then stored in a "cool dark place."

I came to see that my mother's preoccupations with Christmas cards, with decorating the house, with the details of a Christmas feast—brought us gusts of instant happiness because they formed part of a series of rituals. That was why we loved and were comforted by them, these repeated ceremonies, always performed in precisely the same order. And now my own immediate family, my son and four daughters, have sifted through the traditions of two sets of grandparents and have fixed on their own tradition—*what we always do*.

And so it was unexpected that we should all gather in Vancouver a few years ago for Christmas. Vancouver was not a Christmas city; it had no snow, no atmosphere, no traditional context. It was too green, too balmy. A cousin lent us his house since he and his family were to be in Mexico, which was infinitely less Christmasy even than Vancouver. I had not remembered that particular year to make a carrot pudding. We had forgotten to order a turkey. "What about spaghetti?" my oldest daughter suggested.

Spaghetti for Christmas dinner?

It was delectable. We spooned it up greedily in an orgy of renunciation. We ate it with happiness. We ate it thinking how liberated we were by our random decision not to be bound by ritual for once. We ate it thinking that this dish before us might become our new ritual—pasta for the birth of Christ, a ceremonial cement binding the family together, something that we would probably be doing every year from now on, *ad infinitum*.

Coming to Canada[14]

A good many American girls of my generation—the '40s, the '50s—led predictable lives: off to college if we were lucky, marriage in the weeks following graduation, a baby the next year, a new house even farther out in the suburbs, a plunge into menu planning or home sewing, then probably joining the PTA or a symphony auxiliary. An American idyll.

What I hadn't counted on was meeting and marrying a young Canadian engineer and spending all my adult life in a different country, that geographical blur at the top of the map, coloured always a bright pink to match Rhodesia, Australia, and, of course, England, the Mother Country. (How solemn that seemed to my young ears—the Mother Country.) Canada was said to be America's "friendly neighbour to the north," a subtitle that sounded both dismissive and bland, although it was oddly comforting in those Cold War days to think that someone out there liked the United States.

What did I know then of this northerly good neighbour? Almost nothing. Once I'd been taken to see Barbara Ann Scott, Canada's darling, skate on a tiny square of ice at the old Chicago Theater. And like others of my era, I'd grown up with *Life Magazine* photos of the Dionne Quintuplets. People went to Canada for their honeymoons, I knew that, and came back with tales of avid tea drinking, formal table manners, and a queen who was somehow involved in the life of the nation, even though she actually lived thousands of miles away in Buckingham Palace.

There were those handsome Mounties with their red jackets and broad-brimmed hats. And people who spoke French and people who didn't. And what else? The Canadian Rockies, which were somehow cleaner and more photogenic than our Rockies; in my mind's eye, these mountains merged with an image of a virile, plaid-shirted male standing hip-deep in a sparkling stream, expertly casting for trout. Winnipeg, Montreal—I knew these were the names of Canadian cities, but I couldn't have placed them on a map. Toronto, I believed, was located somewhere off in the mists of northern Ohio.

I immigrated on a Sunday afternoon in 1957, twenty-two years old, arriving at the Bellingham, Washington, border point, and handing over my clutch of documents and my full-sized chest x-ray, which "on no account" could be folded. The troublesome x-ray had accompanied us on our one-week honeymoon through the western states, riding atop a pile of wedding presents in the back seat of the car. The immigration officer, yawning, scratching, stamped my papers, and in the blink of an eye our wedding gifts were transformed into "Settler's Effects." And I had become a "Landed Immigrant."

"Wasn't it a terrible wrench?" people ask me. "To leave the country of your birth?"

It didn't seem so at the time. I was deeply in love, for one thing, and, in the daze of newly married life, I was oblivious to national borders. The highway that carried my young husband and me from the state of Washington into British Columbia seemed smoothly uniform and continuous, and the green fields and forests we glimpsed from the car windows travelled along with us over the frontier, an unbroken landscape. I do remember stopping for a final cup of American coffee, making a ritual of it, but I was reassured to see as we entered Canada the same chain of supermarkets I'd known all my life. Everything was familiar, everything was fine. We were driving along in an old blue Ford, but it felt as though we were flying.

Years later I understood what it means to cross a border.

There was so much to learn—beginning with the words of the national anthem, never mind the tune. Canadian allusions, Canadian jokes; they flew past me. What were the origins of this new country, and how did its government work? What lay behind the mysterious initials I kept hearing: CBC, NRC, NFB, PNE? How do you apply for a driver's licence? What was the difference between a premier and a prime minister? Public entertainment figures—did they exist? Were there any Canadian writers, and, if so, what did they write about? There was so much to absorb, so much mystery and strangeness. Moving to a new country was like falling down a dark hole, but for a long while I was too busy to notice.

It takes no time at all to memorize the names and locations of Canada's ten provinces or even to learn the provincial capitals. The river systems, too, are easily enough mastered and the lists of natural resources. This is schoolgirl stuff. But it takes years of on-the-spot habitation to assemble the details of a society, years before there is any feel for how a country functions, how much cultural weight, for instance, the Canadian Broadcasting Corporation carries (enormous), or the real importance of the railway in Canada (also enormous but declining), or how many degrees the mind bends while hearing such names as Gordie Howe, Nellie McClung, Margaret Laurence, C.D. Howe, Pierre Berton. (Pierre who?)

And then there are the nuances that make up the texture of daily life. I noticed that most Canadian households had an electric kettle or at least a kettle of some kind. (My own family in Chicago had made do with a saucepan.) Canadians go on holidays, not vacations, and instead of buying a round-trip ticket they buy a "return." They cover their heads in the winter with a knitted hat called a toque—a necessary indignity, given the climate. They're very big on a game called curling, especially in small towns, and they say "eh" at the end of their sentences instead of "huh." They end the alphabet with "zed" instead of "zee." And sit on a chesterfield instead of a couch. And, yes, they do drink a lot of tea, though they've never taken to ice tea the way the Americans have.

I've spent a lot of time thinking about the ways Canadians differ from Americans, but the minute I come up with a theory it seems I'm presented with an otherwise example. Americans are popularly characterized as flamboyant and Canadians reticent, but these generalizations are absurdly difficult to prove. America is first at the starting gate; Canada is the country that doesn't get asked out on a second date. We point to Americans as being larky, upbeat, and out for a buck and Canadians as dour compromisers with no sense of humour. A joke Canadians like to tell themselves goes like this: Question—Why did the Canadian cross the road? Answer—To get to the middle. Jokes, metaphors, simplifications—none of these serves to pin down elusive differences.

It is true, though, that Canada claims fewer heroes than America. There are no Washingtons or Lincolns nor even the likes of Gloria Steinem or Phil Donahue. Something determinedly democratic or else grudging keeps us from honouring those who dare speak louder than others. In somewhat the same way, and for perhaps the same reasons, Canadians are quietly moderate about their country's virtues. I've heard Canadians say they're proud of their history and content to be citizens of a decent country, but I've never once heard the word *patriotism* voiced. Even the concept is somehow embarrassing.

Like every other country, Canada is changing. Its nearly thirty million people have a vibrant multicultural profile. (The city of Toronto sends out its tax bill in six languages and offers emergency translation services in 150 other languages.) And it is more and more an urban country, with something like ninety percent of its people living on a long narrow industrialized ribbon that borders the United States. There are the usual problems of violence, pollution, and health, but generally Canadians speak optimistically of their relatively low crime rate and of a medical plan that hits them in the pocket but gives them a longer and healthier life.

It took me a dozen years to decide to become a Canadian citizen, but I knew my perspective had shifted when I returned to Chicago for a visit and heard myself bragging to my American relations about our winter weather—exaggerating the height of the Canadian snow drifts, lingering over our wicked sub-zero temperatures, and providing anyone who would listen with the fascinating details of our most recent fuel bill. And now, after living for periods of time in Vancouver, Toronto, and Ottawa, I find myself settled in Winnipeg, where there is no need to inflate the meteorological facts. Winnipeg really is the coldest city in the world, colder than the most northerly point of Maine, colder than Moscow. Some days it's colder than it is at the North Pole. Now that's something to be proud of, something to warm the heart. And it offers an opportunity to join in Canada's favourite sport, which is complaining about the weather.

The summers, of course, are glorious, as Canadians are pressingly eager to tell you. During the warmer months, the 49th parallel seems to soften in the sun, and steady streams of tourists, Americans and Canadians, begin crossing and recrossing the border, looking for change, for the otherness that foreign travel allows. Canadians take for granted that they'll be welcomed in the U.S. since the epithet "Friendly Neighbour to the North" is so enshrined it has prevailed over tariff tangles or occasional rumbles at the border. Many American travellers, however, are somewhat less at ease, having tuned in to vague floating rumours about anti-American feelings and cool receptions in Canada.

It's true that there is a certain Canadian wariness when it comes to the Great-Power-to-the-South, a country with ten times the population and many times the wealth. But this wariness seldom translates into hostility. As anywhere else in the world, polite, respectful visitors

are greeted politely and respectfully. They are greeted, in fact, enthu-
siastically since Americans tend to bring with them not only a freshly
sharpened perspective but a sizable contribution toward the balance
of payments.

My advice to American visitors is not to try to "do" Canada during
a single vacation (we're talking about five and a half time zones) but
to concentrate on one of its regions, the Maritime provinces in the
east, Quebec, Central Canada, the Prairies, or the West. The train trip
through the Rockies is spectacular, but so, in a different way, is the
less-known train ride—the Polar Bear Express, it's called—between
Winnipeg and the town of Churchill on the shore of Hudson Bay.
Anyone interested in gardens should head for the Butchart Gardens
in Victoria or the famed Montreal Botanical Gardens. Those who grew
up with Anne of Green Gables, as I did, will find that Prince Edward
Island has honoured all of Anne's favourite refuges. There are architectural treasures in Montreal and Ottawa but great charm too in the
smaller Ontario city of Kingston. The Exchange District of Winnipeg is
another architectural wonder, and the Inuit sculpture and art collection
at the Winnipeg Art Gallery is the largest in the world. But now I'm
boasting, something Canadians aren't supposed to do.

Do I consider myself a Canadian after thirty-six years in the country? The equivocal and very Canadian answer is yes and no. I still carry
two passports and have friends and family on both sides of the border.
My novels are published in New York, but also in Toronto, and these
novels are set in Chicago, Ottawa, Vancouver, Philadelphia, Toronto,
Manitoba, Indiana, and Florida. It feels natural and also fortunate to
have one foot planted in each country and to be able to say, definitively,
noisily, here is where I live.

Did Anything Much Happen to You in the Fifties?[15]

High school, university, going abroad, marriage, immigration, the birth of two children—that's all.

But, even though I lived during the '50s in the much-maligned territory of suburbia, I was unaware of belonging to a decade characterized by dullness, blandness, puritanism, and hypocrisy. Our lives may have been unfolding according to a plan, but that plan was full of richness, excitement, possibility. I gazed at the paintings of Jackson Pollock reproduced in *Life Magazine*—that holy bible—and read some of the work of the beat poets—this work generally presented to us with a wink of the eye, meaning these guys are kind of crazy, but, well, as a passing fad, they're rather—you know—fun. We were convinced, or almost convinced, that life in the '50s was the way it was always going to be.

But there were flickerings on the wall. In the mid-'50s, my hand trembling, I signed a petition in support of the first black graduate student to enter the University of Georgia. In England, in the mid-'50s, I looked around and observed a transition toward a surprisingly multi-racial society and wondered if perhaps the world was in for a good shaking up. In 1956, at a bridal shower, I met a woman who told me that she intended to keep her own name after her marriage. In the same year, I met another bride-elect, as they were called then, who revealed she would abjure the tradition of a wedding veil. Wedding veils were, after all, pretty pagan, she announced off-handedly. This was for me a new, startling, disturbing thought. In 1958, I read a discussion, either half page or full page, I can't remember which, in *Chatelaine Magazine* on the subject of whether or not one should oil the skins of potatoes before they were baked, and I recall being puzzled and a little overwhelmed—not that I voiced this—by such close attention to the rightness or wrongness of domestic detail.

Betty Friedan had not yet written *The Feminine Mystique*. I had never heard of Simone de Beauvoir. I did read a great deal, though, choosing my books from what was available in the bookmobile that visited our far-flung Toronto suburb—that is to say, I read mostly male writers. I did read my way through Pearl Buck and Edna Ferber but always with a disappointment that I couldn't pinpoint.

I hope it will not sound like dramatic exaggeration to say that Virginia Woolf rescued me. I am talking about her novels rather than her diaries, because, difficult as it is to believe today, her diaries were not then widely available. What Virginia Woolf did was to instill in me an impulse to be serious. Later, in the '60s, Margaret Laurence amplified this through her novels, saying, serious, yes, but not, God forbid, solemn.[16] And Alice Munro, much, much later, stirred me to life with a passage from one of her short stories, confessing that the real work of life was not brightening the house with lemon Pledge or getting the laundry Downy-soft: the real work of life was, as she said, "a sort of wooing of distant parts of myself."[17]

In the '50s, I was largely unaware of Canadian writers. And with some reason. Most Canadian writers were men who were trying to write like American or English male writers and a handful of women writers who were trying to write like men. I had no sense in Toronto, where I lived then, of a community of writers. I had never met a writer. There were no provincial writers' guilds, no Writers' Union of Canada. The reading, as such, was virtually unknown, though I did hear rumours of coffee houses where poetry was shouted out. Somehow I stumbled on the *Canadian Forum*, and I sent them a poem, which they accepted, possibly because I signed my name—and that was how my first publication appeared in print—C. Shields. It seemed the best idea.[18]

No one told me Canadian literature was the preserve of men, but I nevertheless perceived it. University English departments were staffed by men. The poetry editor of *The Canadian Forum*, Milton Wilson, who wrote me a charming gentlemanly note on the acceptance of my poem, edited a mid-century anthology of Canadian poems with ten poets in its pages, only three of them women, and my sense is that was real parity for the time.[19] A.J.M. Smith's *Masks of Poetry: Canadian Critics on Canadian Verse*, 1962, lists on its cover Edward, Archibald, James, Earle (as in Birney), Northrop, another James, Milton, and Irving. That's it. The boys. Hugo McPherson in Carl Klink's *Literary History of Canada: Canadian Literature in English*, 1976, devotes twice as much space to Charles Israel—who?—as he does to Adele Wiseman.[20] The renowned F.R. Scott, in the mid-'50s, organized and presided over a conference on Canadian writing at Queen's University. If you read the reports of this conference, you will be excused for thinking it a male consciousness-raising event—for not one woman is mentioned in the press accounts.[21]

And yet Canadian women *were* writing. Preparing for this talk, I came across a 1955 Alice Munro story in *The Queen's Quarterly*, her name misspelled. Ethel Wilson and Sheila Watson published books in this decade. And from Manitoba alone there was Adele Wiseman's *The Sacrifice* in 1956, Dorothy Livesay's many books of poetry, Miriam Waddington's *The Season's Lovers* (1958), Laura Goodman Salverson's *Immortal Rock: The Saga of the Kensington Stone* (1964), the early, scattered publication of Margaret Laurence's African stories, and, at the threshold to the new decade, 1960, Patricia Blondal's *A Candle to Light the Sun* set in Souris, Manitoba. Why this outpouring of work from our own province? If you have a theory about Manitoba writers, I'd be grateful if you would share it with me.

And yet these women of the '50s seldom appeared in anthologies, almost never in university departments, or on the mastheads of literary publications. They did not head publishing companies, edit book pages, or write reviews; they were not, in short, taken seriously. They wrote about neighbourhoods, about families, about love. They were accused of using the domestic idiom. This was a period, you will recall, in which domesticity—the cult of the perfectly baked potato—was the bedrock of society but an embarrassment when it intruded in the arts.

The 1960s—Laurence, Atwood, McEwen, Engel, Munro—changed everything, making it possible for women to write with the kind of radical closeness that the women's movement sanctioned. We all relaxed about categories, and work was shaped and kneaded into new forms. We agreed that possibly we ALL possessed a domestic life, a reflective life, a life in which the subtleties of all human relationships might be spoken of without the risk of triviality.

In today's writings, I see the '50s being reassessed. A certain amount of anger is bound to erupt from a period as insular, parochial, and restrictive, and we're sure to hear about it; it's a good thing that we hear about it. But there is also a new recognition of this period as one of transition, of infinite complexity, and—dare I say it—of radical progress.

Writers Are Readers First[22]

A character in my first novel, *Small Ceremonies*,[23] says this: "All girls like me who were good at school but suffered from miserable girlhoods were sustained for years on end by the resources of the public libraries of this continent." A rather glib generalization as I see it now. All childhoods, privileged or not—and mine was privileged—are miserable to some degree.

As a child, I read a lot, but I had only three books of my own.[24] Of course, there were books in the house, my father's old Horatio Alger books (which I adored), a girlhood book of my mother's called *Girl of the Limberlost* (also adored), and a set of the *World Book Encyclopedia*, which I read throughout my childhood, as other people read novels, I suppose. This set, plus another set called *Journeys through Bookland*, seemed a promise to me that there was a larger world outside the town where I lived.

The town was Oak Park, Illinois, home of Ernest Hemingway, not that he ever returned there, even when invited, and not that he ever claimed it with much pride. It was in many ways a fortunate place to grow up in. The schools, parks, and playgrounds everywhere were excellent. Oak Park was called in the Chicago guidebook "The town where the taverns left off and the steeples began." The library, Carnegie style, had a children's room with miniature rugs and tiny tables and chairs, and, best of all, it had a Saturday-morning story hour. What I felt the first time I was taken to story hour was pure enchantment. One of the librarians, a kindly unmarried middle-aged woman—all of the librarians and schoolteachers of my childhood were unmarried middle-aged women—stood up and told—not read—but told a story, the story, the twelve dancing princesses, presented as both story and drama, a combination which left me dizzy. All the Saturdays of my childhood were spent at story hours, and I remember one terrible cold and stormy Saturday when only four or five of us turned up. Instead of going down to the library basement where there was a tiny theatre, we sat around one of the little tables. I looked into the eyes of those other children at the table, ardour clearly stamped on their faces, with fanaticism too. We were different. Other children loved these Saturday mornings, too, but we, for some reason, needed it.

I think what we shared—but had no way of knowing—was a wish to escape the confines of the life we lived in, this relatively affluent suburb of Chicago, almost totally WASP, which, for all I cringe, was a little like living in a plastic bag. The stacks of books we carried home under our arms—never less than the legal limit—and the ones we piled in the wire baskets of our bicycles—these books were our assurance that beyond this parochial cheerful world lay another. I can remember once walking home from the library on a summer evening—in those days, we walked unafraid at night—and passing a house not two blocks from the house where I lived. Through the screens, I could hear the people in the house talking, and they were talking—to my astonishment—in a foreign language. Hearing them, I felt a bolt of happiness, the same kind of happiness I experienced from the mysterious rhythms of poetry or the circuitous turnings of stories I was reading.

I read everything I received—Bobbsey Twins,[25] comic books; I even loved my first-grade reader *Dick and Jane*, though I have since been told, and I suppose convinced, that the buoyant middle-class image—the mother in the apron, the father in his necktie—was damaging.[26] They weren't for me, of course, but I loved Dick and Jane for their goodness and for their almost insane enthusiasms, which seemed an antidote to early premature stirrings of ennui. But I chiefly loved them because they were the key that opened the door into the world of reading, and, for writers, learning to read is, I think, the prime spiritual experience of childhood.

When I was thirteen, I read my first adult book, called *A Tree Grows in Brooklyn*. It was my ticket to the grown-up world, a book which was considered to be controversial in its day. Actually, it still is, but for completely different reasons. I never read another children's book again. There is a period in one's teens when one reads more purely than ever again, truly bonded with the material, willing to read uncritically, willing to suspend disbelief indefinitely.

I was lucky. No one ever said to me, "How come you've always got your nose in a book?" No one ever made fun of me by calling me a bookworm, for living in a make-believe world. Instead, because I clearly loved books, people said to me from time to time, "Why don't you write a play for the grade sevens?" or "Why don't you edit the school literary magazine?" or "You're just the one to be class poet." It was others, not me, who first saw this line between reading and writing, a line which, now that I look back, seems to have been self-evident.

When I was in university, I earned a little extra money by working a few hours a week in the university library. By the time I was in my fourth year, I was allowed to choose the hours I wanted, and for some reason I chose Saturday morning as my work slot and was given a key and the responsibility of opening up the library. Another friend and I would arrive at 8 or 8:30—I've forgotten the exact time—and for a manic three or four minutes we would amuse ourselves by running from room to room and filling that hallowed, silent, book-lined space with what I can only describe as primal screams. Why this brought us such intense pleasure—for we were in revolt against nothing that I can think of—I can't say. Then the doors would open, the first people would arrive, and we would stand sedately behind the main desk with our rubber date stamp in hand, models of young womanhood.

When I married and we had children, we, of course, took them regularly to the library, and it seems to me that for years I was always fishing around under someone or other's bed, looking for the book that had been missing for months. I paid so many library fines for a few years that, when we moved from Ottawa, I went into the library to say goodbye, and I asked the librarian if we were really the worst family on her rolls. "Well," she said, sparing me, "there is this one other family. . . ."

Now we chiefly come on Sunday afternoon, a good time, a little like going to a party. You're almost sure to run into someone you know. There's a smell of wet raincoats, and you can lose yourself for hours in the stacks of old magazines. I wish sometimes there was more going on, a discussion group, a reading, free coffee once in a while. There were a couple of women painting china the other Sunday, not something that interests me, but I can think of similar things that might. And I wish, but this is impossibly nostalgic, that the librarian at the desk would say, as Miss Mays in Oak Park used to, "Well, how's your mother keeping?" or, at the very least, pat one of my books and say, "Now that's a good one. You're going to love that."

Books that Meant[27]

Dick and Jane, who starred in my first school reader, were boring, white, and middle-class, and today they are no longer welcome in the primary classrooms of America. But how I loved their uncomplicated effusions. Brave Dick, who never picked on the little kids. Solid Jane with her clean white socks. Sunny baby Sally and the family dog, Spot, so lively and house-broken. Mother in her apron, clapping her hands over her children's minor triumphs, and Father—what a father!—exuberant, compassionate, proud.

Curiously enough, I came from what might pass as a Dick-and-Jane family, lived in a leafy suburb with a sister and brother, an apron-garbed mother, and an employed, white-collared father. Our house, though, like every real house, held shadows, silences, deposits of anger, and unanswered questions. Safe in the realm of Dick and Jane, I found a projection of perfect idealized goodness which no danger could threaten. Isn't this what every child wants?

But more important was what was revealed behind the cipher of ink. Through the agency of Dick and Jane's mild adventures, a permanent code was unlocked, and it was one that I realized could unmake my most stubborn fears and rethink my unthinkable lot. I could be brave, too, as brave and as good as Dick, Jane, Sally, and Spot.

Learning to read was like falling into a mystery deeper than the mystery of airwaves or the halo around the head of the baby Jesus. The mechanics were disappointingly easy, sounding out the vowels and consonants, and I remember that I made myself stumble and falter over each new word, trying to hold back the rush of revelation. No spiritual experience has since struck me with the same force I encountered the moment I understood what print was and how it could speak. I felt suffused with light and often skipped or hopped or ran wildly to keep myself from flying apart.

There is a time in our reading lives when we read anything, when we are unsupervised, when we are bonded to the books we read, when we are innocent of any kind of critical standard, so innocent and avid and open that we do not even bother to seek out special books but read instead those books that happen to lie within easy reach, the family books, the in-house books. These books have a way of entering our bodies more simply and completely than library books, for example, which are chosen, or school texts, which are imposed.

My parents' library was a corner of the sunroom, a four-shelf bookcase stained to look like red maple, which had been "thrown in" with the purchase of the 1947 *World Book Encyclopedia*. This bookcase also had room for a set of *Journeys through Bookland*, black binding stamped with gold, published in the early 1920s, and ten books, oddly uninviting, with cheap red covers and an absence of illustration, entitled *The World's One-Hundred Best Short Stories*, put out by Funk and Wagnalls in 1927. There were two volumes of poetry, the works of James Whitcombe Riley, and, next to it, *A Heap o' Living* by Edgar A. Guest. The rest of the shelf space, only a few inches, was filled with my parents' childhood books.

My father was represented by half a dozen Horatio Alger titles, *Luck and Pluck*, *Ragged Dick*, *Try and Trust*,[28] and so on, which I read, loved, and never thought to condemn for didacticism, for didn't I attend a didactic Methodist Sunday School, sit in a didactically charged classroom at Nathaniel Hawthorne Grammar School, and absorb the didacticism of my well-meaning parents? This was the natural way of the world, half of humanity bent on improving the other half. Nor did it seem strange that I, in the 1940s and 1950s, should be reading books directed at a late-nineteenth- and early-twentieth-century audience. I scarcely noticed this time fissure, entering instead a seamless, timeless universe, scrubbed of such worldly events as wars, elections, and social upheavals, with which we mark off periods of history. Occasional archaisms were easily overleapt since the child's world is largely a matter of missing pieces anyway or concepts only dimly grasped.

Horatio Alger aside, it was mainly the books of my mother that I read. Four in particular: *Anne of Green Gables*, *A Girl of the Limberlost*, *Helen's Babies*, and *Beautiful Joe*. No Shakespeare, Hawthorne, Poe, no Virginia Woolf, Gertrude Stein, Willa Cather—just these four absorbing, popular chronicles. I didn't waste a minute worrying about the sentimentality in my mother's books. Sentimentality, like coincidence, seemed to be one of the strands of existence; it could be detected every week, after all, in the last two wrap-up minutes of *Amos 'n' Andy*; it was a part of the human personality.

Childhood, it often seemed to me, was a powerless interval during which one bided one's time, preparing for a confrontation that might or might not occur, though its possibility, shining in the future and winking off the pages of books, gave promise. I never dreamt then that my own confrontation with a baffling world would take the form it did—in the writing of novels.[29]

The Reader-Writer Arc[30]

Even if we did *not* believe that our literature reflected the norms of our society, or interrogated our communally held notions of the good, or possessed the power to open new moral dimensions, then it would still be of value for us to think about what our literature might look like in the twenty-first century.

Our ability to use language makes us human, and what we do with that language, how far we push it beyond essential grunts, determines, I think, the degree to which we have evolved. We use language to connect with each other concerning simple tasks, to debate issues, to prognosticate about public policy—as we have been doing these last few days, but we also use language for its own sake, turning it into a game, a toy, a human pleasure, an *art*, shaping and making *new* what we like to think of as permanent forms—of course they're not—forms that arrive through certain combinations of euphony, melody, allusive echoes, layers of time and consciousness, the distillation of idea and yearning, formal design combined with an unlimited range, and perhaps, above all, the creation or preservation of narrative.

Let me talk first of poetry, which is thought to be our oldest literary form, springing from the rhetoric of prayer and incantation, twin impulses which may be in decline, for all we know. Poetry's end rhymes—moon, June, September, remember—which have survived right into the early part of our century, are believed to be echoes of early human hands clapping or drums beating or perhaps the ringing of bells. We have seen the diminution of rhyme, what some call an outmoded artifice, and I believe we will continue to see that decline. In recent years—another artifice perhaps?—the arrangement of language into distinct lines and stanzas has been challenged with the introduction of the prose poem and a number of other hybrids, posing the question of what constitutes form and genre, how rigid and isolated they really are.[31]

I remember once being hired to teach the writing of poetry to young schoolchildren in the Ottawa-Carleton school district. My greatest fear was that they would ask me one day what was the difference between prose and poetry and that I wouldn't know what to say. I asked my husband to help me rig up a demonstration. Poetry I would demonstrate by setting off a camera flash, indicating that this form was more concentrated in its force, that you saw it all suddenly or not at all. Prose I intended to illustrate by the use of an incandescent light bulb which bathed its subject, lighted it from several angles, allowing time for the absorption of details.

It happened, though, that none of the children ever asked the dreaded question, and it occurred to me that the conundrum was an imposed one. Poetry carries narrative elements; good prose carries much the same rhythm and movement that we ask of poetry. Poetry puts a certain torque on language; it is in some ways a tissue of surprise, but then so are particular paragraphs (which are really stanzas) or phrases in a prose work. It is sometimes surmised that there are more poets in Canada than readers of poetry. My guess is that poetry will live on as an art form with a small readership, as it has today, but that a poem will cease to be a mystery which must be unlocked with a set of specialized critical tools. In other words, it will become what it once was—accessible, meaningful, with all the force of a photo flash.

Theatre. It may be that we have been asking too little of our dramatists. Often in this last half century we have been satisfied that they base their narrative on some real event or person or that they explore some relatively narrow social issue, like unemployment compensation. What we want from our playwrights, what I want, is invention, not adaptation. Both these directions—adaptation and the focus on highly particularized and localized concerns—may be a form of special pleading for this threatened art or may indicate that drama is going to function very differently in the future. I am thinking of street theatre, the exercise of ceremony, or pedagogical function.[32]

The playwright Alan Bennett[33] sees as the most dangerous aspect to contemporary theatre the fact that the middle-class members of the audience—and they are mostly middle class—are almost never represented on stage except in a satirical mode. He identifies this as a smoke screen, a deliberate avoidance of those issues which are nearest to us.

Our dramatic sensibilities do change and will continue to change. Last year I was lucky enough to see two major modern plays of our times, *A Doll's House*[34] and *Death of a Salesman*.[35] Neither of these plays had lost its overall intensity, but each contained one or two scenes that the audience found mawkish and sentimental. The directors, quite rightly, left these scenes intact, but it seemed clear that audiences were less willing than earlier audiences to be manipulated and charmed by unearned effects.

We're born, it seems, with an appetite for narrative. I can remember that as a child I was not gifted in mathematics but that I did relish what we called story problems. If Mary Brown is sent to the store to buy three pounds of cheese at two dollars a pound and six apples at eight cents each, how much change will she get from a twenty-dollar bill? My non-numerical brain shifted immediately into narrative mode: who was this Mary Brown? And what was she going to do with all that cheese, and how did it happen she was trusted with a twenty-dollar bill, and what of her wider dreams and aspirations? The lives of others, others like ourselves, are compelling. We need their shared drama, it seems, since our own lives are never enough.

We usually think of 1740 as the date when the novel burst upon us.[36] Immediately, it established itself as the primary literary form, at least in English. It was in some ways an astonishing invention—and like many successful inventions it brought together dozens of strands that were *already* part of our culture—those narratives, for instance, we once called the lives of the saints, or the French and Italian novellas, which were really early tabloid reports of local events, the epics from history, myth, from poetry, the polite conventions of letter writing, and, of course, the oral tradition of storytelling. Still, the novel as such was something new. It was distinguished by characters who more or less resembled people like ourselves in predicaments that more or less resembled our own predicaments—all of this signalling a demi-shift from the narrative of high art to popular art. We could all read novels, and novels could tell us not just what people did but how people thought.

The instant and almost universal acceptance of the novel in the West tells me that we are not about to witness the death of the novel in the next one hundred years. Its shape will change; it has always been in a state of change. The problem-solution set-up of early-twentieth-century novels was too formulaic; it did not relate to the lives of women or minorities; it trafficked too freely in artificial moments of revelation, too neatly in terms of closure. Today films perform the world of action superbly, leaving to the novel, by default, that more interesting world, to me, anyway, of how people think.

We began around 1960 in the West to question the meaning of meaning, and I, for one, think this was a necessary phase in our reflective life. We were living in an age that valued scientific achievement, and because of that it perhaps seemed only natural that those of us interested in critical theory should leap into the postmodern experiment and attempt through the so-called tools of deconstruction to quantify our literary forms. This experiment has been called by some "The Beautiful Nonsense." By others, a useful reassessment of how literature gets made, how it is valorized, and whether it can be measured and ranked. Not surprisingly, prevailing theories of economics and politics, of feminism and alterity, filtered into this reassessment, and this led at times to a mechanized image of literature's formation—that we writers could make it from a boxed kit if only we'd digested the requisite French philosophers—but also to the altogether useful notion that literature is not grown in vacuum tubes, that narrative hunger[37] is, in fact, a strand of existence.

If our literature continues to grow, will there be readers to complete the writer-reader arc? This is perhaps the most interesting question for the next century. Most of us sense that the book-as-we-know-it will change, though we're not quite sure how. But the survival of writing, and the reading of text, demand an effort of concentration beyond almost all other human activities, and you may have noticed that you cannot do anything else when in the act of writing. The conversion of little black marks into words and the secondary cognitive shift of converting words into ideas is so complex and so uniquely satisfying a process that it is difficult to imagine the disappearance of print.

Finally, in a world which thinks more and more in terms of mass audience, the movement of print between writer and reader remains one of the most intimate of connections. We talk about mass-market books or bestsellers, but we should be talking about the real enchantment of the written word, however widely disseminated—one consciousness speaking directly into the ear—or eye, if you like—of another single consciousness. Who could ask for a more sublime form of human communication?

The Writer's Second Self [38]

Writers of fiction are frequently challenged by reviewers who accuse them of having incorporated biographical material into their books. There is often a gleeful pouncing on this fact, as though they, the critics, have caught the writer out, have found him guilty of major trespassing. Sometimes the critical tone is openly accusing; more often it is simply revelatory comment, a self-serving tribute perhaps to the critic's own cleverness in ferreting out these literary infringements.

In much the same way, writers of autobiography are pinned to the wall for having bridged a synapse of memory with a fictional connective. Or he may have incriminated himself by "touching up" his portrait. His point of view—if it deviates too wildly from recognized fact—may leave him open to charges of bias or even untruth. One thinks immediately of Hemingway's *A Moveable Feast*, in which the author's vision has become almost grotesquely distorted;[39] what is sometimes forgotten is that the truth an autobiographer is obliged to observe is his own truth, however idiosyncratic that truth may be.

This sort of critical comment—which often carries with it more than a hint of outrage—extends perhaps from an oversimplified view of literature, from a compulsion on the part of critics and academics to categorize the forms of writing and a desire to impose on literature definable and teachable genres. The effect of this insistent cataloguing then leaves critics with the additional task of naming exceptions and making allowances for minor variances. And it makes them responsible for pointing a knowing finger at those who trespass. For it is not the writer who coaxes his work into the narrow confines of genre, and it is not the writer who willingly suspends his disbelief; the writer knows that the self can never be washed out of his storytelling, just as his creative and imaginative impulse can never be separated from his personal history.

If one subscribes to the theory that it is not a writer's self which is revealed in his writing, but a sort of second self,[40] then the onus upon

him to distinguish between the separate spheres of fiction and autobiography will all but disappear. At the very least, the boundaries will
soften to a less arbitrary and more flexible interpretation.

It has always been acknowledged that diaries, whether intended for
publication or not, reveal that side of a writer which he wishes to reveal;
just as one turns his most interesting profile to the photographer's lens,
the writers of diaries project themselves as they would prefer to be seen.
Of course, some writers may use diaries or memoirs as exploratory ma-
chinery, an attempt to understand themselves or the period in which
they lived, but these explorations are almost always undertaken with
conscious shaping and deliberate selectivity, the writer controlling the
direction of the quest and imposing on it his own conclusions.

Many of the boundaries in literature appear to be collapsing. Is
Margaret Laurence's *A Bird in the House* a novel or a collection of short
stories?[41] Is Margaret Atwood's *The Journals of Susanna Moodie* a long
narrative poem or a series of lyrics?[42] The definitions are in question,
not the quality of the writing, and one asks whether the definitions are
not overly subscribed to or insisted upon. Have these rigid distinctions
ever, in fact, been valid?

Various approaches to autobiography, too, have become blurred.
When does a diary become a memoir? When does a tale based on an
actual personal event become reportage or essay or story? The refining
of these distinctions may, in the end, be exhausting and futile.

Most laborious and futile of all may be picking apart of the elements
of fiction and reality, laborious because an infinite number of statements
must be questioned, and futile because no one but the author will ever
be able to settle the question, and even he may find himself helpless in
the making of final distinctions.

The Writing Life[43]

All writers, I suspect, even the cocky and arrogant, dread the period immediately following publication. This is the "fragile time," when we writers are at our most vulnerable. A book has been written, edited, published, and sent to the first line of critical appraisal. There is no way, it seems, to circumvent this painful process.

I'm often asked whether I read my reviews. Of course, I read them.

My rule is to read through them twice, then put them away. If they're good, they warm your shivering limbs but make you big-headed and a pain to those you live with. If they're bad, they make you grumpy, then bring on a paralyzing fit of public embarrassment, which shades, a few minutes later, into courage. Who does this person think he/she is?

If the official reviews are awkward, personal reviews are a torment.

Those seldom come from family members.

Family members are more than pleased to display your book on their coffee tables, and they *do* expect a free copy. They demand a warm inscription, but, beyond that, they have elected, for the most part, a no-comment stance.

This used to worry me. Had I embarrassed my family in some way? Are they fearful and protective for my sake? I've decided, finally, that family members refuse to comment on a book simply because they haven't read it, and they haven't read it because they know me, the author, in a particular way and prefer not to know me in any other, perhaps more dangerous, way.

Friends and colleagues, on the other hand, feel free to offer a range of comments.

"Interesting approach," you will hear, and that word *interesting*, so neutral and meaningless, a pellet so carefully considered and tactfully delivered, alerts you to the fact that your book has been found worthless.

"I've bought your book," a friend says, "but haven't got around to reading it yet." You what? You mean you have it in your possession, and you haven't been compelled to rip open the covers at once? What is the matter with you? Or with the book? Or with me? Are you trying to tell me something?

"I love it but love your other book(s) better." This comment comes in a number of versions. "It didn't hold my attention quite the way your last book did." "I had a little trouble relating to the main character this time, but otherwise. . . ."

Full-blown paranoia has arrived. When a friend tells me she has read my book between dinner and bedtime, I can scarcely keep the whine of injury out of my voice. This happens to be a book I spent two years writing, I want to say, and you're telling me you scarfed it down in one evening!

"I've bought your book for my mother-in-law/for my sister in Florida/for my daughter." These comments come from men, the same men who tell me their wives/mothers/daughters read all of my books.

"I would have bought your book," a colleague tells me, "but it came out far too late for my wife's birthday."

"I read so much during the day"—this is a favourite of lawyers and businesspeople—"that I can't concentrate on anything but junk TV in the evening."

"Robert really wanted to come to your launch tonight, but he felt he should stay home to—I know this sounds silly—to paint the fence. While the weather holds, I mean. You know what September is like. He knew you'd understand, and he sends his best wishes and love. And admiration."

The post-pub period, luckily, lasts only a short while. The authorly skin thickens, as it must. The book itself recedes, and probably you are already thinking of the next project.

And, after all, there was that one friend who wrote to tell you that every word in your new book felt weighted with rare gold. Hang on to that; never mind whether it is a genuine response or a slice of royal baloney. It's better than the other thing.

Making Words/Finding Stories[44]

When I was first contacted to come to Vancouver for this talk, I was told that they would like a title. Now, this was many, many months ago, and so I rather desperately picked a title called "Making Words/Finding Stories," thinking that, if I was going to talk about "the writing life," these two components would have to be in anything that I talked about. There is the whole business of language, there is the whole business of narrative. These are what we always think of as the two parts of the recipe for writing novels.

Language is probably more important to me than narrative, but tonight I'm going to talk about narrative—where our narratives come from, the fact that we're born with a kind of narrative hunger we never quite fill up. In fact, I was one of the very few children, I think, who loved those Dick and Jane stories. You know, those terrible, white-bread, American stories? I felt very warmly toward Jane with her little white socks and Dick, who was the perfect brother, of course. The narrative was just as thin as could be, but it nevertheless captured me. The whole mystery of learning to read was the central transcendent moment of my life, when I realized that those little marks on the paper meant something.

I grew up in Oak Park, Illinois, which you may know is the home of Ernest Hemingway, but Ernest Hemingway got away as fast as he could from this lost stronghold and never returned.

I started my schooling in Nathaniel Hawthorne Public School,[45] and when I got a little older I transferred to Ralph Waldo Emerson Public School.[46] I knew who these gentlemen were because their portraits adorned the corridors of our school with their frock coats and their tiny little glasses and their beards. They were white, and they were men, and they were dead. So it seemed to me, growing up as a child, that I was locked out of the whole world of being a writer. It also seemed very much like wanting to be a movie star to go around saying that you wanted to write a book. It was a bit presumptuous in the puritan

Midwest that I knew. So, of course, I didn't. It was a secret—a secret I kept—that I wanted to be a writer, though I had no idea what I would write about or who my audience would be.

Even after I began to publish novels, I didn't quite know what I was writing about. But I soon found out because I read the reviews. And the reviews said that I wrote about ordinary people. That was something of a shock to me because I never thought of myself or my friends as *ordinary* people, and it's a word that I still don't understand perfectly, although I'm trying to. There is a sense in which you don't know what you're writing about. It's said writers shouldn't let their right hand know what their left hand is doing, but there are some times when the right hand doesn't know what the right hand is doing. One example of this that occurs to me—I've often read, usually in scholarly articles because this isn't the sort of thing that newspaper reviewers tackle—is that, in fact, most of the fathers that appear in my novels are rather distant and inarticulate people. That's something I'll have to think about. You don't know the patterns you're creating. I recently had a letter from a woman in northern California who is actually a columnist for the *National Journal for Dental Hygienists*. I'm sure this isn't a periodical you are likely to have come across. She wanted to know why there were so many teeth in my novels. She had gone through everything I had ever written, meticulously, and she cited—with page numbers—every reference to teeth. She wanted to know what it was about teeth that I was so drawn to. I simply wrote to her that teeth are a part of life, and that's about as well as I could do with it.

Another interesting interview was with a French journalist who, again, was a very well-prepared interviewer. She said, "There are no animals in your books." And it's true, but it's something that I didn't know. My mother didn't let us have cats or dogs, and I married someone who was allergic to cats and dogs, so I suppose I have been out of the world of family pets for a long time.[47]

This is what I mean when I say we don't quite know what we're writing about, what we're putting in, and what we're leaving out. One thing that I knew that I wanted to write about, when I started to write novels in the '70s, was that I wanted to write the novels that I couldn't find at that time. I couldn't find novels about people who lived the kind of life that I was leading. And I felt hungry for those kinds of novels. I wanted to read novels about women who were reflective, who had a moral system, who had ties of loyalty to their community and to their families. The novels that came out in the '70s, at least the early '70s, were all about freedom—striking out for freedom—about leaving home, about trying to find oneself. (I was interested to read in the Vancouver paper today a headline that said "Freedom Isn't Free" in the article about Martin Luther King's daughter. "Freedom Isn't Free"—I thought it was a very nice way to put it.) I learned, at that time, or instinctively felt something which I should have known earlier, that writers should probably write the book they can't find in the bookstore, that they can't find on the library shelf, the book that they want to read themselves.

I also knew the kind of book I didn't want to read or write. I didn't want to write about my family and friends because I wanted them to remain my family and friends. I made that decision fairly early in my writing life. And I also knew I didn't even want to write about acquaintances—you know the old fear of being photographed and having your soul stolen—I think there's a certain amount of rationality to that theory. When I was writing my first novel—called *Small Ceremonies*—I happened to be out shopping one day in a neighbourhood mall, and I met, not a friend, but an acquaintance of mine, and she was in a great rush. She had just bought herself a beautiful, spruce green nightgown. She opened the bag, and she showed me this nightgown. And she said, "Now, I might rush off because I want to buy some candles to match all my nightgowns." My jaw must've dropped, because she said, "Oh, I have candles to match all my nightgowns." I couldn't resist putting this into the novel I was writing, but when I was reading proofs I thought, "I'll have to take this out because she'll read this book, and she is probably the only person in the Western Hemisphere who has carried colour coordination to this extent."

Often it's terribly tempting. On the other hand, we can use what we overhear on the bus—and, by the way, I think it's very important that writers take public transportation all their lives and do a lot of sitting around in coffee bars, too, to see what people are talking about, what they're sounding like, what they're interested in. My favourite eavesdrop of all time—which I've just managed to use—was in a café in Winnipeg, of all places, where I was caught between two conversations. It was a kind of narrative cross-draft. At one table, two women were speaking about their love affairs. At the other table, there were two businessmen with their shirts and their haircuts and ties, and the older one leaned over and said to the younger one, "We'll cross that bridge when we get to the bottom of the barrel." It was exactly the kind of psychic moment that I like to get down quickly in my notebook. The whole world is up for sale, but I try to stay away from those people that I might cause injury to.

I thought I'd talk a little bit about where narratives come from. This is always a great question because people who don't write novels think that we have experienced everything in our novels; the fact is we really make a lot of it up. The imaginative part of the recipe is the part that's always harder to explain. I'll talk a little bit about some of the things that I've written and how the ideas for them came to be.

Ideas, by the way—and I always try to get my students to understand this—are all around us. There's not a day in our lives where something doesn't happen to us—something to do with the weather, or the dream we had, or a snatch of conversation—something that gives us not a whole narrative, something that starts us off thinking.

I'll begin with the first novel that I wrote, called *Small Ceremonies*. I had just finished my master's degree, and my subject was Susanna Moodie, the Ontario pioneer.[48] I think she's much better known in eastern Canada than western Canada. What happened is something that happens often to people who do academic work: not all the interesting material can be used, because it's conjectural. You're forced, really, to use the more conventional material, the material which has already been sanctioned. And so I finished my thesis, and I had all this stuff left over. Well, I'm my mother's daughter—my mother would never throw out a quarter of a tablespoon of frozen peas if she had them left over after dinner. I saved all my notes for my thesis and decided to write a book about a woman who was writing a book about Susanna Moodie. In this way, I could use my leftovers, my interesting material on Susanna Moodie. That's how that novel came into being.

I always worry, of course, about putting too much of my academic interests into my novels, and I once wrote a book called *The Republic of Love*.[49] The heroine is a folklorist, and her specialty is mermaids, which just happened to be something that I was passionately interested in at the time. I was reading about mermaids, collecting pictures about mermaids; I was interested in the whole iconography of mermaids, looking at mermaids from a feminist point of view, which I don't think anyone has done yet. I had one of my daughters read the manuscript—it's my daughter Anne, who lives in Vancouver—and I said, "Anne, have I got too much mermaid stuff in here?" And she said, "Well, let me put it like this—don't put any more in." I always feel that I have to be a little careful about weighing down novels with my own particular passions and trying to remember that this has to be a story about people engaged in something other than their academic interests.

My novel *Swann*,[50] in a way, came out of Susanna. I have a lot to thank Susanna Moodie for and, actually, Margaret Atwood, who originally led me to Susanna Moodie. When I was writing about Susanna—as you know, she wrote two wonderful Canadian books, *Roughing It in the Bush* and *Life in the Clearings*, but she also wrote a whole pack of execrable novels, novels set in England—set in an England that no longer existed, melodramas. Actually, they were the Harlequin romances of their day. And because they were disposable, not many of them have survived. But there are a few, and they're in special university archives. I found the books I wanted at the University of Western Ontario, and I sent for those books through interlibrary loan. They arrived, I read them with my hair standing on end, sent them back, and then, just before my thesis defence, I panicked, as one is wont to do in these situations, and I ordered the books back again to have another look. I received the message that all of the Moodie material had disappeared. So I tucked that away in my mind. I thought that was an interesting thing to happen to such rare material. And then, two or three years later, I happened to be listening to the radio, and there was a young economist speaking who had actually conducted a rather innovative experiment. He had cornered the world market on Mexican jumping beans, and I realized at that moment that, if you choose a commodity that is small enough, you can corner the market on just about anything, which is what I felt that the thief who had plundered the library at Western must have done. By the way, that material is still missing from Western, and nobody knows quite where it has gone to.

So *Swann*, which is a novel about a disappearing manuscript, a disappearing work of a minor poet, really came straight out of this experience, which I recorded not on paper but in my mind. That's one of the plots, the mystery of the disappearing manuscripts. The larger mystery is the mystery of who makes art, who gets to name the culture. The trick was to get those two mysteries moving together like a set of gears, and it took me a little longer to figure out just how to do that.

A couple of others: there are some short stories—I can usually look at a short story when I write it, and I can find the moment that was the original yeast that started it going. There's a story called "Chemistry,"[51] and this came out of my first-year teaching experience. To my surprise, the University of Ottawa, when I finished my MA, hired me to teach an evening course in creative writing. I'm sure many of you here have taken evening courses, and you know what they're like—they're very different from day courses, especially in a cold climate like Ottawa. People come through the cold and the dark to be together, and there's a special spirit in those classes. In this first class I ever taught, it became a kind of lovefest. We all adored each other, and we all loved each other's work. Everyone got an A+, of course. I could never quite explain why this was, whether it was because it was my first exposure to teaching, whether it was the climate, the darkness, or what it was, but I put it down to chemistry. Many professors will talk about this. Certain classes, certain gatherings of people, have a particular chemistry, and we can't really analyze that too closely. I moved this story, called "Chemistry," to Montreal to a YMCA, I changed it from creative writing to a course in the recorder, and the story became something different, but it was still about this mysterious chemical nature that bonds people together.

There is another story called "Hinterland,"[52] about a couple who go off to Paris, and it was based on an experience that I had in Paris in 1986. If you remember, that was a period of great distress in Paris. There were bombings almost every day, and, in fact, there were a number of people killed in these bombings. Everywhere we went, we had to have our handbags checked. We found ourselves in a museum one day, and the guard came over to us and said very quietly, in French, "You must leave the museum." So we began to saunter toward the doorway, and other people were sauntering toward the doorway, and then someone started to run, and then everyone started to run, and people picked up their children under their arms and ran as fast as they could, and people were stumbling over each other. And it turned out to be a false alarm. I felt ashamed afterwards that we had joined into, and contributed to, the panic. The story was written out of that sense of shame.

There's another story called "Fuel for the Fire,"[53] which is the first story I wrote set in Winnipeg. We moved to Winnipeg in 1980, and I was a little worried about going there. The real reason I was afraid to go to Winnipeg was because, in all the years of my long and happy marriage, I have never lived in the same city as my in-laws. But it turned out to be a fine experience. They used to love to come to our house for dinner, not just to see the children but because we had a fireplace. My father-in-law, who was a working-class man, had never had a fireplace. He used to like to sit in front of the fireplace, and he'd say, "Better than TV." But because he was a very practical and resourceful man, he believed that he should bring fuel for our fires. He was horrified at the thought of Prestologs. So one day he turned up with a bunch of old lilac roots that we burned. He also found some old railway ties full of nails that he chopped up and brought over for our fires. But one night he came with a cardboard carton filled with bowling pins, and I don't know if he found them or was given these, but he looked at them, and he must have thought "they're wood. They'll burn." So that evening, it was Christmas Eve, we burned these bowling pins one after another. Now, if you ever get a chance to do this, you should try it because a bowling pin is not what you think it is. It is not a solid lathed object. It's made in four quarters—lateral quarters—which are glued together, and there's an oval emptiness in the middle—a hollow spot. So first the fire burns off the paint—in a gorgeous blast—then it finds its way into the hollow place where it glows a beautiful golden, and then, bang, it just cracks open. So one after another into the fire went the bowling pins. The story is about this, but it's really not about burning the bowling pins. It's about someone making an offering, and the story came from that moment.

One of the stories is called "Hazel."[54] I'm very interested in writing about work, by the way. It's the one thing that I find missing from most novels. I don't know if you saw the movie *Four Weddings and a Funeral*, but in fact I came out of that movie in a rage because everyone had pots of money and nobody went to work. It seems to me that what we spend most of our waking time doing should enter into our fiction. So I do like to write about work—what people are actually doing. You probably notice that novelistic events happen on weekends or in the evenings. But our lives don't. This story came to me when I was living in Vancouver. I was in one of the downtown department stores, and I saw a woman demonstrating cookware. You know, one of that sort of magic slicers that those women are always dicing vegetables with. There's something about those cooking demonstrations which is very dramatic to me. These women gather these huge crowds around them when they dice their carrots and onions. And I'm always right there, right in the front row, watching them do it. I wanted to know what the lives of these people are like, and, when they go home, where do they go home to? I always wanted to go up to them and say, "How did you come to be here and doing this at this moment?" But of course our society doesn't allow for those kinds of questions. So the story called "Hazel" is my attempt to try to construct an imaginative life about something that I don't really know—something that I can only guess at. And that brings me to *Larry's Party*, which is also about something I don't really know, and that is men.

There was a bit of a gap between *The Stone Diaries* and *Larry's Party*,[55] and I was trying to think of what I wanted to write about. I've never had that problem before—the subject for the next novel has always risen up earlier, and I've had to set it aside. This time I didn't know what to write about. I have lunch every Thursday with three women friends. We call ourselves the Critical Theory Group. And it is true that once or twice we have talked about critical theory, but mostly we talk about how to lose five pounds or other interesting subjects. One day one of these women said, "I wonder what it's like to be a man at the end of the twentieth century." And so our two-hour lunch stretched to about three hours, but I don't think we solved anything. I began to think about this, and I began asking some of my men friends, especially men who may be younger—men in their thirties or forties—what is it like? I knew some of this, of course. I knew that men were threatened in the job market. I knew from my New York editor that publishing a novel by a white male is asking for a very low readership these days. Men are in a period of transition, I think. Most of the supports that men have enjoyed have been withdrawn—their role as breadwinner, their refuge in those lodges, the Elks and the Rotary—I know membership in all those organizations is going down. And even the kind of hunting and fishing life that men have enjoyed makes women roll their eyes.

I wanted to write about a man who was born in 1950 so that he would be fifty or so at the turn of the century. I like the neatness of the arithmetic. I wanted him to experience the major existential questions, such as Is this all there is? or How did I get here? I wanted him to be introspective, a man with limited education but an inquiring mind, someone who was always thinking, thinking and never stopping. It was an interesting exploration for me. I don't know if I learned a lot about men, maybe one or two things. I used to think that when men talked about sports and cars they were using a metaphor, but now I just think they're talking about sports or cars. I also think—and I have to be very careful how I say this—that many men most of the time tend, more than most women most of the time, to compartmentalize their lives more than women. I think I knew this before I began, but I ended up believing this more than ever. There's something Darwinian about that—something that is hardwired into the male body. I wanted to try to understand that a little bit. That's why the novel is in compartments—in compartmental chapters such as "Larry's Love, 1978," "Larry's Folks, 1980," "Larry's Work, 1981," "Larry's Words"—so that it moves along in time. But it also moves in what I think of as CAT scan slices. When I was writing this book, I was invited to one of our large hospital research facilities for a tour. I was shown these beautiful pictures that come out of CAT scan machines—these wonderful slices of heart and liver, kidney and vein, aortas, and so on. And I found them very beautiful. I decided to slice up his life into these sections and see if I couldn't catch something in those particular categories.

Now, the whole business about women writing about men is an interesting one—and men writing about women too. I think inevitably we fail. Women can get right up to that male body, but they can't get inside it to really understand it. I think men, and you must know this if you've ever read a male novelist writing about childbirth, get things wrong. They get things wrong about women's lingerie. They get a lot wrong. I nevertheless think it's worth doing, otherwise we're going to end up with a separate literature for men and women. And, to a certain degree, I think we already have that. If you don't believe this, you can ask this question to your men friends: Who is Jo March? It's a question that almost all women can answer but very few men.

I wanted to write about a man who was not a buffoon. You may have noticed, if you put on the TV or go to films, that men have become the buffoons of our age. They are the ones who take the pratfalls; they are the fools. They are the ones who slip on the banana peels. It was very different when I grew up in the '50s with mother-in-law jokes. I thought there was nothing wrong with mother-in-law jokes, or maybe I sensed something wrong but couldn't put my finger on it. The dumb secretary joke, the various ways in which women became figures of fun.

Women who went out to buy hats when they were depressed. Women who wore certain kinds of aprons. I think men have taken this role, and I didn't want my Larry to be a buffoon. When I finished the novel and read it, it felt as if I were going over it with a fine piece of sandpaper to get rid of those particular edges that I didn't want to be there. (By the way, I should tell you that, when this novel was launched in New York at Barnes and Noble, a man came up to me after the presentation and said, "I want to show you my business card." He put it down, and it said, "Larry Weller—Consulting Engineer." Born in 1950, as he confided in me. And I said, "I hope this isn't going to spook you." And he went straight into his male talk and said, "I can handle it.")

I'm going to read you just a short piece. Larry grew up in a work-ing-class family in Winnipeg. His parents had immigrated from England, as many people did at that time in the late '40s and early '50s to work in factories. There's a secret in his family, and the secret is his mother's sense of guilt. She has accidentally killed someone. Her mother-in-law, in fact. Her name's Dot Weller. This part takes place when Larry's about thirty years old.

> The history of Dot Weller, and how she killed her mother-in-law, came to her son Larry in small pieces, by installments as it were. He can't remember a time when he didn't know at least part of the story, and he's not sure, in fact, if he's ever been presented with a full account, start to finish, all at once. . . . (47).

> But it wasn't a heart attack that brought her mother-in-law's cataclysmic end. Oh, if only it had been, if only! Mum Weller's death—as was revealed later through laboratory testing—was caused by severe type C botulism. The source of the botulism was Dot's stewed runner beans, inadequately sealed, insufficiently heated—the same beans that had been standing in their pretty glass jar for the last two months, as purely green and sweet as innocence itself (51).

I should tell you that I have three English-language editors. One is in the UK, one in the U.S., and one in Toronto. They all belong to different companies, and they don't always agree on things, and I'm always trying to make peace between them. Some of the editing for this was done in the UK and by a freelance editor who lives in the wilds of Oxfordshire. We did this by email, a wonderful technology perfect for editing—back and forth, back and forth. One day I had an email from her that said, "We've got a problem." At this time, the Sunday dinner was in August. She said, "You have an August dinner, and you can't have Brussels sprouts until October." We either had to change the month or the vegetable. I got in touch with the New York editor, who said that she hated Brussels sprouts, but when she did eat them she bought frozen ones, and she could have them any month of the year she wanted. However, we did come to an agreement. We moved the dinner to October, but it made me think: you work on a novel for maybe two years, maybe more, and you think perhaps there's a vision there; you like to think that. But it really comes down to getting the right vegetable in the right month.

My Back Pages[56]

We shouldn't do it. It's incestuous. It's arrogant too. It's parochial in the extreme. It's tiresome to read, an offence to those outside the club, a public stroking of our own professional plumage, a preening, a strutting. But we do it anyway. We insist on writing books about writers and their struggles with the task of writing.[57]

We know perfectly well we ought to be writing about bus drivers and dentists and people who manufacture knife sharpeners. These individuals have valid lives, after all, and built-in narratives that may be every bit as meaningful as that of the misunderstood novelist suffering in his Brooklyn basement. Snappish critics tell us we should buckle down and produce fictions that centre on dedicated manicurists or those folks who design the drainage beds for interstate highways or make canoes out of natural materials. A certain amount of research would be required, naturally—some personal interviews or else serious grind sessions in the public library. Only think how the range of fiction would widen out.

Instead, we write about failed writers and (rarely) triumphant writers. About the minutiae of writers' block and the horrors of writers' promotion tours. About the first stirrings of the writerly impulse, or the "long littleness," to use writer Alan Bennett's phrase, of a life spent affixing small words to large empty pages, the heartbreaking futility of the enterprise, and the euphoria of occasionally getting it right.

We write—and we might as well be honest—about our own writing doubts or those of our literary friends and enemies. No laborious research is required, just an airing of observed angst or, as fascinating to us, analysis of the "process." No one can shut us up. We're like those radiant new mothers who can't stop talking about their infants; we know the writer's existence is irrelevant to the general reader—whoever he or she may be—but to us it's the richest territory we can know or imagine.

There *are* novelists who go to the trouble of cloaking their heroes in loose, crossover garments, turning them into painters or architects, but no one's fooled for a minute.

V.S. Naipaul doesn't even apologize. His remarkable 1987 novel *The Enigma of Arrival* opens with the firm assumption that the young narrator will become a writer but that he must first search for what his material will be. In the middle years of our century—in Trinidad, in New York, in London, and, later, in rural England—he observes, records, and discovers, finally, that he is a privileged witness to huge new migrations of people in the world, that he is himself part of the global phenomenon; this will be his subject. The elements of Naipaul's novel are diverse, episodic, and seemingly random, and there were times when reading the book that I doubted he would be able to bring it all together. He does. Brilliantly.[58]

John Updike is a novelist who has put more energy than most into understanding and conveying the texture of alternative work choices. Over the years, he has "done" a physicist, a building contractor, a car salesman, even a cult leader. But his two Bech books are my favourites. In *Bech: A Book*, 1965, and *Bech Is Back*, 1975, we meet Henry Bech, a novelist who is more celebrated for his writer's block than for his creative oeuvre. Updike's observations on literature and those who produce it are spiked with pungent cynicism and expressed in a loving syntax. "Bech talked of fiction as an equivalent of reality, and described how the point of it, the justification, seemed to lie in those moments when a set of successive images locked and then one more image arrived and, as it were, superlocked, creating a tightness perhaps equivalent to the terrible tight knit of reality" (*Bech: A Book*, Fawcett, p. 158). These two comic novels shine with writerly integrity, even as they hover on the cusp of farce.[59]

I read Michael Frayne's novel, *The Trick of It*, when it was first published in 1989, and I had the good fortune to read it in "a single sitting," which is how we are supposed to read short stories.[60] In this book, Mr. Frayne allows himself full presumption, writing about writing about writing, employing a loose-jointed but pulsingly intimate voice. "Are writers somehow different from other people?" he asks. How can we explain the "inventedness" of fiction (102), for surely we have to be able to "relate these figments to the figment-tree they came from" (102). The real trick of *The Trick of It* is that its author makes these questions hilariously absurd and also touchingly relevant.

There are those who found A.S. Byatt's *Possession*, 1990,[61] the work of an academic imagination, but for those of us who are both academics and writers—and there are quite a lot of us—this book felt like the real world as we know it, a sprawling, spewing world of books and those who create them. Ms. Byatt's solidly furnished universe is further anchored by the inclusion of actual writings of her fictional poets, Randolph Henry Ash and Christabel LaMotte. For a year or two after reading this exuberant literary novel, everything else I picked up felt watery.

Women's Voices in Literature[62]

In Muriel Spark's novel *Loitering with Intent*,[63] there is a woman character who pauses and addresses the reader: "What a fortunate thing," she says, "to be an artist and a woman in the 20th century." I can, without blinking, paraphrase this thought and bring it home. "What a fortunate thing to be a writer and a woman living in Canada at this moment."

Our literature has never been healthier. We are, perhaps, still colonial enough in our posture to measure that health by the international stamp of approval. Almost no one missed the fact, for instance, that two Canadians appeared on the Booker List this year. And on the *New York Times* list of the best books, fiction and non-fiction, published in 1996, two of the eight were by Canadian women, Alice Munro[64] and Mavis Gallant.[65] I was delighted to see our two senior writers honoured, but I was also pleased that Canadians took this honour in stride; it is almost as though such recognition has come to be accepted.

When I was in the UK a couple of years ago, every journalist I talked to put one question to me: "Why are we seeing so much Canadian writing, suddenly, and why so much writing from Canadian women?" Now, there's a part of me that resents this question since no one would think to ask, "Why is there so much Canadian writing by men?"

But another part of me, the more honest part, is curious about the perceived phenomenon. And it *is* only a perception. Men are still producing more novels than women in this country, more men are reviewing those novels, and more men are receiving our highest honour, the Governor General's Literary Award for Fiction. Since 1936, there have been forty men to win the prize and only seventeen women. The names of Robertson Davies,[66] Timothy Findley,[67] Guy Vanderhaeghe,[68] and Michael Ondaatje[69] ring loud across the land. Yet the myth, or truth, persists that Canadian literature is dominated by women.

But if, at the moment, our four or five strongest and most widely disseminated writers are women, let's look at possible reasons.

It is possible—and I'll just throw this out as a thought—that the preponderance of women is a coincidence, rather like those unaccountable localized outbreaks of brain cancer or longevity. Every statistical pattern pulls away from an average.

Or it could be that women are not necessarily writing better novels but novels about the kinds of things women readers are anxious to know about. So much has been left out of our fictions—childbirth, female sexuality, the angry woman, the sad woman, the marginal woman, as well as the middle-class woman—and the record demands to be set straight. One of my friends, going through a bad time herself, is looking for the serious menopause novel.

Or—another theory—it could be that women novelists are in the ascendancy around the world. The novel, after all, is the one literary form whose birth—around 1740—took place at a time when women were, for the first time, being educated in large numbers. Women, then, have been writing novels from the beginning, but they had to learn what territory was available to them. Denied the novel of action, the novel of ideas, they fell heir to the novel that reflected the daily life of ordinary people. This kind of novel was one shunted off into a corner called "domestic fiction," until it was realized, and not that many years ago, that everyone, men as well as women, possesses a domestic life.

Another reason we see so many women writers, and I think this theory is far more likely, is that seventy percent of those who read novels in our society are women, or so the booksellers tell us. Women, it seems, are hungry for the lives of other women. Perhaps we've always known this, but we needed Simone de Beauvoir[70] and Betty Friedan[71] to tell us that the narratives of our lives had value. We needed Kate Millet[72]—in 1970, I think—to remind us that we didn't have to take Henry Miller seriously any longer, and what a relief that was. I had always felt locked out of certain texts at the heart of the Western canon—Hemingway comes to mind—because they projected a world in which I did not hold citizenship, a world of action, revenge, ideas, politics, war.

We think of the women's movement as an epic of demonstrations and marches and consciousness-raising groups, but it was also an era in which women could read about the real life of women. As a friend of mine says, "They also serve who only sit and think." She might have said, "only sit and type" or "only sit and read." There really is a network of women readers—ask publishers—in which one woman says to another, or to ten others, "There's this book you've just got to read." Often that book will be by a woman and will present something ostensibly simple, which is the substance of women's lives.

We need that substance. It feeds us courage. It normalizes the marginal, brings to the centre those voices which have been so long on the edge.

The edge, of course, can offer a privileged perspective, the geographical edge, the gender edge. It can be free of cynicism, if not anger. And it can bring forward a real or a willed innocence of vision, which is what I think every writer needs to maintain.

Virginia Woolf[73] (like one of the characters in one of my novels, I have a Woolfian bias) invoked in me an impulse to be serious. And then Margaret Laurence said to me, through her writing, "serious, yes, but watch out for earnestness." Mavis Gallant shows how it is possible to be intelligent on the page without being pedantic. Margaret Atwood,[74] who is, I suppose, Canada's first international star, is just plain brave—she'll tackle any orthodoxy and almost always with wit. Alice Munro describes in one of her stories what real work is. It's not just housework or looking after husband and children; my real work, the narrator says, is "wooing distant parts of myself." These distant parts, these concealed layers of existence, shame or ecstasy or whatever, are what every writer works to get to the heart of.

Part of the appeal of women writers may be the intimacy of voice. I often think how women writers sitting at their desks are speaking not to the ages or to Humankind but to individual readers, as though those readers were in the same room, and what they are speaking about is the texture of their own lives. Women writers often seem willing to engage with vulnerability, including themselves *in* that vulnerability. As a woman who has elected a writing life, I am interested in writing away the invisibility of women's lives, looking at writing as an act of redemption. In order to do this, I need the companionship, the example, of other writing women.

The writer Kennedy Fraser, in an essay on Virginia Woolf,[75] confesses that she once suffered a time in her life which was so painful that reading about the lives of other women writers was the only thing that comforted her. She claims she was slightly ashamed of this, pretending to her friends that she was reading the novels and poetry of these women, but, in fact, it was their lives that supported her. "I needed," she says, "all that murmured chorus, this continuum of true-life stories, to pull me through. They were like mothers and sisters to me, these literary women, many of them already dead; more than my own family, they seemed to stretch out a hand." I've seen this passage from Kennedy Fraser's essay quoted a dozen times and can only guess that it summons up for others, as it does for me, the reader-writer relationship that so many of us know and are indebted to.

It may be, too, that women's writing today is more aware of itself, more inclusive, less oppressed by male patronizing or erasure, less in danger of its substance falling off the edge. As recently as 1988, one of our finest writers, Bonnie Burnard,[76] was taken to task by *Globe and Mail* critic William French.[77] Her book *Women of Influence* was unacceptable to Mr. French. "The melancholy tone is unrelenting," he wrote, "and we want to escape the emotionally frigid world she portrays with such power. . . . Burnard has undeniable talent, and the women's problems she explores in these stories undeniably exist, but I hope in her next collection she can make me laugh at least once."

Like a performing seal. Like a courtesan. No wonder women's books became a refuge for women readers. There they found themselves; there they could be themselves. There they felt the distance shrink between what was privately felt and universally known. Women, I think, were hungry for their own honesty—they'd talked about it (women have always talked), but they needed to see it written down.

I'm always a little thrown when people ask me what I write about. I shuffle my feet and explain that I *don't* write thrillers or mysteries or science fiction or historical fiction. I write, more or less, mostly, some of the time anyway, hmmmm, about women's lives.

And at this point I can put away my typescript because I'm going to talk about some of these women. You all know that you don't need notes to talk about your children.

Not that I really *do* see them as children. They are closer to being sisters or close friends, and probably, though I am *very* hesitant to admit it, they are chips off my own psyche. To start with, there is Judith Gill, her friend Nancy Krantz, Charlene Forrest, Brenda Bowman, Sarah Maloney, Rose Hindmarch.[78]

Women and the Short Story[79]

I am going to begin by begging your special indulgence. I'd like you to receive my thoughts on women and the short story for what they are—a few unconnected, unframed ideas which happen to be drifting through my consciousness at this particular time of my life—spring, Ottawa, 1986. To discuss the short story, there's something audacious about this, when I've not fully articulated, even to myself, what a short story is, and I'm anxious, above all, not to pronounce, since it's the burden of pronouncement which has sometimes made the lot of women writers a difficult one.

We're always hearing, to deal with a major myth, that there are more women writers than men around, as though women were somehow engaged in an aggressive conspiracy to take over. It's interesting that no one ever goes around saying how odd it is that there are so many male writers. This has been going on for a long time. In 1853, J.M. Ludlow[80] advised his British readers, "We *have* to notice (regard the coercion) the fact that at this particular moment of the world's history, the very best novels in several great countries happen to be written by women." And a CBC producer remarked to Margaret Atwood a few years ago, "A number of us are upset because we feel women are taking over the Canadian literary scene." Is this paranoia? And what is it based on? There are eighty-seven writers represented in the widely used *Norton Anthology of Short Fiction*[81]—only twenty-two are women. In John Moss's *Reader's Guide to the Canadian Novel*,[82] there are write-ups of 110 novelists—only thirty of them women. Only twenty percent of Governor General Awards have gone to women, and only twenty percent of review space in Canadian newspapers goes to women writers. Moving around the world a little, there are forty-eight short stories in the *World Classic Edition of Australian Short Stories*[83]—seven by women. In a recent *TLS*,[84] one picked up at random, the index revealed Johnathan reviewing Parker, Harold reviewing Jeremy, Otis reviewing Laurence, on and on, seventeen major reviews, just two involving women. *But wait*: In *The New*

Press Anthology #2,[85] we find eight men and eight women. And in Robert Weaver's new anthology,[86] eight men and *ten* women. Somewhere there is a tide turning, and it may just be here.

And if this is so, let me move quickly away from arid statistics (sadistics) to the question of quality. Why does it seem—and again this is difficult to prove—that the Canadian short story is flourishing around the world and that the women are contributing to that flowering? Some of it must be put down to a random dispensation of talent which makes it presumptuous to speculate on the why and how of an Alice Munro or Mavis Gallant—we just have to be grateful to have them. On the other hand, we're all familiar with the history of the short story as we know it. It began with Poe[87] and Hawthorne,[88] a child of the New World. It's almost as though newly opened regions clamour, not for old tales and myths, but for an account of present moments of experience. Maybe now the frontier has shifted, shifted northward and westward, but shifted most dramatically to that previously unfranchised half of the human race whose experiences were mostly buried in journals and letters and in that perverted but courageous old creature, the potboiler.

There are a few myths about women's writing that can be put under the sod. That women excel at the short story because they write out of fragmented experience, between batches of biscuits or tubs of laundry. That women write short stories because they're forever signing up for creative writing courses down at the Y which concentrate on the short-story form. That something diminutive about the size of women, and something unspoken and fluffy, predispose them to shorter forms and prohibit them from diving into more epic work. That the precision, dexterity, compression, and frugality of the female imagination serve the short-story form, as does something else called the female voice in literature.

The female imagination is problematic because it brings to mind something monumental and eternal when, in fact, it is only what is concerning women at a particular time, a constantly changing and developing pool of ideas or images or whatever, which *some* women, *in general, from time to time, may* share.

And I would be happy to embrace the altogether attractive myth of the feminine voice. It is tempting to believe that delicacy, fluidity, subtlety, and elegance are more pronounced in the writing of women. We would be gladly served by the belief that women are masters of rich language patterns, intricate clustered metaphors, or a syntax which is artful, supple, and suggestive—but can we prove it?

What we do often find in women's work is a time which we may describe as present and personal and urgent. Often, too, the emotional range is wider. There is perhaps less exaggeration, less mythologizing. Settings tend to be simple but universal: enclosures, rooms, houses. And crossing borders, in any direction, we can find a commonality of subject matter, subject matter made accessible by the fact of its being rooted in the lives of women and easily translatable from one culture to another. It is a universal truth, for example, that the majority of women have been mothers and therefore witnesses to the growth and development of human personality. And until recently, there has been the universally shared problem of confinement and expectation; cut off from the world of affairs and from a history of their own, women have turned instinctively to the present moment and to the immediate concerns of what it means to be a woman, of sometimes surrendering power in order to remain human. But do these writers of universal themes find a universal audience? Are they taken seriously? Less than five years ago, a Canadian reviewer described a novel which illuminated the subject of motherhood as a "diaper" novel. With this term, he attacked not the way in which the novel was written but more basically the validity of the experience and its rightful place in literature. It has been a struggle for women writers to persuade themselves that their experiences are relevant. Other people who must be persuaded are the following: publishers, editors, Canada Council juries, teachers of creative writing, reviewers, booksellers, and finally readers—those readers who sometimes shuffle their feet and apologize for the fact that they mainly read women writers.

Women writers—everywhere—share what Isak Dinesen[89] called the "business of being a woman," those demands which cut into a woman's time. It is only, women often think, at the expense of others that they can give themselves permission to write. Listen to Katherine Mansfield[90] writing about the early days of her relationship with John Middleton Murry:[91] "This house seems to take up so much time. I get frightfully impatient and want to be working. Well, someone's got to wash dishes and get food." Washing dishes may seem a feeble whine, but the key words in Mansfield's complaint are "frightfully impatient," because impatience leads to frustration, and frustration to *anger*, and if we listen to Virginia Woolf *anger* often creates a distortion in a work of art, robs it of wit, blurs its edges, provides nothing but a dumping ground for the emotions.

It seems to me we're at an interesting period here on the *frontier.* A certain amount of dumping has taken place, and a certain amount of permission has been given. Women are feeling more secure in the literary world, and we can even imagine a time, twenty or thirty years down the road, when someone will appear on a panel like this and address the question of why so many of our stories are—but I see that my time is up.

The Feminine Line[92]

With your permission, I would like to trace a fast, ludicrously simplified line of descent in Canadian women's writing. There will be just three brief stops on this 220-year tour, but each of them is representative as well as substantive.

First stop, 1769, a book by an English woman called Frances Brooke, *The History of Emily Montague*. Frances Brooke came to the garrison of Quebec around 1763 in order to join her husband, who was posted there. She stayed, as far as we know, about five years. Her novel, and it is generally considered the first Canadian novel, is, like many others of the time, epistolary in form and *very very* long. You've heard of the triple-decker Victorian novel; this book consisted of four volumes. How did she fill so many pages? What on earth did she write about? A great deal about the manners, customs, and fashions of the culture of the Québécois. Some spirited, romantic observations on the culture of the Indians. Rather a lot of extravagant scenery description. Surprising quantities of political commentary and, yes, a love story, teasing, witty, amusing for the most part, quite polite, with some mild embarrassments and standard setbacks, affording Frances Brooke the opportunity to express her not very revolutionary views on male-female relationships. The book was very popular in its day, running to several editions and translated into Dutch and French.

And now I want to jump ahead with you almost one hundred years to Susanna Moodie's *Roughing It in the Bush*. Instead of four volumes, there are now only two. Instead of the letter-writing form, Mrs. Moodie uses a mélange of essay and that peculiar hybrid, the sketch, but most students of Canadian literature have agreed to call this odd book a novel. It, too, was popular, running to several editions, one of them still in print today, though it excited its share of outrage too. With what, then, did Mrs. Moodie fill her pages? Like Frances Brooke, she had an eye for scenery and local customs. She had a number of rather conventional political theories and a compulsion for comparison so overwhelming that it can only have been the result of profound personal shock and also a preoccupation with human anomaly, oddity, irregularity, singularity; in other words, the ineffable mystery of human personality, and very often the ways in which men and women accommodated each other and divided what power they possessed.

And now another jump forward on the timeline, 1985, the publication of a slim single volume, eighty-seven pages to be exact, by a Manitoba woman, Smaro Kamboureli.[93] From Greece originally, educated partly in the U.S., and about to move to British Columbia, she will no doubt continue to be claimed by Manitoba. The book, called *in the second person* (1985), is written in the form of journal entries, but some of the entries, Smaro Kamboureli explains, have been recast or fictionalized in order to make them more accessible. The book has been called variously a book of poetry, a work of autobiography, a meditation, and a novel. What does it deal with? It touches on the manners and mores of the contemporary world, though with a far greater degree of personal voice than either Frances Brooke or Susanna Moodie permitted themselves. There are also observations concerning nature—food, growth, sexual politics, and love between men and women. The book has been read with interest in Canada and may, like the other two books I've mentioned, go into several editions and enter the literary history of the country.

And so we have Smaro, Susanna, and Frances—I feel friendly enough toward all three to use their first names. Imagine, if you will, these three gathered together for, shall we say, a cup of tea and some conversation or, if you insist, discourse. Will Frances, that prodigious writer of quadruple-deckers, monopolize the conversation? Will Susanna, always quick to take offence, a bristling (some would say neurotic) woman, feel herself the odd one out? Will Smaro, by far the best educated, intimidate the others with her learning or puzzle them with her critical vocabulary?

I think not. This tea party, this discourse, is going to be a success, as such things are measured. I imagine a generous exchange of ideas, an excited acknowledgement of each other's predicament, system of values, historical context, creative yearning and frustration, and sources of energy. Once the initial silence is broken, and this silence may be seen to be inversely related to the numbers of pages in each of these three women's books, conversation will flow, *because* what these three women share is greater by far than what separates them. I have already mentioned the fact that each of them wrote fiction, that each expressed her fiction through whatever form lay readily at hand—the letter, the sketch, the poem, the journal. That each dealt in observation and reflection, and each wished to understand something of the world and particularly those tensions between men and women, between the self and the expression of the self. And each of them—and this is what will eventually enliven their hour together and seal their friendship—each of them wrote about the shock of dislocation.

Frances Brooke, to be sure, came to Canada with the assurance of a return ticket. She underwent other risks, illness for instance, drowning at sea, political unrest, but hers was an extended visit and not an immigration. She was not obliged to embrace or be embraced by an alien society. She could afford the detachment of the transient and temporary. *Everything* was interesting to her because she had power over it. Behind her were the bulwarks of family, money, prestige—for she had already published a novel in England—and expectation: Samuel Johnson[94] himself is said to have seen her off on her voyage and wished her godspeed.

Susanna Moodie immigrated without the return ticket and with a full set of false expectations. She and her husband came to Canada out of ignorance, with insufficient capital and experience. She suffered social as well as geographical dislocation, moving from the large, comfortable, Jacobean house of her childhood to a hastily converted pigsty in Ontario, from the liberal and literary salons of London, where she had just begun to get her feet wet, to the raucous, hostile banalities of her Yankee neighbours. That she made the best of her difficult lot, transforming with her imagination her experience into comedy and drama, will certainly win her the admiration of both Frances and Smaro.

Smaro Kamboureli, though she doubtless arrived in the New World by means of jet aircraft, seven hours in the air instead of seven weeks at sea, suffered, it could be said, an even more profound displacement, entering not just a new culture but a new language. The immigrant experience, she says in an introductory essay, is a form of abjection, that is, of humiliation. "But," she continues, "my immigrant condition affords me the perverse pleasure of a double view. Life, for those who change their language, splits itself down the middle. Every object has two names instead of one. Every person belongs either to the old self or the new self, to the old world or the new home. The doubleness can never be escaped, and the fact that it is possible to travel back and forth fairly easily between the two points of reference, switching tongues and cultures, makes it all the more difficult to surrender *one* self to the other. Something is gained, something is irrevocably lost."

Why, you may ask, did these three women decide to write about their experiences? We don't know what drove Frances Brooke, but we know her characters and can imagine one of them saying, "Well, one must keep one's self amused," but do we believe this—that these thousands of words were merely self-distraction? Mrs. Moodie is more forthright, or is she? "I hope only," she says, "that this little book will help some reader while away a rainy afternoon."

We have to remember that in the eighteenth and nineteenth centuries women rarely described their literary work as a means of discovering what was central to their own lives, and these two early books are *very very* long, perhaps because they carry with them the burden of additional texts, secret texts, unconscious texts, the diverting, placating strategy employed by a marginal culture, the need to protect itself by a deliberate understanding of intention.

It's very tempting at this point to offer you the following theory: that women's writing, in Canada at least, is still being written from a point of view that derives its energy and edge from its position of dislocation. I am going to resist that temptation out of a belief that such theories ignore experience that cannot be accommodated.

Furthermore, dislocation fits the present situation less well than another, more positive, word: *relocation*. There have been a number of interesting shifts in women's writing in recent years, too various to be concentrated neatly under one heading or even within national categories. I want briefly to mention some of these relocations, and then perhaps we can open it up into a discussion. I would welcome a discussion much more than a question-and-answer session since I find, as an immigrant, a woman fiction writer in mid-life, that I have more questions than I have answers.

To begin, then, there are a *lot* of women writing in Canada today, more than ever. There is even a myth—perhaps you've heard it—that Canada is *over*-represented by women writers. But is this true? You only have to stop and count—and question. Would anyone ever say, for instance, that there was a disproportionate number of *men* writing in the country? In fact, about sixty percent of novels in Canada are written by men. And, parenthetically, let me say that about seventy percent of novel *readers* are women, which may account for something male critics have mentioned—a kind of complicity between women writers and their readers.

Two interesting historical coincidences have affected women and the writing of novels. One of course, and there is nothing new about this notion, is that the growing literacy of women came during the eighteenth century, which was also the time when the English novel came into being, a new form without rules and classical definition, allowing women a natural entry. The second important coincidence occurred more recently when feminist critique of our dominant cultural structures collided with a postmodernist critique in the arts. Feminist inquiry on all levels has challenged and relocated previously unquestioned and unassailable ideas of what literature *is* and what it is *for*.

Women have, in a sense, been given permission to speak their own language—they gave *themselves* this permission, appropriating what was theirs. Some women writers—I am thinking of Canadian poets Daphne Marlatt[95] and Betsy Warland[96]—feel the need to go back in history and reclaim the lost language memory of women that predates the dictionary and other institutionalized concepts.

Whether or not this is wholly possible I don't know, but I've been interested in watching women affirm the importance and validity of their experiences in fiction in recent years. Twenty years ago, it was thought frivolous and inessential and even distasteful for women to write about their bodies, about childbirth and child-rearing, about the texture of the quotidian. These fictions were often derided. They were thought to belong to a sub-genre, to be precious, to provide housewives with role models or propitiating pats of approval. Though these novels were sometimes called Austenesque or miniaturist in the Katherine Mansfield manner, they were not considered serious in the same way that books about war or race relations were considered serious. It was as though the experience of half the human race lacked value.

At the same time as women legitimized this material, they entered into a radical critique of settled forms, questioning such sanctified polarities as tragedy and comedy and even more successfully challenging that terrible tyrant *unity of sensibility*.[97] Whoever decided that unity of sensibility was a good thing? Whoever possessed such a thing as unity of sensibility or would even want to? In the interest of *disunity*, women have been finding new ways of telling stories—some of these new ways are really old ways: letters, diaries, oral tales in which the voice is present and personal, discursive and very often circular. Stories are frequently told in clusters, in which the so-called side stories are as important as the so-called main story. You can see this very clearly in the legends Margaret Laurence uses to enrich *The Diviners*[98] or the way Alice Munro uses two stories or three and plaits them together into one. *Digression* is also important in women's stories, not in the old self-protective way of Susanna and Frances, but because digression provides depth, texture, surprise, and truth. Linearity has never had much to do with women's lives, which were always considered interruptible, and the break in linearity in women's fiction occurred naturally. Think of the way Alice Munro stops the timeline in her stories by saying, "I forgot to tell you that. . . ." Or the way Margaret Laurence uses her Memory Bank paragraphs, again in *The Diviners*. Or Joan Barfoot's novel *Dancing in the Dark*,[99] which begins at the end of the story. Closure or resolution—whatever you choose to call it—often seems artificial and contrived and untruthful in women's stories, which tend toward the circular, the spiral, or simple openness. Women have also questioned the referential element of writing, the need for universality and larger extended meanings, insisting more and more on the quirky, anomalous singularity of their individually operating, unguarded, untutored, separate, and worthy experiences.

But there is a communal side to women's writing, too. I will mention, since this is a Manitoba gathering, a group of seven young women writers in Winnipeg who have formed a collective which they call Hiatus—so named because it fills a gap. It is a group, says one of its members, the poet Pamela Banting,[100] that works together but without submergence or denial of identity.

And at a more radical edge of the critical community there is, as you know, a denial even of the old idea of originality. Linda Hutcheon,[101] in a recent *Canadian Forum*[102] article, sees so many literary echoes, direct and indirect, in Audrey Thomas's novel *Intertidal Life*[103] that she concludes, along with other critics, that community has replaced individualism, that writing is no longer a single, unique inscribing but a kind of parallel script.

You may well ask is this true? And, if it is true, is it conscious or unconscious? And you might also ask whether or not this is a temporary communal need on the part of women or a permanent and healthy feature or an acknowledgement of what has always been but never admitted or a dangerous cul-de-sac. Smaro Kamboureli and Susanna Moodie and Frances Brooke may, in their discussions of women's writing, agree to disagree, as Kristjana Gunnars,[104] one of the members of Hiatus, says about her experience in that group. Yes, says another member, Kathie Kolybaba, "but by coming together at least we have eased the pain of disagreeing."

I like to think that women writers have the power to create new forms but also the power to conserve what is best, and has always been best, in their writing. In one of the letters in Frances Brooke's novel, the protagonist, Emily Montague, writes from Quebec these words: "In my next letter I will send you a frost piece." What, you may ask, is a frost piece? A frost piece[105] is a little bit of self-conscious, embroidered prose work, a carefully worked paragraph of descriptive lyricism, a winter scene transformed into a literary doily. I think it is important to note that even in 1769 Frances Brooke was using the term ironically. I hope that, in the imagined discourse between Smaro, Susanna, and Frances, irony will get a good word, that it will continue to be a part of women's writing, moderating earnestness and providing that rare commodity, humour.

And I hope, too, that Susanna Moodie's rainy afternoon reader will be remembered. *And* the late-night reader. *And* the reader at the back of the bus, or in the hospital bed, or sitting under the apple tree. As everyone knows, writers need readers, and readers need writers, and both readers and writers need the bracing, regenerating force of criticism.

But we need to ask ourselves where criticism is taking us. Marilynne Robinson, the American critic, in a remarkable essay called *Language Is Smarter than We Are*,[106] reminds readers that, before the world was entirely known—and we only have to go back to the time of Frances Brooke or even Mrs. Moodie—maps were left unfinished at the edges. Where knowledge frayed, so did the oceans and land masses. At the mysterious corners, mapmakers put sphinxes, satyrs, nymphs, serpents, and the like. Readers of old maps knew that the symbols stood not for theoretical projection but for the unknown.

"Bad assumptions," Robinson says, "are never better than no assumptions at all. Among all the constellated forms of describable relationships in the world, there are mists in which we do not yet see configuration. These should neither be denied nor subsumed in other ways of perceiving."

Theory is a tool, she reminds us, but not a belief. It can blind critics, throttle writers and alienate readers, and lead us away from the knowledge that the making of art is mysterious and its powers of transformation probably unknowable.

Marilynne Robinson's point of view seems to me to have the same freshness of approach that I see in much Canadian women's writing. A very quick list would include Merna Summers, Edna Alford, Aritha van Herk, Joan Clark, Margaret Clarke, Sandra Birdsell, Joan Barfoot, Joy Kogawa, and Susan Kerslake.[107] I needn't mention Atwood, Laurence, Munro, Gallant, Rule,[108] and Thomas since these writers are well known to you.

Quite a number of these writers are nearing or have passed their fiftieth birthdays and have begun sending fresh reports from this new frontier. Along with other Canadian readers, I'm watching with interest.

The New Canadian Fiction[109]

I'll begin this talk with a four-letter word: *Whew!* Whew, for a while there, I worried about the future of fiction, which resembled nothing so much as an invalid thrashing and writhing on an ever-narrowing bed. But the threat of other media—films, video, and particularly television—each wanting a slice of narrative, has brought to the novel and short story a flush of health, perhaps even the beginning of a new default tradition in which the written word does what only the written word can do.

It was a close call. The patient nearly died. There was a lengthy period in which we endured a crisis of meaning so traumatic that we began to think that, since words could mean anything, they could also mean nothing. Luckily, the world kept intruding, and linguistic skepticism remained a theory. Besides, only a few writers—Barthelme,[110] Gass,[111] Calvino,[112] DeLillo[113]—seemed able to squeeze any juice out of the thing. On the whole, what is labelled postmodernist writing has been far too generously forgiving, and during the worst of the plague a great deal of fast-food ambiguity, in love with its own slight muscle tissue, passed itself off as the real thing. Video fiction, some called it, because it so resembled the short, randomly juxtaposed scenes of TV shows. Some writers, like Ann Beattie,[114] really did succeed in obliterating the boundary between high and low art and found a huge audience; other writing was so frozen in its self-consciousness that it went unread. Some that *was* read and genuinely delighted in—I think of Barth's *Lost in the Funhouse*,[115] for instance—now seems only mildly provocative or merely cute. The questioning of the book as book led, as we know, to acts of adolescent rebellion—for instance, leaving the page numbers off or, in one case, having two page 90s. Why?—to show it could be done, and so what was sensible, logical, and satisfying in our texts was overturned.

Nevertheless, the idea of treating language as play seemed for a time to offer a new perspective. Writers were relieved of the responsibility of creating a believable world and of investing that world with meaning—there *was* no fixed meaning—and telling a story that derived its tensions from the springs of cause and effect, from psychological motivation or moral consequence. Writers could lean on the absurdity of the endeavour, and their *texts*, that curious but useful word, could be crisped and refreshed by the knowledge that this was, after all, a game.

But how anxious theory is and how arbitrary; today's heresies become tomorrow's orthodoxy. Theories about literature, the text and the text makers, often prove too tendentious, too labyrinthine, and it is disappointing to find that even a theory that illuminates and delights the intellect can fail to convince—and, more important, fail to produce. A postmodernist perspective was inevitable, emerging as it did from high-consumption capitalism, which demands a ceaseless transformation of style, from scientific discourse, which enshrines the discontinuous, from the passivity of a television age, from the recognition of a multi-ethnic society, from the exhaustion of post-positions (that is, postwar, post-hippie, post-'60s), from the homogeneity of our times, which assumes worldwide acquaintance with such artifacts as shopping centres and pop stars, not to mention the rapid ceaseless shifting of computer bytes. The postmodern mode is compilation, writing as patchwork, as pastiche. But writing held captive by other writing neglects to see what hasn't yet been written. There may be nothing new under the sun, but there are portions of our human experience that have not been embraced by our literature, not by the traditionalists, nor by the modernists, nor by the postmodernists.

Curiously, and perhaps thankfully, there has been amongst postmodernist thinkers, and from the beginning, a disparity between theory and practice that signalled a certain effort of accommodation and an easy forgiveness of imprecise expression or ironic aloofness—some would say elitism. Language which might have been liberated often shrank from our touch; we have seen how writers, strangled by theory, become incomprehensible. The Canadian writer Don Coles[116] has written a wonderful poem about a tragic Portuguese child who was kept by her parents in a chicken coop and who, when finally rescued by neighbours, was found to "talk" like a chicken.

Just as serious, because it came about the same time, was the apparent exhaustion of realism in fiction, already badly nibbled away anyway by other media that could often do it better. The old problem-solution trick began to seem like a set-up, and writers started asking how much realism there was in realism. The experience of women, for example, was insufficiently represented and honoured. And valued and listened to and published and read and respected and taught and elected to the canon. Most of what we called realistic fiction began to look like a photo opportunity for catching people in crisis. (If you think divorce statistics in our society are alarming —half of all marriages doomed—you should look up the figures in contemporary fiction.)

The so-called real world was too often shown as fragmentary, a sort of secondary lesion of the senses, interrogated on every side by technology, unwilling to stand still long enough to be captured by definition. Language itself, our prized system of signs and references, frequently appeared emptied out or else suspiciously charged. Realism focused too compulsively on those phantom polarities, comedy and tragedy. It trafficked too freely in catastrophe, leaned too lazily on mental aberration. (Mental illness, after all, is an illness like any other except that it is particularly unsatisfactory fictional fuel because it deprives its victims of a moral sense, and without a moral sense there can be little tension.) Realistic fiction also imposed artificial structures—extraordinary rules or prohibitions such as, to give an example, a major character must not be introduced after the first third of a novel. And why not? a few bold writers began to ask. Suspicion eventually gathered around fiction that was unimpeachably composed, arranged in those classic tableaux of conflict or sailing under the various banners marked farce, comedy of manners, or novel of ideas. So-called realistic fiction searched too diligently for metaphysical resonance and too preciously for graceful epiphanies. It banished certain parts of our language to certain emotional parts of the house. The people who appeared in "realistic fiction" were almost never allowed the full exercise of their reality, their daydreams, their sneezes, their offended appetites, their birthday parties, their toothaches, their alternating fits of grotesque wickedness and godly virtue. Their meditative life was neglected. Realistic fiction passed too quickly through the territory of the quotidian, and it dismissed, as though they didn't exist, those currents of sensation that leak around the edges of vocabulary. The realist tradition stressed—why? because it was more dramatic?—the divisiveness of human society and shrugged at that rich, potent, endlessly mysterious cement that binds us together. The historical background was shaded in, another set-up. Big, heavy themes were painted on top of flimsy material. William Styron,[117] with extraordinary naïveté, confesses sitting down and going through a list of major themes, counting them off on his fingers, as it were, before deciding that the Holocaust[118] was the theme for him. (I'm trying hard to keep the disgust out of my voice.) The Holocaust was big, it was weighty, its passions could be borrowed.

Writers became frightened or else exasperated—no wonder—and retreated for a time into what became known as minimalism, a post-age-stamp realism so restricted that entire novels were composed of media syntax, brand names, and infantile expletives. Novelists, it seemed, were always out buying cheap underwear at Sears, or else they were down at the 7-Eleven hanging out. Cynical, we seemed to lose faith in our culture, which is diminished at the level of language as well.

Nevertheless, these are interesting times for a writer. The crisis of meaning, and we nearly died of it, has brought us a new set of options. The strands of reality that enter the newest of our fictions are looser, more random and discursive, more attentive to language, more respectful of the reader, more willing to connect word with world. More altogether seems possible. The visual media, television and the cinema, have appropriated the old linear set-ups, leaving fiction the more interesting territory of the reflective consciousness, the inside of the head where nine-tenths of our lives are lived.

The new new fiction—for what do you call what comes after postmodernism?—seems to me to be letting in some of what Annie Dillard[119] calls particles of the world, but hanging on to the boldness and linguistic daring that the best postmodernists showed us, a new spoon of grammar stirring its bowl of words in a different way. A return to realism, perhaps, but a reality that is enormously expanded so that those private areas of human consciousness have found a way into our fictions. We spend, after all, most of our lives submerged in a kind of watery silence which is almost never reflected in literature. It gets forgotten, it gets overlooked, it gets dismissed, even while it whispers and snuffles and nags and informs us of what we share.

The evidence is accumulating—in some British writing, in much American writing, very occasionally in Canadian writing—and recently in the dropped remarks of some of our critics and reviewers—that we are coming into brave new fictional territory. But I should also confess that my thoughts about the direction of the new new new fiction are based not just on what I see but what I would *like* to see. In other words, the name of this talk should not be "The New Canadian Fiction" but "What I Would Like to See in the New Canadian Fiction."

What I would *not* like to see is what the American writer Tom Wolfe advocates in his widely read and just as widely discussed essay titled "Stalking the Billion Footed Beast: A Literary Manifesto for the New Social Novel." Many of you will be familiar with this piece that appeared in *Harper's Magazine* last November.[120] The writer, he says, must document what he calls "big rich slices of contemporary life." The second half of our century, he reports, is going to fall through the mesh of history because not one writer has come forward to document—this is his favourite word, *document*—America's "racial clashes, the hippie movement, the New Left, the Wall Street boom, the sexual revolution, the war in Vietnam." Who will the messiah be, he keeps asking throughout the essay, and then announces "the messiah has come, and it's me." (I'm quoting, of course, indirectly.) In his *Bonfire of the Vanities*, he claims to have rescued both history, which might otherwise have leaked away, and literature, which was being minimalized by a pseudo-elite bent on transforming itself into a European-style intelligentsia who believed that, since the social structure was crumbling, the realistic novel was pointless. He comes down hard on Calvino and Márquez and Robert Coover and John Hawkes.[121] It was John Hawkes, you will remember, who said, "I began to write fiction on the assumption that the true enemies of the novel were plot, character, setting and theme."

Wolfe writes this gang off as a temperature blip, saying that "the introduction of realism into literature in the eighteenth century by Richardson, Fielding, and Smollett was like the introduction of electricity into engineering. It was not just another device."[122] And one of the specialties of the realistic novel, he goes on, "was the demonstration of the influence of society on even the most personal aspects of the life of the individual." So let's get back on the Zola[123] and Sinclair Lewis[124] track, Wolfe says, doing what a writer must do—which is report on his society, not his personal psyche or the playful possibilities of language.

Wolfe's remarkably self-serving manifesto brought, as you can imagine, a storm of protest, many echoing Alison Lurie's comments that Wolfe seems utterly unaware of women writers.[125] Mary Gordon[126] accuses him of being the "thinking man's redneck and speaking from a position that comforts the uneasy." The most eloquent response comes from Scott Russell Sanders,[127] who says that fiction, deprived now of its original role as chief reporter of the news, has turned in other directions, directions the camera and microphone cannot go, "exploring past and future, measuring our familiar world by projecting alternatives, speculating on fundamental questions, challenging our notions of what is 'real' and renewing our vision." He lists a few practitioners: Russell Banks, Nicholas Delbanco, Don DeLillo, Louise Erdrich, Ursula Le Guin, Toni Morrison.[128] "In their pages," he says, "the life around us is richly examined, refracted and illuminated." Wolfe, uncowed, replies that these writers were turned from realism by an "intellectual fashion no more profound than a fashion in clothes."

The proof of the pudding, of course, is in the eating, and in eating Wolfe's book, *The Bonfire of the Vanities*, one finds some undigestible lumps and a good many missing ingredients. His world without women, a world without reflection, a world where that precious material *thought* is missing, a slickly observed world of almost obscenely pragmatic hucksters, bankers, fundamentalist preachers. He has no notion of domesticity—the fact that each of us possesses a domestic life seems to have escaped his reporter's eye. The realism of Tom Wolfe is a kind of arrested explosion.

But in another kind of contemporary fiction, fiction I hope is pointing to new possibilities for the form, we can see an *implosion*. The astonishing American writer Nicholson Baker has written a whole novel, *The Mezzanine*,[129] about a lunch-hour sortie to buy new shoelaces. He begins by describing the weightless, helpless, surprising sensation of breaking a shoelace, how it comes flying loose in the hand—a tactile sensation we all recognize but have never seen put into words, and furthermore—this is a kind of test, it seems to me—it can't be done on television. Baker tells us, viscerally, exactly what it feels like to be alive at this minute, what our small sustaining pleasures are, just how the delicate synapses of memory function, telling us by showing us—and how universally felt these sensations are. His second novel, *Room Temperature*, just published, is about what passes through the mind of a man during a twenty-minute period while he is giving his baby daughter her afternoon bottle. The richness and precision of language set it apart from the minimalism of recent years, *as* does its power to move us. *The Remains of the Day*[130] says, "We wait in vain for a drop of honest feeling to ripple the calm surface and touch the reader's heart." This article, I think, with its brave open talk about the reader's heart, that neglected organ, points beyond Ishiguro's novel to the new new fiction.

The New Yorker has published three astonishing stories this year by a new writer called Mary Grimm.[131] Two of them in particular, titled "We" and "Before," deal with material so domestic, so simple, so human, so precise in voice that their enormous impact on readers has come as a surprise to everyone. The magazine, which was beginning to grow elderly and polite and arch, has been inundated with letters, a flood of letters that comes close to the 1950 response to Shirley Jackson's story "The Lottery."[132] Yes, yes, these letters seem to say, this is what we've been waiting for. Mary Grimm is writing, I think, the new new new fiction. The whole noisy buzzing world is in it, but it is not Tom Wolfe's slackly, slickly observed, gentleman-around-townly world.

America's Mona Simpson in *Anywhere but Here*[133] and Jane Smiley in *The Greenlanders*[134] have revised and humanized and made new the old family saga novel. These two writers are as attentive to interior landscape as to external incident. Neither book is likely to be made into a miniseries.

In Britain, Michael Frayne's delightful novel *The Trick of It*[135] takes thick slabs of realism but arranges them in dazzling new ways, as letters, as meditations. The voice is bright, intelligent, and moving. It's more, a lot more, than a bag of tricks.

The best parts of Margaret Atwood's *Cat's Eye*,[136] those that deal with childhood terror and persecution, belong to the new new new fiction. The gaze is direct, the voice is controlled, the narrative urgent—and the focus particularized.

Canada's Alice Munro has been described by the American writer Cynthia Ozick[137] as "our new Chekhov," and her new book, *Friend of My Youth*,[138] has recently been reviewed by Bharati Mukherjee,[139] who claims that Munro has "*deepened* the channel of realism," that her sentences "stick to the rough surfaces of our world." Rather puzzlingly, she goes on to say that Munro has "persevered through periods when her writing was unfashionable"—but I am not sure this was ever true. Munro has written, to be sure, about the K-Mart world of the minimalists but always with elegance and fullness of language. In addition, her stories are powered by the discontinuity and surprise and edge of the postmodernists but not the insulatingly ironical.

Where *does* irony surface in the new new new fiction? Perhaps because of the breakdown of binary ways of thinking, irony can no longer simply attach itself to the flip side of the felt moment. It is forced to be much more *subversive*, to take on disguise, to form temporary alliances with such former oppositional forces as, I suggest, verisimilitude. Not that we are likely to go back to the old realism, the old innocence. Fiction's odd ability to stop and stare at itself—which has always lent a special charm to the form—is now everywhere acknowledged.

In the new new new fiction, I see first a use of language that possesses an accuracy that cannot really exist without leaving its trace of deliberation. I see, too, a risky, respectfully offered articulation of what I recognize but haven't yet articulated myself. And, finally, I see evidence of fresh news from another country, which satisfies by its modesty, a microscopic enlargement of my own comprehended sense of the world. I wouldn't dream of asking for more.

All a writer can do is deposit some small part of herself or himself into the vastness of the universe. But small does not mean insignificant. The new offerings seem to me to be full of promise. The new new new fiction lets the reader in, and—writer and reader—we live in our new creaturely dust, our own cracks in the world, thinking our unclassifiable, irreducible thoughts.

Crossing Over[140]

Fiction writers, doing their part to promote their books, welcome the chance to appear on a certain national network show. The host is genial and intelligent, and in fact it seems he actually reads the books. Nevertheless, the interviews almost always become a game of gentle cat-and-mouse in which the host attempts to link the work of fiction with the life of the writer, who is driven into cries of "No, no, this is fiction, I made it up." "Well, yes," the host agrees, "but it must have really happened, if not to you then to someone else."

There is a curious opacity here, perhaps even a kind of honourable innocence, which prefers to believe that people on the whole tell the truth and refrain from telling lies. This attitude, which seems to me to be very widespread, acknowledges the experience-plus-imagination recipe that makes fiction possible but for some reason devalues or distrusts the role of imagination.

Imagination, to be sure, is hard to talk about, this amorphous, transparent ether of the senses. We resort to metaphors, saying it is a kind of elementary wooden spoon with which we stir, blend, and generally rearrange life's offerings. Or we claim to lift it from the lint trap of our dreams or our unconscious. Or find it beneath a trapdoor labelled "What if—."[141] Or describe it as a species of wistful daydreaming or the artful resculpturing of actual experience to conform to a more satisfying aesthetic pattern. Alice Munro talks about "real" experience being a lump of starter dough, and everyone here knows how little that small damp yeasty lump resembles the risen loaf with its lightness and fragrance, its imaginative dimensions and substantiality. Russell Hoban,[142] speaking to the Manitoba Writers' Guild a few seasons back, encouraged us to *expand* our realities, to include in the realm of the real those not-so-rare moments of madness or transcendence. Audrey Thomas once declared in a radio interview that "everybody writes autobiography," but I wonder if she wasn't using the word *autobiography* as a filter that concentrates and refines the comprehended world and makes it legible to the individual consciousness. When Oonah McFee's first, and I think only, novel was published in 1976,[143] she was asked if the book was autobiographical. "Well," she admitted, "there's at least an arm and a leg of me in it."

Just how much arm and leg gets into the writing varies enormously from one writer to another, but I don't believe there's a writer alive who hasn't struggled with the alchemy of reimagined reality and the moral questions it poses. To write is to raid, the saying goes, although I suppose you might also say to live is to raid, life being mainly a kind of cosmic lost-and-found bureau or an everlasting borrowing and lending of communal experience.[144]

Writer as thief, writer as scavenger—almost all writers feel the sting of such charges, even, I've noticed, beginning writers or writers who have published nothing or writers who are only just *thinking* about writing. The question generally arises early in a creative writing course, how can we deal honestly with the experiences of others without injuring them? How, too, can we deal with our own experiences without exposing ourselves unmercifully? My advice is always to write first and revise later (or *disguise* later, as it were) since it's unlikely that a writer hobbled by the fear of giving offence is going to write at all. As my friend Sandy Duncan[145] says, there's no need to let facts get in the way of truth. The essential core of *truth* (that problematic word) need not necessarily be diminished if names are changed or if the short fat bond salesman becomes the tall thin lumberjack. In the same way River Heights can be renamed and moved to Nova Scotia if you like or even to Mars or Baloneyland. The fictional variables can be moved forward or backward in time, or else the timeline can be fractured or even smudged. (By the way, an astute interviewer once fixed me with a steely eye and demanded to know why the women in my novels were invariably tall and large-boned, with heads of thick, dark, curly hair.)

I would defend the rights of writers to use *any* experience they choose in their fiction, but I have come to think that it is more charitable, kinder that is, to refrain from embarrassing others or borrowing their stories without permission or else dramatic revision or, especially, redemption. Like everyone else, writers need to sleep easily at night. "I don't write about my family members or friends," says American novelist Barbara Kingsolver,[146] "because I want them to remain family members and friends."

But beyond the ethical questions of exploitation, beyond the simple respect for the privacy of others, is the work itself, and I am convinced that the increased weight of the imaginative element contributes to the aesthetic power of a piece of writing. Colouring outside the lines may be harder to accomplish but can yield more in the end than simple follow-the-dot transference. (Yes, I do recognize this as a botched metaphor, but I give myself permission to use it.)

On the other hand, I think we owe our work the texture and taste of the apprehended world, and it seems to me ungenerous to withhold those few insights we may have gathered along the way. The writer Kennedy Fraser, in a recent essay on Virginia Woolf,[147] confesses that she once suffered a time in her life which was so painful that reading about the lives of other women was the only thing that comforted her. She claims she was slightly ashamed of this, pretending to her friends that she was reading the novels and the poetry of these women, but in fact it was their lives that supported her. "I needed," she says, "all that murmured chorus, this continuum of true-life stories, to pull me through. They were like mothers and sisters to me, these literary women, many of them already dead; more than my own family, they seemed to stretch out a hand." In particular, she says, the brave autobiographical writings of Virginia Woolf answered her, as they also helped heal Woolf's own pain. In her fifties, shortly before she died, Virginia Woolf set down the history of child abuse she had suffered and wrote that "By putting it into words . . . I make it whole; this wholeness means that it has lost its power to hurt me." "Honest personal writing," Kennedy Fraser concludes in her essay, "is a great service rendered the living by the dead." What we need to establish, perhaps, is a new form, a form that invites the personal without risk to the self or to others and one that incorporates the author's voice without giving way to self-indulgence. One thinks of diaries or certain forms of memoirs or docufiction, forms that attempt to place the self in time.

Think of the loss to history if we fail to record the full and authentic lives of people, their private lives, their domestic lives. When Canadian writer Peter Ward began working on his 1990 book *Courtship, Love and Marriage in Nineteenth Century English Canada*,[148] he came, he says, "head-on into the frustration shared by all who want to know what the silent Canadians of the past thought and felt. The evidence of personal experience and feelings, of private conduct and personal relationships, is at best fragmentary." English historian Theodore Zeldin,[149] recording the history of France, could find only one account of eighteenth-century peasant life, though peasants at that time accounted for some eighty-five percent of the French population. The "Maps and Chaps" recording of history, as it is sometimes called, has carried forward only the sketchiest outline of society. It is no wonder that novelist Margaret Drabble[150] has been called a true chronicler of the late twentieth century; her novels hold the randomness of felt lives, the diurnal rub and drub of existence as it is experienced by at least a segment of our population. The eccentric but captivating fictions of Nicholson Baker rather bravely, I think, risk triviality in order to record what we all experience but hesitate to enter on the page, the sensation of a shoelace breaking loose in the hand, for instance, or the precise colour and muscular flicker of a baby's eyelid. The sensations, recordings, and reorderings of these writers, and others like them, add up to more than the sum of their small parts. This kind of writing takes time. You have to pay attention. You have to have the patience to move the words around until they are both precise and allusive. I believe it is worth the effort. You can think of such fictions as entries on a ledger that push past print into an expanded reading of our world in all its intricacies and mysteries.

Writers' Gender Swapping[151]

V.S. Pritchett[152] considers that the first duty of a fiction writer is to become someone else, and, as it happens, women writers, in an effort to create a fully furnished universe, are often called upon to write about men, and male writers to write about women. They go even further at times, not just writing about them, but speaking through their consciousness, using their voices. The question can be and often is asked, how successful is this gender hopping? Does any truth at all seep through? Maybe more than we think. Oscar Wilde[153] had the notion that we can hear more of the author's true voice in his or her fictional impersonations than we can hear in his or her autobiography. (Not that he bothered with all this his and hers frippery.) This is what he said: "Man is least himself when he talks in his own person, give him a mask, and he will tell you the truth." A mask, he said. He might just as well have said, or perhaps a skirt.

This is not to say that crossing gender consists of trickery or sleight of hand; nor is it a masquerade, as Anne Robinson Taylor in her new book *Male Novelists and Their Female Voices*[154] would like us to think. To believe this is to deny the writer the powers of observation and imagination and also to resist the true composition of a universe real or created, in which males and females exist in more or less equal numbers.

However, having said this, the general rule in literature, with some startling exceptions, seems to be that men are better at creating men and women at creating women—this despite the fact that as early as 1905 Freud was thinking about the possibility of the bisexual disposition. Jung went even further in his writing about the mixture of male and female which makes us human, and this is an idea which has found widespread acceptance. But, despite this, it is still considered a rare achievement for a man to have created a believable woman and a woman a believable—and morally balanced—man. We point to these as exceptions. Isn't it wonderful, we say, that Brian Moore could get inside the brain of Judith Hearne[155] and make us believe in her. And

Flaubert—how was he able to understand the temperament of a French housewife, her yearnings and passions?[156] And let's see, there must be a couple of others out there. And what about male characters created by women. Hmmmmm. Lots of villains. And lots of men who are just plain silly. Take Aylwin Forbes, the male hero of Barbara Pym's book *No Fond Return of Love*.[157] Aylwin is a man who describes his hobbies as wine and conversation—clearly, he's doomed. At least in Barbara Pym's sly eye. Jane Austen created a few men who were worth waiting four hundred pages for, but there's a chilliness about even the best of them. Margaret Atwood is always hearing complaints about the meanness of her women, but she says, in a recent essay, "Writing the Male Character," that novels don't come out of a vacuum.[158] There are flogging scenes in *Moby-Dick* because there was flogging aboard nineteenth-century ships. There are mean—or, rather, insensitive men—in modern fiction because there have been quite a lot of them around for quite a long time. She also makes the point that her villainous female characters go uncriticized; when men show the male character unfavourably, it's the human condition, but if a woman does it she's being a castrator. Just as George Orwell can get away with saying that every man's life viewed from within is a failure, but a woman saying the same thing might be leaving herself open to a charge of sexism. We would all agree, I think, that it's necessary for men to write about women and women to write about men, but it would seem they are required to tiptoe rather more carefully than when writing about their own sex.

Writers who attempt a radical change of persona are doomed to risk-taking but may reap unexpected benefits. Defoe,[159] Richardson, Dickens, Henry James, and James Joyce have all written from within the consciousness of women—with differing degrees of success. Indeed, Defoe's women, Moll Flanders[160] in particular, is considered by many to be a male character in skirts. Some writers have even used that most dramatic and challenging convention, the first-person voice, becoming the "I" of the women they write about. Perhaps it is, in a small way, easier for a man to write from a female point of view rather than the other way around, since femaleness is traditionally thought of as a state of mind, a mode of consciousness, rather than a simple "category," which is what "male" writing has been called. And writing in the female persona can offer a male writer some advantages. It may even occur quite naturally; a case can be made that writing itself is a feminine activity.

Writing has a passive side; writers are cut off from vigorous activity, the out-of-doors, the active life that we often associate with maleness. Traditionally, writers have led precarious, unprotected lives, dependent on patrons, and, of course, art itself is a sphere of life which has conventionally been seen as feminine.

But there may be a further reason that men have been drawn to writing these women characters; choosing to use a female persona has availed men a greater range of emotional experience—women may weep, faint, scream; they are allowed a measure of melancholy which would ill suit a man; they are permitted fits of narcissism that might look absent on a man. But there are problems: women characters who depart radically from the female stereotype, becoming scolds and shrews or strumpets, for example, are said to have a "masculine" side. And the mainstream women, Richardson's Clarissa[161] and Dickens's Esther Summerson,[162] for example, are stifled by a sense of decorum, which their authors feel is part of their womanhood.

Women writing through the consciousness of men have been relatively rare until recently. Fanny Burney[163] in her epistolary novels stuck almost exclusively to the female point of view. Charlotte Brontë uses the male voice in *The Professor*,[164] but the tone is painfully awkward. Brontë says: "In delineating male character, I labour under disadvantages; institution and theory will not adequately supply the place of observation and experience. When I write about women, I am sure of my ground—in the other case I am not so sure." Joyce Carol Oates[165] once remarked that she did badly with male narrators because the angle of vision was too restricted, and too much feeling and self-awareness had to be sacrificed. Mary Shelley[166] only partly succeeds with her Frankenstein—he is too much a demonstration of an explicit theme—males demand power and ruthlessly seek it. We often think of Flaubert as the master of the female psyche, yet Baudelaire[167] saw in Madame Bovary "an unlimited urge to seduce and to dominate, including a willingness to stoop to the lowest means of seduction, such as the vulgar appeal of dress and perfume and make-up, all summarized in two words, 'dandyism, exclusive love of domination,' which is more commonly male than female." In this country, we point to that rare exception, Brian Moore, whose Judith Hearne, and others, does ring with remarkable and terrifying authenticity to women readers as well as men. Leon Rooke's *The Fat Woman*[168] is also, I think, successful. On the other hand, we have Hugh Garner,[169] who made the gigantic blooper of having one of his women characters first remove her slacks and then her half-slip, a misunderstanding of surface detail which points to a more basic failure of understanding.

If few Canadian men have written about women, the question may be asked, is it because it is too difficult, or is it because it is considered to be lacking in interest? Women are still outside the power structure, and to write about them seriously not only requires intimate knowledge but a belief that their lives have value. Ordinary women—and I am setting aside dusty, old, eccentric "dames" or precocious and nubile teenagers—ordinary women may be perceived as being fluffy.

And why have so few Canadian women written—written well, I mean—about men? A few years ago we could point to a lack of experience in the world of men. As recently as 1950, Elizabeth Hardwick[170] had this to say about the difference in experience:

> If women's writing seems somewhat limited, I don't think it is only due to psychological failure. Women have much less experience of life than a man. *Ulysses* is not just a work of genius; it is Dublin pubs, gross depravity, brawls. Stendhal is a soldier in Napoleon's army, Tolstoy on his Cossack campaigns, Dostoevsky before the firing squad, Proust's obviously first-hand knowledge of vice, Conrad and Melville as sailors, Ben Jonson's drinking bouts. Experience is more than going to law school or having the nerve to say honestly what you think in a drawing room filled with men. In the end, it is in the matter of experience that women's disadvantage is catastrophic, and it is very difficult to know how this may be extraordinarily altered.[171]

But, of course, it has been extraordinarily altered, by legislation and a revolution in the way of thinking. And what has furthermore been altered is the sort of experience which can successfully be brought to literature, the sort of experience which deserves to be taken seriously. Mary Gordon, the American writer, complains that some people still think that Hemingway writing about boys in the woods is major, while Mansfield writing about girls in the house is minor. Exquisite but minor. (*Exquisite* is, by the way, a word often used to denigrate women's writing.) Mary Gordon goes on: "It was all right for the young men to write about the hymens they had broken, the diner waitresses they had seduced. Those experiences were significant. But we were not to write about our broken hearts, about the married men we loved disastrously, about our mothers or our children. Men could write about their fears of dying by exposure in the forest; we could not write about our fears of being suffocated in the kitchen. Our desire to write about these experiences only revealed our shallowness; it was suggested we would, in time, get over it."

Mary Gordon, though fearful of being thought trivial, admired writers like Brontë, Woolf, Mansfield, Lessing.[172] She says, "I discovered that what I loved in writing was not distance but radical closeness; not the violence of the bizarre but the complexity of the quotidian." I have no statistics to prove it, but my guess is that Mary Gordon is read much more by women than by men. The same might be said for Anne Tyler, Alice Walker, Gail Godwin, Margaret Drabble, Muriel Spark.[173] It seems a little sad in this day that there are so few men and women writing well about the other gender and also that they are not writing for the other sex.

We are always hearing that there are more women writers than men. This is a statement which is seldom backed up by any statistics, and it is interesting to notice that no one ever says how odd it is that there are so many male novelists around. This conception, or misconception, whichever it is, goes back almost to the beginning of the novel as a form, and it may be directly related to the fact that women have apparently always read more novels than men—at the moment, it is believed that seventy percent of novel readers in Canada are women. Yet occasionally we hear that women are engaged in a kind of aggressive conspiracy to take over the audience for fiction. In 1853, J.M. Ludlow advised his readers, "We *have* to notice the fact that at this particular moment of the world's history the very best novels in several great countries happen to have been written by women." A CBC producer said recently to Margaret Atwood, "A number of us are upset because we feel women are taking over the Canadian literary scene." Is this paranoia or what? And what is it based on? There are eighty-seven writers represented in the widely used *Norton Anthology of Short Fiction* edited by R.V. Cassill. Only twenty-two of them are women. In John Moss's *A Reader's Guide to the Canadian Novel*, there are write-ups on 110 novelists. Only thirty of these are women. Thus, we believe that women writers speak mainly to women, and, if we believe that seventy percent of the people who read novels are women, then we have less than a third of the writers in Canada speaking to two-thirds of the readers; perhaps this is responsible for the idea that women are swamping the market. There are some other interesting statistics in John Moss's book. There's a list of the fifty-six Governor General Awards for Fiction—sixty-five between 1936 and 1980. Of the sixty-five winners, twenty-one are women. There is another list of novels called "Novels with a Moral Vision or Significant Moral Concern." Moss lists forty books here, only seven of which are written by men. I don't want to point too much at this statistic because the choices are obviously highly subjective, with one man doing all the choosing. But the suggestion is there that women are scarcely in the running when it comes to writing significant books. There may be a double standard here or some serious confusion about what is significant—confusion which, for all we know, comes from one of the myths that adhere to women's writing: that there is a specific thing called the female imagination and something else called the female voice in literature.

What are some of the problems facing women writers? The first I've already alluded to; the fact that women have to be persuaded that their experience is relevant, that it is important. The people who have to be persuaded are the following: publishers, editors, reviewers, booksellers, and finally readers—those readers who sometimes apologize that they mainly stick to women writers. Another problem—and there is no easy way around this—is what Isak Dinesen calls the business of being a woman. By this she means those demands which cut into a woman's time—motherhood being a very large one, but also the demands of being "feminine"—that old mythical figure "The Angel in the House."[174] It is a fact that there have been very few great women writers who had children and few who had demanding marriages. Tillie Olsen[175] has written at some length about this problem, reminding us of various silences in literature. There are the silences which occur in certain periods of one's work when for some reason the creative imagination is atrophied. There is the silence before achievement. But worst is the total silence of the would-be writer who never wrote. We can go on at great length about the reasons for this: the problem of insufficient education, the problems of expectation and so on, but there is also the problem of simply having too many dishes to wash. It is only women who often think, at the expense of others, that they can give themselves permission to write. Here is Katherine Mansfield writing about the early days of her relationship with John Middleton Murry: "The house seems to take up so much time. . . . I mean when I have to clean up twice over or wash up extra unnecessary things, I get frightfully impatient and want to be working. . . . Well someone's got to wash dishes and get food." Washing dishes may seem a feeble whine, but the key words in Mansfield's complaint are "frightfully impatient." Frightfully impatient is akin to frustration and frustration to anger.

I would like to say a few words about anger and what it can do to writing. Virginia Woolf heard in *Middlemarch*[176] and in *Jane Eyre* the voices of women who were resenting their treatment and pleading for rights. Woolf sees it as a distortion and frequently the cause of weakness. She says, "The desire to plead some personal cause or to make a character the mouthpiece of some personal discontent or grievance always has a distressing effect, as if the spot at which the reader's attention is directed were suddenly two-fold instead of single." This kind of novel she saw as a dumping ground for the personal emotions, and only the happy few—Jane Austen[177] is one—are free of the sin of dumping.

It seems to me we are at an interesting period for women writers. We are really past the point now where we can take a novel like *The Woman's Room*[178] seriously, and yet that may have been a novel that was necessary. A certain amount of dumping has taken place, and a certain amount of permission has been given. Women are less likely to see fiction as the "only kind of writing they are capable of" and think of it, instead, as the expression of a personal vision—not hanging their head or shuffling their feet when they come to that troublesome word *personal*.

I would hope that women writers, feeling more secure in the literary world, will explore the male side of the world just as I hope that they will find the male readers they need.

The Unity of Our Country

Ladies and Gentlemen, *Mesdames et Messieurs*, and all these good friends I see in today's audience—I am honoured to be here to talk about what concerns us all—the unity of our country.[179]

I was also asked to say a few words about what it's like to be a writer in Canada today. So let me start at the beginning. Where I grew up, in Oak Park, Illinois, I attended Nathaniel Hawthorne Public School. Later I transferred to Ralph Waldo Emerson Public School. I knew who those gentlemen were because their portraits hung in the corridors of those schools. They peered down at us, bearded, frock-coated, and stern. They were writers. They were men. And they were dead.

It seemed impossible that I could follow in their wake, but nevertheless I formed the resolution to become a writer. I didn't know who my audience would be, nor did I have any notion of what I would write *about*. The books I read as a child were set in immense, glamorous cities—like New York—or else on cattle ranches in Wyoming. And there was also *Anne of Green Gables* set in Prince Edward Island, which I believed was somewhere up there in northern Wisconsin. And, of course, I hadn't the faintest idea that I would grow up, fall in love with a Canadian, and, at the age of twenty-two, immigrate—to Canada.

This is, perhaps, one of the easiest immigrations in the world. Nevertheless—and I think you in the audience who have undergone the transplantation experience will understand this—nevertheless, it took me years to understand how things worked in my adopted country: the political system, the intricacies and pressures of geography, the Canadian character, or why on earth Canadians cracked up when hearing the following joke. Here it is: why did the Canadian cross the road? Answer: To get to the middle.

I'd lived in Canada for more than ten years before I read a Canadian novel. It was a good novel—*The Honeyman Festival* by Marian Engel. Then, very quickly, I read Margaret Laurence's *The Stone Angel*.[180] Two years later I found myself registered at the University of Ottawa, taking a master's degree in Canadian literature—*Canadian* literature! my friends and family exclaimed—and writing a thesis on the Canadian pioneer Susanna Moodie.

The year of my immigration was 1957. The tallest building in Toronto was the Bank of Commerce, a lovely old building, but one which is now utterly dwarfed in the city skyline. Juliet[181] sang on the radio. The Happy Gang[182] did their daily gig. Canadian literature was Pierre Berton[183] and Morley Callaghan.[184]

Someone told me an interesting and rather telling story about Morley Callaghan's early novels—that they were published in split editions. For the very small Canadian reading public, a novel would be set in Toronto. The same novel, published in the United States, was set in Chicago. Nobody, it seemed, thought this strange or considered that it reflected tellingly on the important question of Canadian culture.

1957, the same year I crossed the border with my young Canadian husband, all our wedding presents crammed into the trunk of a six-cylinder Ford, was the year the Canada Council was founded. Next year will be its fortieth birthday. In 1957, we became a country that decided it could afford its own culture.

How much of a difference has the Canada Council made to our sense of our culture and, by extension, our sense of who we Canadians are? For this is what culture is: at its simplest, culture is a shared experience or combination of experiences, a vital voicing of self-definition, a belief that what we say and do and express has meaning for us.

What exactly is it that glues a diverse society together? Leadership? Perhaps. A railway system, a postal system? Yes, and yes. A health program, yes, of course. But even more powerful is this body of aesthetic expression that becomes our definition and shared experience.

For this reason, the arts are everybody's business. I want to say what I think needs to be heard in today's political climate: the arts are vital to Canada's economic and social and cultural health. I use the word *health* with purpose. There are those who feel it frivolous to talk about cultural funding when hospital beds are in short supply, but I believe both issues can be on the table at the same time. Art, and the transcendent experience that art provides, can save us from despair. It can make us into socialized beings, give us life skills, show us the possibilities of tolerance. The experience of art enlarges the vision of human capability, adds a few extra notes to our emotional keyboard. The ability to respond to works of art rescues us from emotional bankruptcy. Art lends us a kind of godly oxygen and shortens the distance we must travel to discover that our most private perceptions are, in fact, universally felt.

The arts enrich not only the soul—as most of us accept—but they also enrich the economy of Canada. To be sure, the artistic community must explain how its particular economy operates. It is a positive story. Take a look at this economic fact. The arts and culture sector in Canada employs almost 900,000 people or almost seven percent of the Canadian labour force.

And here's how it looks closer to home. Manitoba's arts and culture industries make an economic contribution to the province's gross domestic product of at least $432 million annually. This represents almost two percent of Manitoba's GDP. The arts sector's contribution to GDP is growing faster than the provincial economy. Occupations in the arts and cultural industries in Manitoba number over nineteen thousand, accounting for almost four percent of the labour force. Over the past decade, Manitoba's motion picture industry has enjoyed significant growth, going from just under one million [dollars] in 1985 to twenty million [dollars] this year. Next to the film industry, book publishing in Manitoba is the second largest cultural industry. Total sales have grown from $378,000 in 1983 to $2,869,000—an increase of 759 percent. And so you can see that art is the stuff of our soul and also a booming business.

Large as it is, the arts sector is not like any other industrial sector. We are accustomed to sectors made up of a few large companies—like the forest industry. The arts are more of a scattered and unorganized cottage industry—an assemblage of small and large theatres, galleries, symphonies and musical groups, publishers, and thousands of individual musicians, composers, writers, painters—each creating a separate vision.

It is important that our overall numbers and importance don't get lost when governments set priorities. We must supplement our arguments on national and spiritual benefits and argue that any dollar invested in the arts will be returned many times over. The money from the Canada Council is a seed, planted to reap a harvest. Concert goers, book buyers, and corporate sponsors nourish that seed. You may be interested to know that Winnipeggers spend more of their own money on culture than any other Canadians. The Winnipeg Symphony receives thirty percent more in private donations than does the Toronto Symphony.

Support comes also from the city of Winnipeg and from the provincial arts council, and, with arts cuts across the country, particularly in Ontario, where thirty percent has been slashed from the budget, I feel proud to live in a province which has held the line in its support to the arts. Is it climate? Is it our relative isolation and fortunate history and population mix that make us here in Manitoba understand that cultural health means a healthy society?

Of course, it's not nearly enough.

Let me state this clearly: the iron rule that governs the Canadian cultural economy is this: the arts we know and enjoy in Canada could not, would not, and never will be able to survive as strictly commercial ventures in our small but interdependent marketplace.

If we are to at least maintain the level of public and individual support for the arts, we have to explain that our cultural enterprise is not structured like our industrial enterprises. The culture of Canada is not a collection of commercial companies but a whole network of interconnected and interdependent elements—and individuals working alone. If any are weakened, the whole is in danger.

It is not possible to downsize culture because culture takes on the world and insists on excellence. Here's an analogy. Imagine an ophthalmologist performing a delicate feat of eye surgery. She brings to her task the best equipment and most highly developed techniques. She does not perform a cheap, cut-rate operation because there is insufficient cash. That would not be good medicine. In the same way, a serious writer does not write a bad book because the audience is small and the compensation paltry. He writes the best book he can.

Arts *administration*, on the other hand, *has* learned how to cut back. The Canada Council's aim is to reduce administrative costs by fifty percent over a three-year period. Better business practices, streamlining of programs, and electronic assistance are making this reduction possible.

Many of the major organizations in our metropolitan centres are endangered. It becomes, without stable public funding, impossible to keep together a critical mass of talent, production, and performance. If you stop that flow of money, our homegrown talent drains outside the country. This repositions the question of how much *do you* value our culture? The Jets' departure split the community, and many of you have accepted that loss. But let me ask you if you would be willing to see the Manitoba Theatre Centre, the Winnipeg Ballet, and the Winnipeg

Symphony disappear. Even if you don't support these institutions with your presence, are you willing to live in a society that deems such activity as dispensable? Imagine Winnipeg without opera, without our art galleries, libraries, bookstores. I suggest that what we would have is mass desolation. Commercial entertainment offers an hour of escape. An encounter with, say, a fine film will change the person you are— minutely or perhaps extraordinarily.

What does it mean to afford your own culture, remembering always that the economy is a player in creative expression? It might, for instance, be easier and cheaper to import American plays than to develop and nourish our own playwrights. The *Free Press* book page divides its reviews between local reviewers and those taken off the American wire services. I know why they do this, and I don't blame them—it's affordable, however much we might regret the policy and feel it compromises our own sense of ourselves.

There is another powerful and topical national reason for the survival of our national arts structure; it's one with a political dimension. Canada Council support makes an important contribution to Canadians' understanding of each other across cultures and regions. That's an important role in today's charged political environment. The council doesn't just assist individuals and organizations. It ensures that their messages reach as wide an audience as possible. We take it as a core part of our mission to forge understanding among Canada's many communities.

We do this partly through touring grants which allow Maritimers to see the Winnipeg Ballet and we in the west to enjoy the Rankin family from Cape Breton.

Our assistance to the two language groups is impressive. In twenty-three years, the council's translation program has facilitated the translation (English to French and French to English) of almost fifteen hundred books, including fiction, poetry, drama, children's books, and non-fiction.

We are encouraging more private sector investment by lobbying for tax concessions. And we have instituted an advocacy policy aggressively explaining ourselves and our mission.

How much has the council's presence stimulated Canadian interest in the arts, and how much have its programs contributed to Canadian creativity? I think the effect has been enormous. Those first two novelists I read in Canada, Margaret Laurence and Marian Engel, were both supported in their writing by Canada Council grants. These women were young mothers at that time, and their grants allowed them to buy time so that their wonderful books could be written.

I don't believe for a minute that art is created by throwing money at artists. But money does provide permission as well as *real* support. I used my first grant of six hundred dollars—this was in 1973 when I had five small children—to hire household help, to send my husband's shirts to the laundry, and to order the odd pizza dinner for the family. In a year, I had a book.

In 1957, under the grants program of the Canada Council, symphonies began to flourish, and Canadian theatres began to produce plays written by Canadians. This was something new. Canadian art filled our galleries, and librarians across the country proudly pasted that little red maple leaf to the spines of Canadian books. We became a country that, this year, took in its stride the fact that two of its writers were on the shortlist for the Booker Prize. We became a country, in short, that made up its mind to own its own culture.

Of course, all this cultural activity has benefited the country in other ways. Here's what Canada Council Chair Donna Scott[185] has to say: "The artist is boosting Canada's exports, bringing tourists to our shores, filling our restaurants and hotels, creating thousands of highly skilled jobs, getting us noticed in the capitals of the world, advancing bold new technologies, bringing joy of all kinds to millions of us, and, by the way, giving us another reason why the world keeps calling Canada the best place on earth to live."

Certainly, I have found Canada a good place to be a writer. And *Winnipeg*, it seems to me, is also a good place to be a writer. By the way, when I was a child in Chicago, I remember looking at the maps and seeing the state of North Dakota, a place I imagined to lie at the end of the world. And today—I can hardly believe it—I live *north* of North Dakota.

Morale is always a problem with artists, many of whom live at or below the poverty level. An artist needs two things. To feel rooted in a community that honours the arts and to enjoy the company of other artists. In Canada, we are fortunate to have both things.

Address to University of Winnipeg Graduands[186]

It is a great honour to be standing here today, June 2, 1996, in front of you, the graduands of the University of Winnipeg.[187] It is also extraordinarily frightening—for what words can I bring you, you who in the closing years of our century will prepare for the next, its thinkers, its leaders, its hope for deliverance from what is sometimes termed the "society of confusion." If I possessed the requisite wisdom, I would offer advice, but I am still, like you, in the process of coping with the world's contradictions and how best to approach them. And so, instead of advice, instead of wisdom, I offer, against the tidal wave of the electronic era, a few thoughts about the reading of books.

Some years ago a Canadian politician, one of our more admirable figures, announced that he was cutting back on his public life because it interfered with his reading. *His reading*—notice the possessive pronoun, like saying his arm or his leg, and notice, too, the assumption that human beings carry, like a kind of cerebral briefcase, this built-in commitment to time and energy—*their reading*.

I'm told that people no longer know how to curl up with a book. The body has forgotten how to curl. Either we snack on paperbacks while waiting for the bus, or we hunch over our books with a yellow underliner in hand. Or, more and more, we sit before a screen and "interact."

Curling up with a book can be accomplished in a variety of ways—in bed, for instance, with a towel on a sunlit beach, or from an armchair parked next to a good reading lamp. What it absolutely requires is a block of uninterrupted time, solitary time—and our society sometimes looks with pity on the solitary, that woman alone at the movies, that poor man sitting by himself at this restaurant table. Our hearts go out to them, but reading, by definition, can only be done alone. I would like to make the case today for solitary time, for a life with space enough to curl up with a book.

Reading—at least since human beings learned to read silently, and what a cognitive shift that was!—requires an extraordinary effort at paying attention, at remaining alert. The object of our attention matters less, in a sense, than the purity of our awareness. As the American writer Sven Birkerts[188] says, it is better, better in terms of touching the self within us, that we move from a state of half distraction to one of full attention. When we read with attention, an inner circuit of the brain is satisfyingly completed. We feel our perceptions sharpen and acquire edge.

Reading, as many of you have discovered, is one of the very few things you can do only by shining your full awareness on the task. We can make love, cook, listen to music, shop for groceries, add up columns of figures—all with our brain, our self that is, divided and distracted. But print on the page demands *all* of us. It is so complex, its cognitive circuitry so demanding; the black strokes on the white page must be apprehended and translated into ideas fitted into patterns, the patterns shifted and analyzed. The eye travels backward for a moment—this in itself is a technical marvel—rereading a sentence or a paragraph, extracting the sense, the intention, the essence of what is offered.

And, ironically, this singleness of focus delivers a doubleness of perception. You are invited into a moment sheathed in nothing but itself. Reading a novel, *curled up* with a novel, you are simultaneously in your armchair and in, for instance, the garden of Virginia Woolf in the year 1927 or a shabby Manitoba farmhouse conjured by Margaret Laurence,[189] a graduate of this university, by the way, participating fully in another world while remaining conscious of the core of your self, that self that may be hardwired into our bodies or else developed slowly, created over the long distance of our lives.

We are connected—through our work, through our familial chains, and by the way of the internet—to virtually everyone in the world. So what of the private self which comes tantalizingly alive under the circle of the reading lamp, that self that we only occasionally touch and then with trepidation? We use the expression "being lost in a book," but we are really closer to a state of being found. Curled up with a novel about an East Indian family, for instance, we are not so much escaping our own splintered and decentred world as we are enlarging our sense of self, our multiplying possibilities and expanded experience. People are, after all, tragically limited: we can live in only so many places, work at a small number of jobs or professions; we can love only a finite number of people. Reading and particularly the reading of fiction—perhaps I really do have a sales pitch here—let us *be* other, to touch and taste the other, to sense the shock and satisfaction of otherness. A novel lets us be ourselves and yet enter another person's boundaried world, to share in a private gaze between reader and writer. *Your* reading—and here comes the possessive pronoun again—can be part of your life, and there will be times when it may be the best part.

This university has made a strong commitment to information technology but without abandoning its *older* commitment to the written text. There is nothing to fear from the new technology—but a written text, as opposed to electronic information, has formal order, tone, voice, irony, persuasion. We can inhabit a book; we can possess it and be possessed by it. The critic and scholar Martha Nussbaum[190] believes that attentive readers of serious fiction cannot help but be compassionate and ethical citizens. The rhythms of prose train the empathetic imagination and the rational emotions.

You are about to enter a wide spectrum of disciplines, but my sense is that almost all of you will be plugged into the electronic world in one way or another, reliant on it for its millions of bytes of information. But a factoid, a nugget of pure information, or even the ever-widening web of information, while enabling us to perform, does relatively little to nourish us. A computer connects facts but cannot reflect upon them. There is no depth, no embeddedness. It is, literally, software, plaintext, language prefabricated and sorted into byte sizes. It does not, in short, aspire; it rarely sings. Enemies of the book want to see information freed from the prison of the printed page, putting faith instead in free-floating information—and this would be fine if we weren't human beings, historical beings, thinking beings—with a hunger for diversion, for narrative, for consolation, for exhortation.

We need literature on the page because it allows us to experience more fully, to imagine more deeply, enabling us to live more freely. Reading, you are in touch with your best self, and I think, too, that reading shortens the distance we must travel to discover that our most private perceptions are, in fact, universally felt. *Your* reading will intersect with the axis of *my* reading and *his* reading and *her* reading. Reading, then, offers us the ultimate website, where attention, awareness, reflection, understanding, clarity, and civility come together in a transformative experience.

I wish you success on this June afternoon in the year 1996. And I wish you, too, happiness and self-discovery throughout *your* reading lives.

Carol Shields

University of Winnipeg Convocation
Luncheon Address[191]

President Hanen, ladies and gentlemen, friends, colleagues, family, I thank you all for being here to share this enormously happy occasion with me, and my thanks go, too, to all who have made this weekend one of festivity and consecration to the future. The happy combination of celebration and solemnity defines, I think, the human balance that this institution represents.

When Dr. Hanen first presented me with the chancellorship idea, my first thought—I confess this today—was: Surely, I'm not old enough to be a chancellor. But after doing some very elementary arithmetic, I realized that maybe I was! I discussed the idea, which was still no more than an idea, with a friend, and her advice was: "Think about who you'll be working with." This was good advice, I thought. I already knew a good many old friends at the university, and now I met others. The working relations between these people is unbelievably warm and easy, familial as well as collegial, and they have extended to me a generous welcome.

I didn't, of course, know what the chancellorship would involve. But I did know that I loved universities. It is a truth universally recognized that academics often complain and carp—perhaps because we're critically trained—but it is also a fact that we are extraordinarily privileged to belong to an institution whose major concern is the life of the mind. And this life is shared with students.

A friend of mine, a university teacher, told me the other day about an incident that occurred on the first day of term as she set off to meet her first of the year class. She was walking rather slowly, putting off that always fearful moment when one comes face to face with a new group of students—a kind of stage fright, I suppose.

In the crowded hall she happened to spot a very small boy of three or four, and, responding to maternal instincts, and perhaps to put off a moment longer her arrival in class, she stopped and asked him if he was lost. Yes, he said; he'd lost his father.

Is your father a professor? she asked. Yes, he said. What does he teach? She asked. There was a pause, and then he said, He teaches … students.

Well, I like to think that this is a university that teaches students. And that in the pursuit of advanced research, new teaching tools and methodologies, and exciting partnerships with other institutions, the student, as partner, is never for a minute forgotten.

When I was walking through Centennial the other day—and, by the way, to leap onto one of Centennial's escalators is to understand the meaning of the word "throng"—I looked around at all those upturned faces, and it occurred to me that each one of these people had made a deliberate choice—elected a particular educational path, chosen a personally congenial ambiance, said yes to diversity, opted for a sense of tradition, but the kind of tradition that has not strangled the forward movement of knowledge.

I should tell you that coming through the doors of Wesley Hall never fails to thrill me. The beautiful stone, the handsome architecture, the plaque that spells out a history of more than one hundred years—more than a hundred because, as you will remember, the building was begun in 1894. Are we influenced by architecture, by the spaces we inhabit? Yes, I think we are. And—and this is important—inside this graceful old building can be heard the busy modern hum of a university which is facing the twenty-first century. This weekend we have been witness to the new shape, the new direction of our university. I can only say that I am happy, and honoured, to be aboard.

Thank you.

Carol Shields

University Leadership and Social Change[192]

Greetings friends, ladies and gentlemen, Professor Michael Osborne, my fellow panel members Professor Conway and President Davis. And special greetings to our hosts at the University of Ottawa, which is—I can't resist saying so—my own warmly remembered and much valued alma mater, welcoming me as a mature student in the late '60s now asking too many questions. There are so many "honoureds" present here today along with their guests, each of you a concerned citizen and leader in the university sphere, that one can feel the intellectual kilowatts bouncing off the walls of this auditorium, and, of course, one also feels a corresponding sense of humility—what can I possibly say about the future of the university, its leadership in society, how it will change and preserve culture and our communally-held values?

I'd like to begin with five short stories, and the first, if you will forgive me, is a personal story. It is one that comes back to me often, especially when in a university setting—the fact that I was for many years haunted by my own university graduation address. It was a very hot June day, the temperature stood at 35 Celsius, not that any of us knew how to convert to Celsius. My girlfriends and I had agreed to wear under our black robes—nothing. This was considered high daring in 1957—before Jack Kennedy was elected president of the United States, before the Vietnam War, before independence arrived in Jamaica, before the tumult of the '60s, the confusion of the '70s, the greed of the '80s, before most of you were born, I lined up with one hundred fellow students at a small Presbyterian college to receive my bachelor of arts degree.[193] On that June day in 1957, our speaker was a young and extremely popular math professor at our college. He put his message squarely but prefaced his remarks by saying that we were highly unlikely to remember anything he said that day.

He was right. I, for one, sat dreaming about my wedding, six weeks hence, but dimly, through faraway romantic thoughts, I heard him say

he would be happy if we carried away a simple phrase from the day—
and this was it: June 1957. *Tempus fugit*.

Now, I don't know how many of you sitting here today have studied
Latin, but in those days most of us had had a smattering. And I knew
what *tempus fugit* meant: it means "time flies." Our speaker was telling
us that, unless we seized the moment, every moment, our lives could
get away from us, could be eroded, erased, wasted, thrown away through
carelessness, lost. I remembered those words.

And in the years to follow, years in which I might be changing
diapers, washing floors, sewing, shopping, cooking meals, writing
thank-you notes, weeding the garden, reading a little poetry on the
sly—those words would come back to me—*tempus fugit*. Time was
hurrying by, brushing past me. I could almost hear the flapping of its
winged chariot. I was standing still—or so I thought. The words *tempus
fugit*, whenever I paused to recollect my graduation day, spooked me.
Scared me. I was persuaded that I was not pushing forward and making
the most of my allotted time on earth.

And so today, fully conscious of my good luck in being asked to
speak, I would like to revise that dictum. *Tempus* does not *fugit*. Time
is not cruel. Given the good luck of a long, healthy life, as most of
us are, we have plenty—plenty of time. It is important, I think, that
universities address the question of time in relation to our projected
working lives. We must examine our concept of our own narrative lives,
and their time frames must be altered. We will examine the *curricula
vitae* of prospective employees and see how they have strange *lacunae*
in their middle years—how was it they leapt from their PhDs to ten,
or twenty, unrecorded years? What happened? Well, we know. Time
was taken. Time to produce and raise a family, or to pursue some other
line of passion, which perhaps came to nothing. Who knows?

We have time. Time to try on new selves, time to experiment, time
to dream and drift, time even to waste. Fallow time, shallow time.
We'll have good years and bad years, and we can afford both. Every
hour, particularly those unrecorded hours on an official CV, will not be
filled with meaning and accomplishment, as the world measures these
things, but there will be compensating hours so rich, so full, so humanly
satisfying that we will become partners with time and not victims of it.

Most of us end up seeing our lives not as an ascending line of
achievement but as a series of highly interesting chapters. In all

probability—because the world is changing so rapidly—we will work in a number of different jobs in a variety of different fields. Serial careers have become almost the norm. One decade, or chapter, or life introduces the next, and the climate of reward, and its nature, moves all over the map. We will be rewarded when we least expect it, even during an epoch when society tells us that few rewards are available or forthcoming.

In addition, the realities of biology and new ways of considering parenthood are more and more listened to and registered, and we know that our professional lives will have, must have, accommodating patterns. Some of this new thinking has been initiated; a new generation will doubtless see its implementation.

This generation, the first of the new millennium, is also likely to question and deconstruct the metanarratives of our society, our social messages which are so deeply embedded that we don't always remember to hold them up to the light and ask what they mean, forgetting that what goes without saying needs to be said. Needs to be questioned. Such things as the bottom line is the bottom line. War equals valour. And—*tempus fugit*.

My second story: once upon a time there was a man who invented buttons and buttonholes. He saw a need: it was important that clothing be held in place on the human body—somehow. Secure fastenings were required, for warmth, for human propriety. These fastenings must be inexpensive so that everyone could possess them. They must be so simple to manipulate that even very young children could make use of them.

Our inventor worked for many years—all his life in fact—perfecting his button idea. He laboured over the roundness of the button, the flatness, the correct thickness of a button, searching diligently for a way in which buttons could be attached and, if lost or broken, inexpensively replaced. The buttonhole was another challenge, for he wanted his mechanism to lock perfectly, easily, so that even those buttons on the back of a garment could be slipped into place. The buttonhole must not fray, and it must not weaken the cloth it opened. He laboured, he succeeded, he was acknowledged and rewarded.

And then someone invented the zipper.

And then someone invented Velcro.

I tell this story not to say that one technology overtook another but to repeat what you already know, that technologies can exist side by side, buttons, zippers, Velcro closings, and who knows what else?

My third story, which I take from the economist Adam Smith,[194] and which those of you who took Economics 101 will already know, is about the making of pins in the year 1776, and I am talking about simple tailors' pins, those shining, slender implements we use to hold a pattern to a piece of cloth or to secure two pieces of cloth together so that we can sew them in place permanently.

Pin making, Adam Smith tells us, had been revolutionized in the eighteenth century, so that one man drew out the wire, and another straightened it, and a third cut it. A fourth pointed it, a fifth ground it at the top for receiving the head: to make the head required two or three distinct operations; to put the head on was a peculiar piece of business; to whiten the pins was another; it was a trade by itself to put the pins into the pin paper. The important business of making a pin was, in this manner, divided into about eighteen distinct operations, which in some factories were all performed by distinct hands. In this way, it was possible to make twelve pounds of pins in a day, with four thousand pins making up a pound. Previously, a pin maker was considered an exemplary worker by producing twenty pins a day, each wrought separately by his own hand.

You can guess what happened. Pins became cheap to buy. They also became more uniform in quality. If a pin dropped on the floor, it was almost too much trouble to bend over to retrieve it. Pin making, previously an art, became an industry. Workers lost connection with individual pins and with the moment of satisfaction that arrives at the moment the pin is completed and set down with other pins. One pin maker was as good as another. Was that a good thing? Was his life happier? Was it more or less frustrating, less or more generously rewarded? Did joining the pin-making assembly line free the worker to devote off-work energies to playing the guitar, to reading works of history, to working in the garden, to enjoying the companionship of family and friends?

A fourth story, a tragic story, concerns the recent slaughter in Bosnia.[195] You in the English-speaking world, a wide web, a former empire, and there are those centrist powers in the world who would consider that most of us live in small nations at the edge of a map, and yet that single word—*Bosnia*—sets an image alight in our minds. We know with surprising intimacy about the atrocities that took place in Bosnia. Famine, rape, random killings, deliberate executions, malnutrition, the hysterical ranting about blood purity with one human group privileged above another. This knowledge, which arrives to us almost simultaneously with the events themselves, is communicated by the new electronic technologies. It is knowledge that is bounced off satellites and beamed into our television screens. It screams at us from electronically produced newspapers. There are pictures as well as text, so convincing, so immediate, that in a real sense we are there. And because of this, for the first time in history, we hold a new moral responsibility. It is useful to reflect on just how *new* the modern conscience is. The universal rights culture is bursting, suddenly, all around us and is not about to go away. This culture embraces the rights of women, workers, and non-whites and a new definition of democratic citizenship.

My fifth story concerns the link between technology and development. That link is a wavy line but one we must look at. Why should people or an institution commit themselves to technology? Technology is not produced in order to fulfill a human need to tinker, though there does exist, it seems, a desire to discover and improve and learn underlying principles. Remember the *Titanic*, how one of the world's first SOS signals was sent to the nearby ship the *California*, which could have saved almost all on board, but—and here the story splits in two—the radio operator was asleep, or else he was awake but needed the permission of the captain, who asked not to be disturbed at night. The human factor is part of technology's cycle. Technology is seen often as a way to produce wealth and to speed up and heighten what is recognized as the gross national product, never mind that many technologies bring pollution and suffering and unemployment in their wake and necessitate the long technological fight against the devastation that technology has brought into being.

Technology and development go hand in hand, and it is development I've tried to look at in the telling of my five stories. We need to look at new ways to deal with time in our lives. We need to hurl ourselves into risky explorations even though we are unlikely to know what will overtake us and when. We need to assess what damage or beauty work can bring us, its creativity, its productivity, its weight in human values. Work is part of our communal existence. There is a branch of the Hutterites[196] who, when they do their bookkeeping, place work on the credit and not the debit side of their ledgers. This is a difficult concept to put one's head around, but, once done, one will be changed.

The workplace today is a major source of tension, depression, loss of self, loss of energy, loss of morality. It need not be so in the future, and here is where the university can take a lead by setting an example. By equity of employment, by new work models, by the understanding that the day of the bossy boss is over, by the incorporating of new, more humane management models, by making the workplace a rewarding and self-invigorating place, by diversity of the student body, by respect for professional and student work, we can see that work needn't be devalued, compromised, or scorned.

We need to assume moral responsibility in a world which technology has made into a global village. We need, in short, to rethink that word *development* so that it embraces the development of a child's mind, the responsibility for moral decisions, the fulfillment of individuals as well as societies. We need poetry, electric light, music, computer programming, the exaltation of drama and dance, and a pure water supply. There is no reason we can't have it all.

Tempus fugit. It is August 17, 1998. Time is passing. The clock is ticking as we sit here. The world is turning. But we, those of us fortunate enough to be part of university systems today and with some opportunity to touch and perhaps ignite the system in the future, are able to think widely, leap into new technologies, revise our concepts of time, undertake new moral callings, and appreciate anew what work means to our society—we are uniquely privileged to decide where universities will go in the future, whom they will serve, and what their ambitions will be.

Idealism and Pragmatism in Two Novels of Sara Jeannette Duncan[197]

In her novels *The Imperialist* and *Cousin Cinderella*,[198] Sara Jeannette Duncan examined the whole range of contradictions presented by the representatives of the Atlantic Triangle. Her Canadian men and women are contrasted, sharply and often amusingly, with the British and Americans of the time. Social and cultural traditions are examined in bright geographical context; history or the lack of history is commented upon; relative attitudes toward possessions and toward such institutions as marriage are peered at through Duncan's powerful magnifying glass. But in the end, she seems to have grown impatient with generalizations based on nationhood, amusing though they were and attractive though they seemed as vehicles of plot. The differences she saw between individuals went far deeper than crude national generalities. These particular differences were rooted in two distinct responses to human events, responses which cut across national lines to a more universal view of human personality.

It is almost as though Duncan in *The Imperialist* and *Cousin Cinderella* discovered two new countries of the mind: in one, the idealist or purist struggled and suffered; in the other, the pragmatist or realist prospered and won. These two worlds collided in much the same way as the Canadian and British worlds collided, producing insights which were more fundamentally useful than the energetically ironic cross-cultural encounters.

The Imperialist written in 1904 and *Cousin Cinderella* written in 1908 share a number of obvious similarities. They are both novels in which Canadians come into contact with the British. In *The Imperialist*, Lorne Murchison visits England as a member of an official delegation. In addition, a number of British personalities arrive in Canada and come into contact with the more open and less class-ridden society of Elgin, Ontario. There is, for instance, the Scottish clergyman, Hugh Finlay, who comes to minister to the townsfolk of Elgin, only to find that his rigidities of spirit have no value. And there is an Alfred Hesketh, who immigrates with the vague idea of finding a profession; he finds it, but it is less a profession than a continuation of his pragmatic self-seeking. Christy Cameron arrives from Scotland with the specific intention of marrying Finlay; she stays but not until her intentions have been iron-ically reshaped by events. Duncan makes countless cultural comments on both societies and on the confrontation between them, and on first glance it would appear that the making of these distinctions is her chief concern. But there is a larger pattern beneath, that of idealism pitched against a realistic and pragmatic vision of life.

On the surface, *Cousin Cinderella* also revolves around the problems and pleasures of cultural shock. Graham and Mary Trent, the son and daughter of a Canadian businessman-senator, are sent to Britain by their father as "samples" of the kind of product Canada produces. In England, Graham and Mary come into contact with a wide variety of English people and with an American, Evelyn Dicey. As in *The Imperialist*, Duncan splashes her novel with references to national dif-ferences, and again Canada is more or less always displayed as a more vigorous and more open society. The viewpoint, Clara Thomas[199] says in an article in *Canadian Literature*, is insistently Canadian.[200] But, as in *The Imperialist*, the national differences are mined mainly for their comic value and political points. The real tensions lie between the forces of pragmatism and idealism.

Duncan seldom speculates in her novels about the reason behind the idealism or pragmatism of her characters. An unnamed something has made Lorne Murchison an idealist. Certainly, it is not a quality inher-ited directly from his parents. Mr. Murchison, Lorne's father, is a man of unquestioned integrity, but his integrity does not preclude a tough pragmatic grasp on affairs. He is a hardware merchant, an active layman in the Presbyterian Church, a stern and loving father to his children, and an affable and amused husband to his wife. Mrs. Murchison does not even possess her husband's reflective sensitivity; she is a woman who is happiest performing the practical tasks involved in a busy household. Lorne's particular brand of idealism, a compulsion toward abstraction, appears to be a mutation, although it is a quality which is apparent to a lesser extent in his sister Advena.

Graham Trent in *Cousin Cinderella* also appears to have arrived at his state of pure idealism by accident. His father is bluff, honest, and down to earth; certainly, he has no illusions about the greatness of England. Graham's mother is an invalid who is scarcely mentioned in the story and whose influence on her two children is minimal. And Graham's sister Mary is the extreme example of the clear-eyed observer, the realist without rancour; her illusions are shed painlessly, even cheerfully; she is open to change, and for Mary change is always in the direction of perception and acceptance. She is, in fact, much like Duncan herself as described by Claude Bissell[201] in his introduction to *The Imperialist*: "Sara Jeannette Duncan was neither repelled nor confused by the society she found around her; she looked at it objectively, yet sympathetically ..." (p. 1).

All that Duncan is prepared to offer by way of explanation for Lorne's eruptive idealism are a few suggestions concerning a special and mystical connection with the past. In *The Imperialist* (p. 22), Duncan describes the citizens of Elgin: "They are altogether occupied with its affairs and the affairs of the growing Dominion, yet obscure in the heart of each of them ran the undercurrent of the old allegiance. They had gone the length of their tether, but the tether was always there." Lorne, apparently heir to particular sensitivities, feels the force of the tether more strongly than others in his family or in his town. It is as though a recessive gene manifests itself in him, for later, when he visits England, Duncan speaks about his having found his "claimed inheritance" (p. 112).

The source of Graham Trent's idealism is more difficult to pinpoint. He and his sister shared a childhood in which there were many British influences. (Mary mentions a particular English teacher, remote and superior, who brought with her an imported blackboard.) Their father's attitude toward the old country was cheerfully ambivalent; he was afraid to go back for fear he might discover he had made a bad bargain, yet he knew, in fact, that he had made the best of all possible bargains. Mary provides a clue by describing Graham as having been "different" from childhood.

Graham was a kind of missionary in Minnebiac, of simple purposes and fine ideas in wood—the people there, though so near to nature's heart, being dreadfully fond of gilt and plush. He would have done well as an *ébéniste*[202] of the First Empire;[203] he had the conscience and enthusiasm. Or as a Japanese cabinet maker with his life before him, and no accounts to keep (p. 6). It is perhaps the combination of "conscience

and enthusiasm" which singled Graham out as one of life's purists. He
had been wounded in the South African war, and appeared to have been
morally wounded, as well as physically, for when discussing it with his
sister Mary he replies to one of her questions with brutal bitterness.
The one thing the common soldiers could do well, he told her, was to
"drop down dead" (p. 4).

If Duncan is somewhat vague about the causes of excessive idealism,
she is absolutely precise about the effect: idealism as expressed in Lorne
Murchison or Graham Trent is a crippling, limiting, blinding disease.
Stricken with the malady of idealism, Graham and Lorne often appear
noble, even poetic, but, in fact, they are highly vulnerable. In the end,
they both prove ineffectual, and both go limping off in surprisingly
similar exits. These two novels, then, may be interpreted as studies in
chastened idealism.

Both Canadian towns, Elgin in *The Imperialist* and Minnebiac in
Cousin Cinderella, reflect the more open attitude of the New World.
But, of course, there are limits. The one thing which the citizens of
Elgin and Minnebiac cannot swallow is an excess of passion. In Elgin,
at least for the Presbyterians, religious fervour is, in Duncan's words,
"reasonable" (p. 60). Hesketh, a character in *The Imperialist*, is perplexed
by Lorne Murchison because he himself grew up in a land where ideas
were "disengaged" (p. 122). Lorne confounds him with his simple zeal.
Lorne's political downfall, which comes at the end of *The Imperialist*,
occurs because he frightened solid stolid Elgin with a zeal which,
Duncan says, "lacked actuality" (p. 223). His speech before Election
Day frightened and disturbed the citizenry and made him an alien,
almost a madman, in their eyes.

Hugh Finlay, the young clergyman in *The Imperialist*, has his own
special brand of madness too, an inward commitment to an absurd piece
of self-sacrifice—the refusal to jilt a woman he doesn't love. The notion
at first sweeps him with an almost religious ecstasy: "Hugh Finlay saw
his idea incarnate" (p. 111). The romantically idealistic Finlay manages
to sell his "idea incarnate" to Advena Murchison, a woman Duncan has
already established as a character poised between the forces of idealism
and pragmatism. Advena's agreement to participate in Finlay's sacrifice
is brought about by her "aesthetic ecstasy," a quality inadmissible in
pragmatic Elgin. Advena, Duncan tells us, was "prone to this form of
exaltation" (p. 218).

Graham Trent's idealism consists of an unreflective attachment to collective ideas. He commits himself to the *idea* of England, turning a blind eye to the savageries of that particular society. He gives himself to the *idea* of Barbara, and, once he is committed, a chivalrous purity prevents him from examining her further.

A small incident in *Cousin Cinderella* shows how Graham's idealism operated in miniature. Surrendering to a burst of passion for antique furniture, he bought one day an octagonal table of the time of Charles the First.[204] Later, discovering that, except for one drawer, the piece was a fake, he insisted on burning the table, preserving only the single drawer. His sister Mary, though affectionately tolerant, believes his action to be wasteful, and Lady Barbara, a genuine aristocrat, is sincerely shocked. This incident may, in fact, have been a warning to Barbara that idealism as practised by Graham might be difficult to live with.

Both Lorne and Graham have exalted feelings for England, feelings which arise from a mystical, almost religious sense; certainly, they are not feelings based on reason or on observation. Lorne Murchison is the only member of the delegation to England who will not permit himself to admit disappointment. Duncan stresses his unwillingness to be enlightened by detailing a number of aspects about England which Lorne found sad and disappointing. These negative details far outweigh those features about England which Lorne was able to admire, but details in themselves, Duncan suggests, are the materials on which only pragmatic minds rest their cases. For a pure idealist like Lorne, details might simply be swept away by the grand vision. At the end of Chapter XV, when the delegation is weighing in a point-for-point fashion the success of the mission, Duncan says, "Only Lorne Murchison among them looked higher and further, only he was alive to the inrush of the essential; he only lifted up his heart." This passage with its almost biblical echoes may at first suggest that Lorne's idealism would lift him above his fellow countrymen. In fact, by looking "higher and further," Lorne avoided an open and pragmatic analysis of the mission and deliberately separated himself from the very people he sought to serve.

Graham too is blinded by his passion. Like Lorne, he is fully equipped with intelligence, and his eye for detail, especially social detail, is very fine. It is often he who points out amusing ironies for Mary's enjoyment, and it is he who is the first to feel a snub. But unlike Mary, he cannot disassociate himself from the idea of England. He appears to be unable to sift the details and arrive at dispassionate judgments. He is, Mary says, "in love with England." The particularity of her own feelings about the English emphasizes the ephemeral quality of Graham's obsession.

> By this time it had grown quite clear to me that Graham was seriously in love. Not with any lady—with England. . . . Wherever we penetrated deeper it was Graham who really cared most; and I think his sensitiveness to the little things was exactly because he did care so much about the big ones. I was always amused in London; Graham was always occupied; where I found spectacle, he found drama and the matter of life. I was in love with England too—clothes and ideas and old china, anything portable. . . . Graham, on the contrary, seemed hardly to have a rapacious thought. What he seemed rather to bemoan was the impossibility of contributing anything. (p. 146)

Later Graham was to fall in love with Pavis Court, a microcosm of all that was England at its best. At Pavis Court, too, he overlooked the details by leaving the repair work to others. What he loved was the *idea* of Pavis Court, that such a house had actually been conceived and built and that it was in danger and must be rescued. For, like Lorne Murchison, he was conscious of his role as rescuer.

With women, too, Graham chose to ignore the telling detail, loving instead the idea of a woman. Mary sensed this vagueness in her brother's attitude toward Barbara when she remarked: "Somehow if she had been insignificant and rather plain like me, it would have been easier to see Graham in love with her—he liked a sketch always better than a finished picture; and Barbara was a finished picture, that left the imagination nothing at all to do" (p. 278). The important word here is *imagination*. Duncan makes it clear that both Graham and Lorne are intelligent men, yet neither was able to assimilate the details of the woman he believed he loved. In Lorne's case, Duncan explains his blindness about Dora by referring to his romantic imagination: "But Lorne loved with all his imagination. This way dares the imitation of the gods, by which it improves the quality of the passion, so that such a love stands by itself to be considered apart from the object, one may say. A strong and beautiful wave lifted Lorne Murchison along to his destiny, since it was the pulse of his own life, though Dora Milburn played moon to it" (p. 147).

Graham's failure in his love affair with Lady Barbara is brought about by his inability to particularize. One of Graham's flaws was his overwhelming desire to fit all the parts into a grand vision of England. It was only later in his courtship that he made a real attempt to get to know Barbara, and the friendship that sprang up between them made each of them less eager to enter into a marriage of convenience. Graham became an actor in his own vision, a fact which Mary points out frequently. "He liked that part of Knight Hospitaller"[205] (p. 189), she says at one point.

Barbara was the first to understand the fact that she was no more than a part of Graham's oversized and idealized picture of England. "Graham," she says, "doesn't care a bit more about me than he does about mother" (p. 327). Peter, Barbara's brother, and Mary meet by accident one day and agree that the love affair is an empty one. Peter asks Mary what on earth Graham is thinking of in entering a loveless marriage. Mary's reply is that Graham is "simply charmed" (p. 304)— charmed, she means, by the whole idealistic picture in which Barbara is only one detail. Graham, of course, is the very last to discover his own true feelings.

Curiously, both Lorne and Graham appear to function as heroes in these two novels, but they are heroes who are inexplicably maimed by idealism. They have, by their wholesale embracing of idealism, violated the code of moderation and pragmatism and severed themselves from the real world. What they have really lost is immediacy of judgment, their own will to act and choose.

The voice of pragmatic opposition is expressed mainly by Mary in *Cousin Cinderella*. In *The Imperialist*, this role is shared between the citizens of Elgin and the unnamed narrator. Mary Trent is devoted to her brother Graham; she opens the narrative by freely offering him centre stage in her story. But, ironically, this is something he never succeeds in taking away from her; her immediacy is such that she is always between Graham and the reader, explaining, allowing, excusing, lamenting, even occasionally worshipping in a sisterly way. Graham merges his will with his idealism; he actually loses himself in his vision of England. But Mary, who in many ways is just as enchanted with England as is Graham, manages to retain her disinterestedness of stance. One evening, driving through London, she had what might be called a transcendental experience.

> Suddenly, without Graham, without anybody, moving through the lovely thronged, wet, lamplit London streets in Mrs. Jarvis's electric brougham,[206] I felt myself realized— realized in London, not only by the person who happened to be near me, but in a vague, delightful potential sense by London. Realized, not a bit for what I was—that wouldn't, I am afraid, have carried me very far—not exactly for what I represented, but for something else, for what I might, under favourable circumstances, be made to represent. The odd part was that seeing it on this lower level made no difference to the thrill, which has its wonderful source in the fact that London should take one into account at all. It was even part of the thrill to know that one would never be obliged, in a way, to hand oneself over. It was even a happier excitement to see that nothing in the matter was to be taken for granted, that I was only a possibility, a raw product, to be melted, or hammered or woven into London, by my leave. (p. 126)

It is, of course, the final three words "by my leave" which set Mary on the other side of the world from Graham. Even when she is transported by the magical effect of the evening, she retains, in the end, her will.

The deliberate abandonment of will is seen even more clearly in the case of Hugh Finlay, the young minister in *The Imperialist*. He had, before leaving the old country, promised marriage to Christy Cameron, a woman he didn't love and a woman who was unsuitable for him in almost every way. In Elgin, he meets and falls in love with Advena; they are spiritually mated from the start, united at first by their love of literature and later by a curious obstinacy of temperament. Finlay persuades Advena of the impossibility of breaking his engagement, and together, rather like over-excited children, they plot to sacrifice their lives to a chivalrous ideal. The ideal is never made quite clear by the narrator: Finlay mumbles something about how he cannot persuade himself to hurt or embarrass Christy, but what he really cannot abandon is his self-image as a moral idealist. Like Lorne and like Graham Trent, he loses his grasp on detail, failing to see what is directly before him, that he is about to ruin three loves, not one. Because it is so painful to lose his self-image, he simply surrenders his will to a moral imperative, and for a time he is warmed in the fires of his own sacrifice.

Lorne Murchison abandoned the last of his will in his election speech just before polling day in Elgin. His prior restraint and political poise melted away in that mystical moment when suddenly the imperialistic idea that he had carried for months began to carry him. "Who knows at what suggestion or even precisely at what moment the fabric of his sincere intention fell away? . . . I can get nothing more of them his colleagues, though they were all there, though they all saw him, indeed a dramatic figure standing for the youth and energy of the old blood, and heard him, as he slipped away into his great preoccupation, as he made what Bingham called his 'bad break.' His very confidence may have accounted for it; he was off guard against the enemy, and the more completely off guard against himself" (p. 228).

The disease which infected the three heroes—Lorne, Hugh Finlay, and Graham Trent—was not self-limiting. That is, they did not arrive by themselves at new insights; they did not work out their own salvations as true heroes, in fiction anyway, often do. Their individual wills were lost to the extent that outside events intervened and brought them once again in touch with reality.

Hugh Finlay was liberated from his obsessional idea of sacrifice by the direct intervention of Dr. Drummond and by the gradual awakening of Advena to the absurdity of the martyrdom. Dr. Drummond, the established clergyman in Elgin, is a man with vision, but his vision is rooted in day-to-day events, in the moderate and pragmatic soil of Elgin. He can talk Greek philosophy with Advena and kitchen stoves with Mr. Murchison, and one feels that these varied conversational thrusts are all of a piece. He is temperate within the code of Elgin, and he sees early in the novel that Lorne is in danger of violating the code. But Finlay's intemperance strikes him as even more dangerous. He makes every attempt to persuade him that he is doing wrong, that he is injuring Advena and himself. He pleads, cajoles, even prays with Finlay over the matter, and in the end he performs the consummate (and somewhat comic) piece of pragmatism by marrying Christy Cameron himself, leaving Finlay free to marry Advena.

Lorne Murchison is cut off from his idealism by the most direct means possible—rejection by the voters of his riding. Like Hugh Finlay, he has held fast, until the moment of liberation, to his ideals. The breaking of his vision is final, sudden, and catastrophic, and it is brought about by exterior forces. Lorne's love affair with Dora is also brought to a close by the intervention of Hesketh, a pragmatist of the selfish sort.

Graham Trent's release is brought about by a letter from Barbara; even then, the contents are known to Mary before Graham sees them. His disenchantment with England, climaxed by Barbara's refusal, is completed by a series of small humiliations; he realizes that he has been used to the advantage of others. T.E. Tausky[207] in his article in the *Journal of Canadian Fiction* calls *Cousin Cinderella* a melancholy book because the Trents sacrifice themselves and are met with snubs. But what Graham is really confronted with is the flaw in his own personality and the realization that a balanced and moderate viewpoint is the most necessary piece of equipment for survival in the modern world.

These heroes—Lorne, Graham, and Finlay—are men of affairs, but none of them is a modern man; their vision is romantic and chivalrous; at times, it is almost renaissance in its richness. As a result, both Lorne and Graham suffer depression and mild breakdown, a peculiarly modern punishment, for their refusal to confront reality. Lorne, when told by Hesketh that Dora is to marry him instead of Lorne himself, listened and "in one consciousness . . . made concise and relevant remarks; in another he saw a spinning dark world and waited for the crash" (p. 266). Ill health, believed by the people of Elgin to be caused by his political disappointment, carried him to the most ironic of places, the United States. Duncan hints in the closing paragraph of the novel that Lorne is to have a second political chance, but she makes no promises about his having arrived at a more balanced view of life.

Graham's disillusionment and depression are more specifically expressed. After his engagement is broken, Mary says: "I never knew him so dull. He had long periods of meditation, out of which he would come with a baffled air, and straightway bury himself in the Toronto papers. . . . [H]e was living, I supposed, in the reaction from his high attempt. There was a kind of flatness in the check he had received which was more disconcerting than the sting of defeat. He was not to be allowed to immolate his heart on the altar of Pavis Court, that was how it summed itself up to me" (p. 331).

Duncan, however, is fairly positive about Graham's future, despite his tattered heroic state at the end of the novel. He indicates a genuine and healthy bitterness about the way he has been treated and shows signs of gaining a clear-eyed grasp on the future. He signals recovery when Mary asks him if he intends to spend the day "mooning about Westminster." He replies, "I'm a landed proprietor now, and I don't much moon as I did. I shall spend it with my agent" (p. 342).

If Lorne and Graham are the losers in these novels, those characters who practise the art of the possible are clearly the winners. Robust, resilient, and possessed of an eye for subtle detail, they adapt to circumstances and exercise their will in their own lives. They are, of course, less than heroic by conventional standards. Dr. Drummond, for instance, has enough vanity to make him occasionally comic, but also has enough experience and warmth to realize exactly how far human nobility can be stretched. Compromise is chief of his talents; one can see by his office fittings, in which he mingles Greek sanctuary with Christian symbols, that he knows to take the best from all worlds. His clerical eye falls gently on the sinner; he is tolerant of youthful enthusiasm; he sees no contradiction between Christian charity and earning a good living. Though he has lived for much of his life in a provincial Canadian town, he is a modern man in Duncan's sense of the word. And he is realist enough to know that heroism can be mere grandstanding, a child's game. From the pulpit one night, he preaches straight at Finlay and Advena: "O thou Searcher of hearts, who hast known man from the beginning, to whom his highest desires and his loftiest intentions are but the desires and intentions of a little child, look with Thine own compassion. . . . [D]o Thou teach them that, as happiness may reside in chastening, so chastening may reside in happiness. And though such stand fast to their hurt, do Thou grant to them in Thine own way, which may not be our way, a safe issue out of the dangers that beset them" (p. 204).

Drummond is the modern man of reason, the kind of reason which Finlay deliberately rejects. In attempting to explain his stance to Dr. Drummond, he says, "The objection to it [jilting Miss Cameron] isn't in reason—it's somehow in the past and in the blood" (p. 162). Poor Finlay, clouded by lack of reason and deformed by heroic gesture, never comes across as a genuine hero. There is always something a little ludicrous about his gesture, a little pathetic about his vision; this may be why Duncan rewards him in the end, rather than taking the kind of toll she exacts from Lorne and Graham.

Advena, too, is rewarded and liberated, but one feels that she has been drawn into the idea of sacrifice by Finlay and is thus less culpable.

Her weakness, Duncan suggests, is a woman's weakness. She had felt and even enjoyed for a time the "aesthetic ecstasy of self-torture" (p. 184), but in the end she arrives at her own deliverance; visiting Christy Cameron for the first time, she moves swiftly toward the sort of insight which Finlay was never to find. Finlay is not really brought to his senses until Dr. Drummond presents him with the *fait accompli* of his own engagement.

Mary Trent, who is the narrator of *Cousin Cinderella*, possesses a brisk but affectionate, pragmatic heart. As the title of the novel suggests, her relationship with England is a little distant, cousinly rather than daughterly. Her Cinderella status suggests innocence but also independence. Her voice flows through the book with cheerful, affirmative strength; it is, in fact, the one thing which holds together the succession of tea parties and travellers' observations. One is informed from the start that her perceptions are to be trusted, while Graham's are not. It is Mary who handles the details of setting up the house, while Graham stands in the background warning and worrying. It is Mary who makes detailed observations on English life, while Graham digests and interprets them into something larger and more meaningful. In the end, Mary is rewarded: she succeeds in what Graham has failed to achieve, acceptance in the British aristocracy. And she makes a love match when Graham has not. Most importantly, she stays afloat psychologically while Graham slowly sinks. Peter, her intended husband, is her partner in reason. Though not a very well-developed character, he consistently demonstrates his attention to details and, by refusing to marry Evelyn, the effectiveness of his will.

It is to Duncan's credit as a novelist that she shows rather than preaches her point of view about idealism and its valuelessness in the modern world. There is no need for her to belabour her concept, for, as in a morality play, those who are equipped to survive do. And those others, who by temperament or by choice surrender to idealism, are brought gently into line and into life.

The Two Susanna Moodies[208]

In many ways, Margaret Atwood's poem *The Journals of Susanna Moodie*[209] follows the pattern of change in narrative poetry. Recent poets who have grown to maturity in a Freudian-influenced age have abandoned linear storytelling. The human personality with its motivations and aberrations makes a more compelling theme. And it is one which is more easily handled in an age where poetry is personal rather than grandiose.

One might look to the American poet William Carlos Williams and his strange poem *Paterson*,[210] which is the name of a man and the name of a place. He attempts to say who and exactly what that man is composed of. An even better example is the poet John Berryman's masterpiece *Homage to Mistress Bradstreet*,[211] in which he contacts, resurrects, and even assumes the persona of the appealing wife of Governor Bradstreet in the Plymouth Colony.[212] These poems explore personalities and at the same time explain them. Or rather they attempt to explain them, for both Williams and Berryman find the single human personality as enormous and complex as a continent.

Canadian narrative poetry seems headed in the same direction. Don Gutteridge,[213] in his study of Louis Riel,[214] is less interested in the historical background than he is in the complicated personality of Riel himself. Michael Ondaatje[215] examines the character of Billy the Kid through the anecdotes and bits and pieces which surround him. Peter Stevens[216] is at work on a narrative poem about Dr. Norman Bethune.[217]

It is interesting to note that all these characters, with the exception of Paterson, who is a wholly fictitious person, sparkle with complexity. Each is given to near-manic ravings or to extraordinarily dramatic contradictions of personality. Even Susanna Moodie, an Englishwoman of great integrity, has been shown by Margaret Atwood to possess a personality bordering on schizophrenia.

There is so much to be said for person-centred narratives. They lend themselves to flexible techniques. They can be handled neatly by clustering "snapshot" poems around one individual. The projection of a central voice-image strengthens and unifies a poem. And the poem's psychological insights can be dramatic and appealing to readers who demand psychological motivation and consequences.

In an afterword to her collection, Margaret Atwood describes her gradual discovery of Susanna Moodie. At first, she had only heard about her. Later, when she read the journals, she was disappointed to find the prose style so decorative and disconnected, although she found the personality of the English lady immigrant to be a unifying quality. She claims to have put the journals out of her mind until she dreamed she was watching an opera which she had written about Susanna Moodie. It was this dream which generated the poems in her series. Thus, she explains, her poems are a mere departure from the spirit of the original journals. Seen at such a distance and through the blur of a dream, it is not surprising that the poems are more the vision of Margaret Atwood than of Susanna Moodie.

Her method has been to take the basic narrative outline of the original Susanna Moodie account and use it as a rough framework. She has divided her poems up into three groups. The first group corresponds with Mrs. Moodie's first seven years in Canada spent on a bush farm. The second group relates to the late years spent as a citizen of Belleville. The third section is an attempt by Atwood to project herself beyond the original accounts and into the twilight territory of great old age, death, and even afterlife.

This, then, is her framework, and on this framework she has hung like ornaments certain incidents in Susanna Moodie's Canadian experience, as well as a large number of purely imaginary ones. These are mingled freely, and even those incidents which are real are so altered that the whole may be said to be a work of imagination.

The woman who emerges from Atwood's account is radically different from the picture Susanna Moodie has unwittingly painted of herself. But a comparison of these two characters is a rather artificial task, since Margaret Atwood denies at the outset that she is talking about the same person.

"I suppose many of [the poems] were suggested by Mrs. Moodie's books, though it was not her conscious voice but the other voice running like a counterpoint through her work that made the most impression on me. Although the poems can be read in connection with Mrs. Moodie's books, they don't have to be; they have detached themselves from the book in the same way that the other poems detach themselves from the events that give rise to them."

After this rather firm divorcing statement, it might seem silly as well as stubborn to force a comparison. Nevertheless, it is interesting to examine the extent to which she altered that personality and the technique by which she created "her" Susanna Moodie. And, in the light of Margaret Atwood's critical work *Survival*, it might even be worthwhile to ask *why* she did it.

Both Margaret Atwood and Susanna Moodie have assisted this examination by recording in a few neat words their separate and divergent motivations. Margaret Atwood felt drawn to the character of Susanna Moodie because she saw in her a microcosm of what was to become the Canadian Character, what she calls a "violent duality," a national split personality, a love-hate relationship with a land of freedom and hardship. Schizophrenia meant not madness but emptiness, the blank desire to endure, to survive. *The Journals of Susanna Moodie* might almost have been written to illustrate Atwood's later theories on the nature of Canadian literature. Her poems shape themselves around these musings. Susanna Moodie fails as earthmother figure but succeeds as schizophrenic citizen.

Mrs. Moodie's motivations are set out at the close of the book *Life in the Clearings*. Her tone here is injured and defensive. Clearly, she has suffered criticism from the Canadian press and has been stung with the injustice of it. "I have written what I consider to be the truth, and as such I hope it may do good, by preparing the minds of immigrants for what they will really find, rather than by holding out fallacious hopes that can never be realized." She may, as was claimed, have discouraged immigrants from coming, but she denies that this was her intent. Even Margaret Atwood has misread her motivation, writing in *Survival*, "One of the first full-length prose works by an English-speaking immigrant to Canada—Moodie's *Roughing It in the Bush*—was written for the express purpose of telling others not to come." Thus, Susanna Moodie was casually misunderstood even by someone who had made a study of her. Mrs. Moodie intended to inform educated people who had had no experience with farming in Canada of some of the pitfalls of bush living. The country, she repeated over and over again, afforded a variety of opportunities for immigrants of all classes. Perhaps her stories of hardship overweighted her stated purpose, causing her to be misjudged.

Certainly, she was misunderstood in her day, and, apparently, she is still misunderstood. But, buried though it might be, her motive shaped her outlook and indirectly framed the picture we have of her. Sincere, earnest, and entertaining, she wrote, "My book is written more with a view to convey general impressions than to delineate separate features." This detailing, she felt, was the special task of men rather than women. Her task, as she saw it, was to amuse, and in her many excellent and highly dramatic stories she succeeded.

If Margaret Atwood and Susanna Moodie had different motives, so too did they write in a different tone. The first Susanna Moodie raced along with an audience in mind, an audience, in fact, which she frequently addresses, scolds, advises. "My friends at home" or "my dear unknown readers" she calls them. She is anxious, she insists, to divert her "weary reader" with a "tale of great amusement." She supplies him with a thousand details in spite of the fact that she feels this to be a masculine talent. She "shared" with him, even debated with him, matters of education and politics.

Atwood's Moodie, on the other hand, never addresses a reader. She is entirely subjective, turned in towards herself. Her glimpses into reality are brief. Images open and close quickly. She returns immediately to her brooding self, sometimes with a question, sometimes with a summation. "I should have known anything planted here / would come up blood," she ends one poem. Perhaps this extreme subjectivity is the reason Atwood uses the device of the mirror-photograph so frequently. In the very brief introductory fragment, she has Susanna say:

> I took this picture of myself
>
> and with my sewing scissors
>
> cut out the face.

Now it is more accurate:

> Where my eyes were,
>
> every-
>
> thing appears.

In her poem called "Looking in a Mirror," she sees herself ravaged after seven years in the bush but comments at the end that it doesn't matter by what process one is changed. "You find only / the shape you already are." In another poem, "Daguerreotype Taken in Old Age," she seems unable to recognize herself. She has become one of the mysteries she ponders, "being / eaten away by light."

In reality, Mrs. Moodie only once mentioned her physical change. When her husband wrote that the family was moving to town, she briefly examined her greying hair and coarsened skin. It mattered very little to her. What she had lost and what she lamented was the pleasure she once found in art. And even this seems mere wistfulness from a woman who painted, studied nature, wrote poetry, and published books. In fact, the moment the snow comes to form the forest road which is to carry her to Belleville,[218] her spirits lift exactly as they had lifted a hundred times before. Margaret Atwood acknowledges this spiritual buoyance in her poem "Departure from the Bush." In this poem, Atwood imagines that the *torments of dislocation* have assumed the fearful shapes of animals, animals which have been absorbed into the pioneer woman's being. She is frightened by their weight and their eyes, although she senses they have something to tell her. And yet, the moment the sleigh comes to take her away, these strange animals leave her:

> and rounding the first hill, I was
>
> (instantaneous)
>
> unlived in; they had gone.

In Mrs. Moodie's account, she comes closer at this moment to revealing her true feelings than she does at any other part of the book. She has lived under great hardship in the bush, but the moment of departure fills her with despair and apathy. Margaret Atwood seems to make much of this torpor but neglects to enlarge upon Susanna's amazing recuperative energy.

This is, in fact, the first of a long list of things about Mrs. Moodie which Atwood has obliterated. Perhaps she is being selective for the purpose of making Susanna a mythic figure of the anguished immigrant. She is far too intelligent to have missed the hundreds of details which show the real Mrs. Moodie as a figure of strength. It seems almost certain that she deliberately focused on Susanna's occasional neurotic moments and from that base built her picture of a lonely and alienated woman.

As Al Purdy[219] points out in his review of the book in *Canadian Literature*,[220] there is no humour in these poems other than satire. There is a witch-like cackle heard in the poems which form the final section but nothing of the warm and generous Mrs. Moodie who loved a funny story and whose sense of humour could be both broad and subtle. The number of times she threw back her head and "laughed heartily" cannot easily be counted. Her humour embraced the broadly comic and crazy friend Tom, who first interested them in coming to Canada. Although horrified by the borrowing practices of her neighbours, Susanna is able to describe the situation with hilarity. She sees comic irony when the local scoundrel turns revival preacher or when a friend preached tolerance for the blacks but couldn't abide the Irish. The scene in which the Scottish serving girl refuses to sleep under the same roof as a Papist is pure farce. And so is the predicament Susanna and her husband find themselves in when they are forced to enter their hotel room through another occupied room. As a keen collector of humorous anecdotes (and there is not one which could be regarded as cruel), she bears little resemblance to Atwood's dour, introspective Susanna.

As an example of their different levels of perception, one might look at Atwood's poem "Visit to Toronto, with Companions." She describes the visit to the insane asylum in this way:

> On the first floor there were
>
> women sitting, sewing;
>
> they looked at us sadly, gentle,
>
> answered questions.

Susanna's own reaction is quite different. The women were sewing, but they were cheerful, and their rosy happiness seemed to deny madness. Mrs. Moodie describes two inmates—one who fancied herself to be Queen Victoria and another who believed he was a famous poet. She speaks of their delusions kindly, even respectfully, but with expansive humour. Atwood's poem goes on from one horror to another until Susanna herself seems to feel the vibrations of madness. One view is balanced and objective; the other neurotic and subjective.

Another way in which Atwood has altered the personality of Susanna is to blur her experiences with dreams. Purdy says, quite rightly, in his review, "Atwood's poems have a slightly-off-from-reality impression." These indistinct dreams veil the brisk, wide-awake Mrs. Moodie. Atwood has enclosed some of Susanna's best stories in dreams, leaving Mrs. Moodie shorn of her natural insight. Perhaps the best example is the poem "Dream 2: Brian the Still-Hunter." In the centre of her poem, Atwood has Brian, the half-mad woodsman who has several times attempted suicide, explain his obsession with hunting:

But every time I aim I feel

my skin grow fur

my head heavy with antlers

and during the stretched instant

the bullet glides on its thread of speed

my soul runs innocent as hooves.

This exhaustion, which is a beautifully stated psychological condensation of Mrs. Moodie's explanation, gives Brian a glowing immediacy, but he fades almost as soon as he emerges, for Margaret Atwood ends her poem by explaining she had only dreamed of him. The hunter's terrible and innocent reality is snuffed out by what seems like a whim. He is also made a little burlesque by uttering what sounds like John Wayne dialogue: "I kill because I have to," and "I die more often than many." In Mrs. Moodie's account, Brian is a failed innocent, suspended between life and the wish for death, whose eloquence underlines his complexity. Mrs. Moodie seems able to resist making people into picturesque characters. Her respect for the mentally deranged suggests a spiritual kinship rather than the morbid curiosity with which Margaret Atwood accuses her in her afterword.

Another incident which Atwood has clothed in dreams is Mrs. Moodie's episode with the bears. In her poem "Dream 3: Night Bear which Frightened Cattle," she writes that the bear is more terrible and real than a real bear. "It absorbs all terror." It is as though dreams are more real to her than actuality, and in this belief she departs radically from the solidarity of Mrs. Moodie.

Atwood has further altered the personality of Susanna by totally isolating her within the bounds of her own thoughts. In Mrs. Moodie's account, Susanna is constantly forming contacts with people and relishing these links. In the Atwood poems, she turns instead to mirrors and photographs of herself, to dreams, and to personal despair. The only character she mentions sympathetically is Brian, and he is half hidden in dream. Her dead children exist as extensions of her tortured self, part of the death she feels in Canada. In one of the most beautiful and moving poems, "Death of a Young Son by Drowning," she refers to her son as "cairn of my plans and future charts." His death roots her in the land she had only "floated on." "My foot hit rock," she said after the drowning, and a final image pins her down: "I planted him in this country / like a flag."

In her poem "The Deaths of the Other Children," her dead children are synonymous with her own death: "My arms, my eyes, my grieving / words, my disintegrated children." In these poems, Margaret Atwood has unearthed events which Mrs. Moodie brushed aside with a few words. Her reason, as she explained it, was to spare her reader her darkest sorrow.

Atwood, quite rightly, perceives that these tragic deaths were central in Susanna's life. What she overlooks is the fact that Susanna was able to carry on with remarkable courage. Atwood appears to have read Mrs. Moodie's books with care and has paid particular attention to the silences in these accounts. Her poems reverse values of importance in somewhat the same way as a negative reverses black-and-white images of a photograph. But she has gambled on what those silences contained and seems to have read weakness where strength was more often indicated.

She seems to have deliberately clouded Susanna's relationship with her husband. In the poem "Further Arrivals," she has Susanna speak to her husband as her "shadow husband." In a deeply felt poem, "The Planters," Susanna watches her husband and another man weeding in the fields. The distance she feels between herself and her husband is enormous. He "denies" the land, she feels. He is clinging to an illusion while she, who is on "the dark / side of light," admits to having been broken. In an extraordinary poem, "The Wereman," she imagines that her husband, unseen in the fields, assumes grotesque shapes. He is possessed with powers, she imagines, and can even change her into strange shapes. She is toying with the problem of illusion and reality, but it seems peculiar that she should make her husband the object of that musing. For in both of Mrs. Moodie's books, the relationship between Susanna and her husband seems to have been close and open.

It does, of course, place a strain on the modern reader to believe that a woman who calls her husband by his last name (for she always refers to him as Moodie) can feel a genuine affection for him. However, it is a peculiarity to which the reader becomes conditioned, and, when read in the context of her accounts, the name acquires the levity of a nickname, something akin to a wife calling her husband Smitty or Jonesy. Their relationship seems to have been modern in the sense that she and her husband shared all things as equals.

Because of the many affectionate references to him, it is difficult to see why Margaret Atwood has distorted this particular relationship. One explanation might be that she has Susanna make of her husband an object of blame, the cause of her parting from home and her alienation in a new country. Or it may be that Atwood, in an attempt to isolate and illuminate Susanna, has removed all others to a great distance, her husband ironically removed further than anyone.

Of the many ways in which the character of Susanna is changed, there is none so devastating as the way Atwood strips away her self-assurance and her resourcefulness. This is apparent from the first poem when Susanna asks

> or is it my own lack
>
> of conviction which makes
>
> these vistas of desolation

In actuality, Susanna's first impression of the new country was rather touristy, and as a newly landed Englishwoman she may have felt conspicuous, but she in no way felt lacking in conviction. "I am a word / in a foreign language," Atwood has her say, but it seems more probable that this forceful woman felt the others to be words in a foreign language. Atwood has overlooked her character's arrogance.

In the poem "Further Arrivals," Susanna says she has entered "a large darkness. / it was our own / ignorance we entered." The spirit of the utterance seems contrary to everything Mrs. Moodie has told us about herself. Her approach to the Canadian wilderness was, at first anyway, one of enormous interest, and, on the contrary, she devoured information, consumed scenery, thirsted after vignettes. No incident, not even the milking of a cow, was too small for her not to be able to extract some element of interest. This was partly her conditioning as a writer, but most certainly it was also the manifestation of an eager intelligence.

For reasons of her own, Margaret Atwood has deprived her character of ingenuity. She has her say in the poem "First Neighbours"

[I] got used to being

a minor invalid, expected to make

inept remarks,

futile and spastic gestures

Her neighbours thought she was overbred and useless, but she watched them closely and picked up their skills. She learned to cook and eat squirrel, to fish in the lake and clean her catch, to make bread in a kettle, to milk a cow, to make coffee of dried dandelion roots, to make salads of weeds. Far from complaining about these new tasks, she rejoiced in her small accomplishments and occasionally crowed over her own ingenuity.

In the poem "Departure from the Bush," Susanna says, "I who had been erased / by fire." The fact was she was not erased by fire, and in another poem called "The Two Fires" Atwood refers to two actual events, a time of sickness in the summer and the burning of the house in the winter. She closes the poem by saying that these fires "informed me." They "left charred marks / now around which / I try to grow." Here Atwood has most truly caught Mrs. Moodie's spirit. The fires became marks on a pattern, the patterns she begs for in another poem called "Paths and Thingscape." These fires, like the drowning of her child, are spiritual events which root her firmly to the new land.

Atwood misinterprets Susanna most by assuming a duality in her nature, a tension which does not really exist. In a poem called "Later in Belleville," for instance, Susanna says, "I wrote / verses about love and sleighbells / which I exchanged for potatoes." Atwood seems to find this extraordinary and untenable, but Mrs. Moodie was far more practical about her art and even cheerful about the irony of poems bartered for potatoes. Writing was the way in which she supplemented her income, and quite possibly she never saw art in the same rarified way that Atwood takes for granted.

In another poem called "The Double Voice," she elaborated on this theme of duality. Susanna, as seen by Atwood, is divided down her Victorian middle. One side has manners and pursues ladylike art forms.

The other is conscious of sweat, drink, messy births, mosquitoes. It is questionable whether Susanna Moodie was conscious herself of this dichotomy. Like any person of her class, she disliked the more brutal aspects of human nature, but, as anyone who has read her books can testify, she never blots them out. We are always conscious of the every-dayness of her society but seldom hear her outright condemnation. In her poetry, she is operating on an unreal level, writing within a genteel convention. In her prose, she seems open, for a woman of her times, to the realistic details of frontier life.

It is in her relationship with the land where Atwood sees her at her most schizophrenic. In a poem called "Thoughts from Underground," she says, "When I first reached this country / I hated it / and I hate it more each year." Later she remarks, "and I felt I ought to love / this country. I said I loved it / and my mind saw double."

Mrs. Moodie's essential ambivalence to the country runs from the beginning of her books to the end. She is one minute praising the natural beauties of the land and the next minute smarting under the bad manners of her neighbours. She enjoys local folk customs while longing for those at home. But how neurotic is this sort of behaviour? Wouldn't one hundred percent consistency be unreal? This is a balanced view of a woman who naturally enough longs for her homeland, who is being exposed to rougher conditions than she ever imagined and to people who really do have appalling manners. If she were to hurl herself into total acceptance, as Margaret Atwood seemingly would have her do, she would be unreliable as a reporter.

Atwood's Susanna emerges more as symbol than person. Having lost her humour, her ingenuity, her insight, and her affection for others, she is a barren symbol of the type of Canadian Margaret Atwood believes to be typical, a person who merely survives. In this respect, Atwood's haunting poems with their musical patterns of sound are entirely successful. But it is to be hoped that someday someone will write a narrative poem about the real Susanna Moodie, whose spirit not only survived but overcame.

The Healing Journey[221]

I think; therefore, I am—you will all recognize this statement from Descartes, Philosophy 101. To live our lives, we must think, and it's always struck me as an impossible task to think while in the midst of a thicket, which is where we seem to be a good deal of the time. We need, in the midst of illness, grief, confusion, in order to understand ourselves, a clear and uncluttered perspective—which is why, I suppose, people seek sanctuary, why they observe silence, why they go on pilgrimages, why they attend retreats, why they fast, why they meditate or pray, why they gather as we are gathered today—to compare our experiences and come again and again to the understanding—for it seems we are never finished learning this lesson—that our most private thoughts and needs are, in fact, universally shared.

People who have pets are allowed to name them. If we have children, we name them. And novelists are privileged to name every creature who enters their pages.[222] I like short, unobtrusive names that don't draw too much attention to themselves. I can also rename towns[223] or even countries. There is something else we can do, I believe, to remove ourselves from the thicket, and that is to imagine a construct of what our lives look like. Constructs—and I'm thinking in terms of a physicality, a reality, an icon or object which is at least roughly congruent with our life narrative—such constructs allow us to stop and stare at ourselves. We can pull them up as you might pull up an image on your word processor. We can touch these objects and feel out their surfaces, their dimensions, their revealed patterns.[224]

Probably, the journey is the most frequently called-upon image. A journey, like our lives, has movement. It also has varied terrain, obstacles, good and bad weather, spectacular views or sloughs of despond, places of rest, the possibility of encountering other travellers—*and* a destination. "I am going on my final journey," Ronald Reagan announced to a television audience when his Alzheimer's was diagnosed; I think it was the most eloquent thing he ever said.

A friend of mine sees her life as a house she is forever and ever building. With her metaphorical blueprints and building tools, she is perpetually adding on rooms. Opening up windows or skylights, widening the stairs, inspecting the roof, the gutters and downspouts, having the chimney seen to, improving the landscaping. She knows every inch of her space but admits there are certain corners too dark to enter. Naturally, she prefers the sun-filled southern exposure rooms, but sometimes nothing will do but the dark passageway where she can pace back and forth and *think*. This is not a heritage building she's working on. She imagines that she and the house will come to an end simultaneously.

We choose the constructs that are useful to us, illuminating and comforting, and often, I think, we employ more than one at the same time.

I'd like to talk a little about images that have been valuable to me and which have helped me to think about the lives of the characters in my novels. I admit to feeling a little uneasy about this, since I grew up in a time when women—girls—were told not to talk about themselves. I apologize in advance both for seizing this opportunity and for risking your impatience. Naturally, I'm taking for granted that we'll have a discussion later on so that we can share our experiences.

Because I'm a novelist, it has sometimes been useful for me to imagine a life as possessing roughly the shape of a novel. I don't mean that I am willing to confuse fact with fiction, illusion with reality. I am talking about the structure of a novel and particularly the fact that novels fall into chapters, separate chapters in time and space, but chapters which are joined by an overriding narrative line or what I like to think of as the spine of the story.[225]

More and more it seems to me that important, life-giving novels are about the search of an individual for his or her real home.[226] You can go all the way back to Ulysses to see this. Or you can look at Stephen Dedalus in *A Portrait of the Artist as a Young Man*[227] or Emma Woodhouse[228] or Fanny Price[229] from Jane Austen's pen. They are all journeying toward that place called home.

Almost inevitably, people are born in the wrong place; they are misassigned, detoured, lost in the dark, and compelled to go forward by that image of home. I'm thinking of home in the way the French use the word *foyer*. To us, a foyer is an entrance hall, but originally it was the centre of the house, and even the centre of the *centre* of the house, the heart of the fire burning in the central hearth, offering comfort, welcome, and the instant recognition of being the only habitable place, the inevitable and ultimate shelter.

When I think about my own life, I am astonished how different these chapters are one from the other, how each had a certain coherency while I was living within its pages, but how each is furnished with its own atmosphere and gravitational pull. Of course, there is the childhood chapter, those first ten years in particular, a time of strong discovery and ever-present confusion. It's a curious fact that children aren't particularly interested in childhood; it is only later that we recall those profound first impressions and wonder how we survived. Parents think they have explained everything to children, but this task is impossible. I tried a few years ago to write about this in a story called "Times of Sickness and Health."[230]

One passage goes

> Kay, who is fifty, has no children of her own, but is interested in the way children think and the questions they like to ask. For example: is a tomato a fruit or a vegetable? Do these querying children, she wonders, really want an answer? Or is there a kind of hopeful rejoicing at the overlapping of categories, a suggestion that the material and immaterial world spills out beyond its self-imposed classifications? What is the difference between sand and gravel? Between weeds and flowers? Between liking and love? It occurs to her that these children may be blurring with their bright, winning curiosity, being playful and sly, and masking a deeper, more abject and injurious sense of bewilderment. There is, after all, so much authentic chaos to sort out, so much seething muddle and predicament that it is a wonder children survive their early ignorance. How do they bear it? You would think they would hold their breath out of sheer rage or hurl themselves down flights of stairs. You would think they'd get sick and die.

In my novel *Small Ceremonies*, the heroine Judith Gill confides to her friend Nancy how she had been frightened for most of her childhood. What frightened her was the suffocating sameness of it all. The awful and relentless monotony, the fear, she says, that it was never going to be over. Quote:

The furnace switching off and on in the basement. Amos and Andy on the radio. Or the kettle steaming in the kitchen. Even the sound of her parents turning the pages of the newspaper in the living room while she was supposed to be going to sleep. Her mother's little cough, so genteel. The flush of the toilet through the wall before they went to bed. And other things. The way her mother always hung the pillowcases on the clothesline with the end up, leaving just a little gap so the air could blow inside them. With a clothespeg in her mouth when she did it, always the same. It frightened her.

Joanie, the younger daughter of Daisy Goodwill in *The Stone Diaries*, lives for the first chapter of her life inside the tent of secrecy that children often construct for themselves. Her secrecy is sly, self-protective, necessary. She often tests the boundaries of that secrecy. Quote:

Joan is so full of secrets that sometimes she thinks she's going to burst. Her mother, putting her to bed at night, leans down and kisses her on each cheek and says, "My sweetie pie," and never dreams of all the secrets that lie packed in her little girl's head. . . .

Already, at the age of five, Joan understands that she is destined to live two lives, one existence that is visible to those around her and another that blooms secretly inside her head.

There's a Decal transfer—a black swan swimming through green reeds—stuck to the top of the clothes hamper in the bathroom. She remembers watching her mother apply this decoration, first soaking the Decal in a sink full of water, then peeling the transparent backing neatly away, centering the swan in the very middle of the hinged lid, and wiping it smooth with a wet cloth. Joan had thought the moment beautiful. Nevertheless, whenever she finds herself alone in the bathroom she scrapes away at the swan with her thumbnail. So far, she's managed to loosen the edges all the way around, and she expects any minute to be accused, though at the same time she knows herself to be full of power, able to slip out from under any danger.

The writer Annie Dillard in her book *An American Childhood* talks about the remarkable watershed of reaching the age of ten. At ten, a child is allowed more freedom from parental observation, more roles to play. It is a time, Dillard says, when a child becomes for the first time fully awake. Patterns form and interlock; understanding is glimpsed; a self is cautiously built in the light of approaching but undreamt-of puberty. Defences, too, are built—what we sometimes call coping skills, tactical solutions for dealing with injustice or sorrow.

And then a page turns to that new chapter, adolescence, a chapter of entrapment and revisualization. Alice, the oldest child of Daisy Goodwill in *The Stone Diaries*, understands this. She has lived all her life in a bedroom in an old house, and on the ceiling of that bedroom is a hideous crack. The crack takes many forms in her imagination, but it is chiefly threatening because it is always *there*, endlessly there. One day she realizes that with a little plaster and paint she can erase the crack, and this is what she, in fact, does. To her surprise, no one stops her. She is allowed this act of recreation. The crack and its repair are emblematic of a larger change in her life. She transforms not just her bedroom ceiling but her self, deliberately leaving behind the bossy, arrogant big sister and becoming someone who is kind and responsive to others. A new chapter has been arrived at, written in the ink of self-invention.

When I speak of my own twenties and thirties, it is often through a haze of memory. The period of having children and looking after them filled two decades, a chapter in which hard physical work prevailed and where reflective moments were rare. But the day I realized, at age twenty-two, the mother of a newborn baby, that I was entirely responsible for the life of another—that was the day when I understood how alert and attentive I must henceforth be. Like Alice, I had to be someone else. Responsibility meant far more than turning in a term paper on time. Responsibility meant life or death, nurturing or neglect. It was frightening, but I remember that I welcomed it, recognizing that I was perhaps involved in the most important project of my life—there would never again be work this hard and this rewarding.

I believed it would go on forever. This was going to be my life. Of course, I was wrong. One by one the children left home, and with each departure all the relationships in the family shifted slightly, introducing new sub-chapters. Until this time, all my books had teenagers as sub-characters—perhaps not the main characters but presences that filled the spaces and redirected the course of action. Suddenly, one day in 1986, as I sat correcting proofs for a new novel, *Swann*, I realized there were no children in its many pages, not one. I was in a new place in my life, one I hadn't thought to recognize earlier.

There is a time in our lives when we say goodbye to the bodies that seem to have been with us forever, and I think it is not surprising that there is a sense of mourning that takes place for that loss. It helped me at that time to think of the other changes of my life, the many changes that, taken collectively, placed me squarely in a new chapter. I had much greater personal freedom. I had a sense of being part of a clan, although I was no longer an overseeing mother with daily responsibilities. There was more space for friendships. I could afford occasional small luxuries. My daily schedule was responsive to my own decisions, and I was free to turn to new forms of work, work that I would choose and develop.

I was sometimes uneasy about this new work—this writing. Women were out marching for peace or for civil rights or for the advancement of feminism, or else they were single-handedly supporting their families. These were the days when I wondered if sitting in an upstairs bedroom and making up stories was a worthwhile occupation for a grown-up woman. One of my colleagues helped me with this. "We also serve who only sit and think," she said. She might just as well have said, "We also serve who only sit and write."[231]

There will be other chapters. I had a moment of self-doubt in the middle of writing *The Stone Diaries*. I had planned ten chapters, and they were the traditional chapters of a life's journey: Birth, Childhood, Love, Marriage, and so on. Now I was only halfway through the list of chapters, and Daisy Goodwill was already old. I think I had always thought of a long life as an arc, with old age occupying a short space at the end of the arc. But suddenly I realized just exactly how long one spends being old. This was frightening at first, struggling to understand this notion.

But it strikes me now that each decade, each chapter to come, will have its own colours and narrative structure. The trick will be to occupy those chapters, to live in them as one learns to live at home in the centre of one's life.

If the construct of life as a novel fails me from time to time, I turn to that more variable structure, the labyrinth.[232]

What I love about labyrinths is their ubiquity. Wherever human society has flourished, on every inhabited continent, there you will find evidence of the labyrinth form. Labyrinths are etched into rocks, printed on coins, shaped from masonry, textiles, and living matter to form temples, fabrics, teasing puzzles. They stretch back as far as we *can* stretch back, even into prehistoric times. But what are they for, these endlessly twisting paths? There are all sorts of theories: they may represent a pathway to God, a pathway to death, a prebirth journey toward life, or toward sexual fulfillment, or the trip to Jerusalem. They gesture toward the search for the self; they provide access to a kind of controlled chaos, which brings us heightened sensations of being grievously lost and then triumphantly found. There is always a centre, a goal, so one is never moving toward the pain of nothingness, though it may sometimes seem just that. Beneath the clipped hedges and strict conformity burn alternative and opposite possibilities. The false turnings, the repetitions, the retraced steps mimic, I think, the workings of consciousness itself. The same places are encountered again and again, but they are seen from another stage of the journey, another perspective opened up with the assistance of all that has been accumulated along the way.

The doubled and retraced labyrinthine path became apparent to me a week ago when I attended my forty-fifth high school reunion.[233] There we were, men and women in our early sixties, joined in time and space by experiences from our teenage years. If you have gone through a similar ceremony, you will understand the confusion I felt. My body remembered what my brain had erased. What was appropriate behaviour under the circumstances? I scarcely knew. I actually babbled. My right foot fell over my left, leaving a bruise. But the experience was exhilarating, an unlooked-for loop in the journey, a celebration, and a reminder that we can multiply our experiences by playing them to different music.

Because mazes or labyrinths exist in every corner of the world, because they have been with us forever, I think we must pay attention to what they mean. Perhaps they are just a game, laid for our diversion. But their antiquity, *and* their ubiquity, suggest otherwise. It seems more likely that they are a correlative structure—part of the racial mythology and memory, humanly recognized and appointed—to give our often meandering and meaningless lives value. And hope. Because a maze takes many forms but always possesses a goal.

It was this interest in labyrinths that formed a matrix for my novel *Larry's Party*. I made Larry a designer of real mazes in order to lighten the symbolic load. (Who was it who said symbols are the fleas of literature?) Larry Weller of Winnipeg, Manitoba, enters each chapter of the novel as one entering a maze, exiting at the close of the chapter to find himself, or to will himself, lost once again. One such maze is his marriage, another his family, another his work, another his friends. In the novel, he reaches the centre, the goal, but this is not the end of his journey. He now must find his way out, and this journey may be longer and more difficult than the journey to the centre—but we will have learned to trust the process.

We may not grow wiser as we grow older—certainly there are no guarantees of this. And we may not know the turnings the path will take. But we do know that turnings exist. There are false corners, too, that lead nowhere—we will not be quite as shocked as we once were to find these treacherous surprises. And probably we will have a fund of positive strategies to call on and to share. We know what rescues us from emotional bankruptcy because we've been there before. Perhaps this fund of possibility really does add up to what the world calls wisdom.

Thank you for inviting me to talk a little about journeys, journeys that heal our pain and distress, and journeys that enliven us by their own expression.

PART 2

Carol Shields's Previously Published but Uncollected Essays

This section includes two dozen essays previously published in travel and women's magazines, journals, and books—essays that focus on subjects from travel to divorce and from petals to purses and thus open up a world of possibilities. Some of them, such as "Living at Home" and "I've Always Meant to Tell You: A Letter to My Mother," are quite personal, whereas others, such as "The Visual Arts," have a cultural focus.

Shields's essays include both memories of home and accounts of travel, conveying the tension between wishing to travel and wanting to stay home. Family rituals, or "small ceremonies," are celebrated in essays such as "Sunday Dinner, Sunday Supper" because "These rituals caught us at our very best, informing us of who we were and what we could be to one another." Such rituals also enrich her fiction: *Small Ceremonies* (1976), for example, opens on "Sunday night" as the family enjoys the "Englishy" ritual of high tea that they have brought home to Canada from their sabbatical year in Britain (1).

"At Home in Winnipeg" conveys her sense of feeling at home in that city. Shields lived in Winnipeg for twenty years—1980 to 2000— longer than she had lived anywhere else. As she concludes in "Living at Home," "This is my *home*, the place I come from," a sentiment that she also expresses in her poem "Coming to Canada—Age Twenty-Two" (*CP* 178), the poem that gave its title to her third poetry collection, *Coming to Canada* (1992). Winnipeg, also the setting for her 1992 novel *The*

Republic of Love, took her to its heart, naming her Winnipeg Citizen of the Year in 2000, commissioning a bronze bust and building a hedge maze in her honour in 2009, and lavishing her with awards.[1]

As Shields affirms in "At Home in Winnipeg," "At home, I yearn to travel; travelling, I hunger for home." Travelling in Scotland, as she records in that essay, she viewed through an open window a woman happily reading. Shields frequently recalls observing strangers glimpsed through windows and her curiosity about them, including in her essay "Where Curiosity Leads" (*SI* 83–92) and in her first novel, *Small Ceremonies*. This epiphanic vision reflects her belief in the magical experience of reading. "Travelwarp" conveys brilliantly the way that reading can transport one to another place that might contrast vividly with one's actual location, as Shields recalls travelling in South America while reading a novel set in Medieval Greenland.

Some of her essays were written for travel magazines, such as *Travel and Leisure* or Air Canada's *enRoute*. Her 1997 essay "A Legacy of Stone" records her visit to the Orkney Islands, where Shields went to research her award-winning 1993 novel *The Stone Diaries*. "My Favourite Place: At Home in Deepest France" was a significant publication for Carol Shields and her husband, Don Shields. Don told me that it was through this article that he and Carol became friends with Bill and Arlette Baker. When Bill read the article in a doctor's office, he was inspired to get in touch with its author. After both Bill and Carol died, Don and Arlette "joined their lives together," in Don's words.

"Others" expresses Shields's lifelong interest in other people, an interest that doubtless inspired her reading and her writing in general and her interest in biography in particular. *Others* is the title of her first collection of poems, published in 1972, before Shields had published a single novel. As she acknowledges in her essay "Where Curiosity Leads," "My 'other' was men" (*SI* 87). Perhaps that is why she elected to compose two novels, *Happenstance* (1980) and *Larry's Party* (1997), about a male protagonist.

"What's in a Picture" demonstrates her interpretive skills as Shields interprets a photograph of an older woman, an example of an "other," who she suspects might be a family member, just as one might interpret a poem or "read" a Hogarth painting.

"Parties Real and Otherwise" reveals her interest in parties, which Shields includes in all her novels, the most important being Larry

Weller's eponymous party. In this essay, she revisits the parties in some of her novels, portraying herself as the uninvited guest—"an authorly mouse under a fictional chair." She also reveals her research on micro-filmed newspapers in her desire to get the historical setting exactly right, as even menus reflect their historical periods. She actually includes menus in some of her novels, including *Larry's Party*. In her interview with Shields, Eleanor Wachtel recalls how Shields prepared the menu from that novel to celebrate her friend's fiftieth birthday. Eating a chrysanthemum leads Shields to reimagine her mother's sisters' gardens in "Rare Petals." Judy Chicago's 1974–79 installation, *The Dinner Party*, which made a considerable impact on Shields, transformed the traditional dinner party into a startling exhibition of feminism.

Some of Shields's essays were written for women's magazines, such as *Allure*. In "A Purse of One's Own" (possibly a play on the title of Virginia Woolf's famous essay), the subtitle—"Other than a Woman's Own Thoughts, a Handbag Is about the Only Inviolable Space that She Possesses"—turns what might be a mere fashion statement into a feminist suggestion. As Shields concludes, "Later I came to suspect that the inside of a handbag is also the single inviolable space a woman possesses, other than the labyrinth of her own thoughts."

In "Divorce," Shields decries the high rate of divorce in recent fiction. She affirms, "I *would* like to see more marital equity in the pages of our fiction." She explains that she has attempted to write the novels that she would like to read, which portray marriage in a positive light, including her *Happenstance* pair and her courtship novel, *The Republic of Love*. Her belief in marriage is reflected in the weddings contained in virtually all her novels.

With "Heidi's Conundrum," inspired by Wendy Wasserstein's play *The Heidi Chronicles* (1988), Shields's implicit feminism, in addition to her interest in contemporary drama, becomes explicit. Shields defines "the Heidi-conundrum" as the problem that women face of how to deal with "the burdens of anger and abandonment." She also notes the absence of women in plays, films, and newsprint, a subject that she addresses in the angry letters that Reta Winters writes in *Unless* (2002).

Even "The Best Teacher I Ever Had" reveals her innate feminism as Shields records how she observed as a child that, with the exception of schoolteachers, only men worked outside the home, whereas she viewed women's housework as her "destiny." She declares, however,

"I love work," adding, "I love writing about work as well as doing it." When she discovered that "my two passions, reading and writing, might become my work. And that my work would ground me in the world," she made several of her heroines into writers, from Judith Gill of her first novel to Reta Winters of her last. She always gives her characters interesting work, from writing biographies through researching mermaids to creating mazes.

"A Delicate Balancing Act" addresses Shields's views on book reviewing. The author of many reviews of books, primarily novels, especially Canadian and American novels by women, Shields believed in treating books respectfully, as Alex Ramon confirms in his essay "'Little Shocks of Recognition': Carol Shields's Book Reviews."

Shields's account of the Booker Prize dinner of 1993 in her letter to Eleanor Wachtel is a triumph of understatement, dramatizing the maxim absorbed by her girlhood self: "If you can't say something nice, don't say anything at all." Underlying her dinner with her Fourth Estate publishers and *Guardian* people, her meeting with Salman Rushdie, Stephen Spender, and Margaret Drabble, is the fact that Shields was expected to win the prize for *The Stone Diaries*. People were shocked when Roddy Doyle's *Paddy Clarke Ha Ha Ha* was announced as the winner.

In "The Visual Arts," Shields addresses the question of "how art gets made," a question that informs her 1987 novel *Swann*, in which a farmwife produces poems of startling brilliance. *Swann* represents "the central mystery of art ... that from common clay ... works of genius evolve" (96), a mystery that Shields also explores in *Jane Austen*. Her essay focuses on Edouard Manet's portrait of a stem of asparagus and segues to the eighteenth-century artists who painted over bricked-in windows to give the impression of light through glass. She discusses this subject in her introduction to the 2001 Modern Library edition of *Mansfield Park* and revisits it in her short story "Windows" in *Dressing Up for the Carnival* (109–20), in which she employs the same words as in this essay: "Not a real light, of course, but the idea of light, which is infinitely more powerful than light itself" is virtually identical to the clause "infinitely more alluring than light itself" (120).

This collection includes introductions, prefaces, forewords, and afterwords that Shields composed for her own and other publications, works that have not previously been collected and that would prove difficult for readers to access. They include her introduction to her pair of sister novels, *Small Ceremonies* and *The Box Garden* (1977), reissued as *Duet* by Fourth Estate in 2003, in which she discusses her interest in "companion novels," a term that also applies to her second pair of novels, her husband-and-wife pairing—originally titled *Happenstance* (1980) and *A Fairly Conventional Woman* (1982)[2] and reissued in 1993 by Fourth Estate in the United Kingdom and Canada as *Happenstance: The Husband's Story and The Wife's Story.* The collection also includes her retrospective foreword to the 2001 reissue of *The Stone Diaries*, which won the Governor General's Award for Fiction in Canada in 1993 and the Pulitzer Prize in the United States in 1995, catapulting Shields to instant fame. She explains how that novel, republished in 2023 on the thirtieth anniversary of its original publication, reflects her continuing interest in biography and her desire to "redeem" the neglected generations of women, as well as her habit of visualizing a structure for each novel, as she explains in her essay "Boxcars, Coat Hangers and Other Devices" (*SI* 23–30)—"a series of Chinese nesting boxes" (26) for *The Stone Diaries* being her most elaborate structure to date.

In her afterword to *Life in the Clearings*, Shields addresses the form of Susanna Moodie's books, concluding that "*Roughing It in the Bush* and *Life in the Clearings* are both books that generously and disconcertingly embrace elements of travel writing, the literary sketch, narrative fiction, meditation, factual material, and poetry." She frequently objects to the academic urge to categorize literary works, complaining that "Trying to place such a text in a governing tradition is to miss the book itself." She affirms, "The form is Susanna Moodie's invention."

Shields composed the afterwords to both editions of *Dropped Threads: What We Aren't Told*, which she co-edited with Marjorie Anderson. Both editions contain unabashedly feminist responses by three dozen women writers—from Margaret Atwood to Betty Jane Wylie and from Maude Barlow to Wanda Wuttunee—that read like a "who's who" of "Canlit" who were invited to "identify the areas of surprise and silence in their lives" (viii), as Anderson puts it in her foreword to the first edition. In her afterword to *Dropped Threads*, Shields reveals, in her memory of burning her saddle shoes and graduating stark naked under her robe, her "nose-thumbing rejection of the suffocating shell of convention" that parallels the "sparkling subversion" (*SD* 337) of literary rules and regulations that characterizes her mature writing

(*DT* 343). She refers to the Latin dictum *tempus fugit* frequently in her essays, citing it only to disagree with it. As in "The Healing Journey," she proceeds to review the "chapters" in her life, her battle with cancer being the last.

In her afterword to *Dropped Threads 2: More of What We Aren't Told*, Shields celebrates her "two favourite things: language and the company of women" (367). She focuses on a personal injury when a senior colleague in the Department of English at the University of Manitoba took over, with the blessing of the department chair, the office that she had made attractive and welcoming for students, explaining how she buried this injury in a novel. Perhaps she buried it in *The Stone Diaries* by having Daisy Goodwill Flett wreak revenge on Pinky Fulham—for the "grave injury" (325) that he did her in taking over her "Mrs. Greenthumb" horticultural column—by imagining a vending machine collapsing and crushing him as he shakes it in an attempt to retrieve his quarter. Addressing the traditional silencing of women, Shields repeats the dictum "*Woman, hold thy tongue*" in her afterword to the first edition of *Dropped Threads* (346). Margaret Atwood's contribution to that collection is appropriately titled "If You Can't Say Something Nice, Don't Say Anything at All" (133–34).

ESSAYS

I've Always Meant to Tell You:
A Letter to My Mother[3]

Dear Mother,

You told me once—I must have been eleven or twelve—that my conception was "an accident." I suppose I could have been crushed, but I wasn't. The way you said it, the look on your face and the girlish way you rolled your eyes, told me that it was one of the good accidents of your life. It was an easy birth too. "You slipped out like a lump of butter," you used to say.[4] I can't think now why I found this announcement so mortifying. Was it the image of butter? Or the unimaginable bloody process and that most intimate of connections?

You said all kinds of things, and many of these sayings are available to me on the long-playing record inside my head. All I have to do is press a button, and your voice comes on. "Always give to the Salvation Army, they do good work." "Never light candles in the daytime, and never have candles on the table if you don't intend to light them." "Always buy from the Fuller Brush Company, they're a fine old company." "Don't make promises you can't keep." "Add a few drops of strong coffee to a chocolate cake." "Never let a boy put his hand on your knee." "Crossword puzzles keep your mind active." "Your skin will turn to leather if you stay out there in the sun." "If you put good things into a casserole, it will turn out good." "Be sure to get your teaching licence, so that you'll have something to fall back on." "When you make a tailored wool suit or dress, send it out afterwards to be professionally pressed." "Pastry toughens if you roll it out more than twice." "Feed your husband nutritious meals, that way he'll live longer and support you."

Sometimes what you said and did were in conflict. "The human body is a beautiful thing," you said before each visit to the Art Institute, preparing us for the sight of nude statues. But you yourself dressed and undressed in your closet. I understood though, even as a child, that there was no hypocrisy involved here, that you were only trying to puzzle out your own feelings.

President Roosevelt[5] was a bad man, you said. He was a threat to America. My brother and sister and I grew up thinking this was true, that Franklin Delano Roosevelt was in the same camp with Hitler and the devil. And so, when the news came crackling over the radio that he had died—I was nine, my twin brother and sister were eleven—the three of us set up a rousing cheer. You spanked us all on the spot, the only real spanking I can remember. Something was amiss here, something not quite logical. And yet an underlying logic made itself instantly known.

You can be anything you want, you told us, even president. Part of me believed this or at least believed that you believed it. But there was a gap always between how you saw yourself and how you were seen by others. You were pretty, you went to teachers' college, you lived most of your adult life in a Chicago suburb,[6] you were innovative in the way you cooked and dressed—that red gabardine pantsuit circa 1946—but you never got over the feeling that you were a gawky girl from the sticks.

You grew up on an Illinois farm, you and your twin sister being the youngest in a family of eight children. I never saw that farm. It was only fifty miles from Chicago, where we lived, and I can't help wondering why, on a family outing, we never drove by and paid a nostalgic visit. I can only guess the reasons. It was probably poor—your parents had immigrated from Sweden at the beginning of the century—and it may have held memories you preferred to forget; not every rural family is as jolly and cohesive as the Waltons.[7]

I'm not sure why I know so little about your childhood. You were not, of course, one of those jolly story-telling mothers, and I was not, sad to say, curious enough to demand information. For your first eight years of schooling, you went to a one-room schoolhouse, and for a number of those years your teacher was your own older sister, our Aunt Edna (the difficult one, as she came to be called in the family). This teacher-sister coincidence seemed wildly improbable to me as a child, the sort of twisted unlikelihood one comes across in ancient folktales.

You went to a nearby town for high school—I believe it was called Villa Park—and while at that school you failed Latin. You told us this, sitting one day at the kitchen table. Your tone and your timing were deliberate. We paid attention. "I want you to know that I failed Latin in high school," you said to me and my brother and sister. Of course, we understood why we were hearing this: so that we wouldn't be afraid of our own failures. None of this had to be explained.

Your twin sister was your best friend—you told us this often—but sometimes you mentioned other girlhood friends. There was Grace, brave Grace, who had to be pushed to school in a wheelchair. Grace grew up, married a man named George, and the two of them lived like a pair of sparrows in a tiny house in Sycamore, Illinois. One day George went down to the basement and shot himself. It was said that his eyes were failing and that he didn't want to be a burden to poor crippled Grace. I found this story deeply poignant as a child but didn't quite believe it. Why not? I wonder.

You had another friend called Lily. She signed her letters "Lovingly, Lily,"[8] one word swimming above the other, the L and y linked with inky tendrils. I never knew anything else about Lily, but this feat of penmanship seemed all I needed to know.

There was Helen, there was Hap, there were the Betchlor sisters (who never married). You kept up with these friends all your life, writing back and forth, dropping in when you were in the neighbourhood. And later there was Mary Organ,[9] your Catholic friend, who cried all night long when Al Smith was defeated for the presidency in 1928. Teaching school in Chicago, Mary Organ got pregnant and in desperation leapt from the top of an upright piano—but this story is oddly unfinished, or have I simply forgotten the ending? Did she succeed in aborting the baby, did she die? In my mind, she is still suspended in that still parlour air, her destiny unknown.

You and your sister Irene finished high school and enrolled in college. Who paid for this education? Who offered encouragement? (You almost never spoke of your parents.) You lived at home, taking the new Interurban back and forth to DeKalb Normal School, and two years later, your diploma in hand, you arrived in Chicago, where you had secured a teaching job.

Then followed what I have always thought of as your great adventure. You and Irene and two other young teachers roomed in the Hemingway house in Oak Park. At this time, Ernest had not yet begun to publish. He was in Paris, living what his parents considered to be a dissolute life—if only he had gone into medicine or into the educational field! The Hemingways were proud; they wouldn't have dreamt of turning over their third floor to roomers if it weren't for the expense of their daughter Sunny's college education. Mrs. Hemingway informed you four young women that you were not to entertain your boyfriends in the house. You could have only two inches of hot water in the bath, and that only twice a week—this was all the Hemingways allowed themselves. Noise would not be tolerated after ten o'clock since Dr. Hemingway was a light sleeper.

The Hemingways seldom referred to their son. "Is he an artist?" you once asked. "He is a time waster," Dr. Hemingway replied.

A year later Ernest Hemingway published *The Sun Also Rises*[10] and became famous, but by that time you and the others had moved to a more congenial apartment on the west side. This has always seemed to me a tragedy of timing, your near-brush with celebrity. I remember badgering you. "Couldn't you have lasted one more year?" "Oh, that drafty house," you said, "we had colds all the time, and Mary Organ came down with pneumonia."

You never read Hemingway. I think his reputation intimidated you. You read the *Reader's Digest* instead and the *Ladies' Home Journal* and *Better Homes and Gardens*. You quit teaching when you settled down with my father and began to raise a family. (Somewhere along the way you took the train to California to visit your sister Edna, and this journey was always spoken about with epic resonance: *the time you travelled all the way to California, and by yourself*.)

After a year or two of marriage, you had a miscarriage, a little boy. "I think of him as Jack," you told me once. "And I think of him every year on his birthday." Then came the twins, my brother and sister, and eighteen months later I was born.

You went back to teach after the war, and I have no idea how you felt about that. (Teaching always seemed to be what you did rather than what you wanted to do.) You ran a Girl Scout troop for years. You sewed for me and my sister, beautiful clothes, though you always told us not to tell anyone they'd been made at home.

On Saturday afternoons, you played bridge with your school-teaching cronies; these bridge parties took place in a local restaurant called The Spinning Wheel, and always, before you drove off for the afternoon, you sat down in the living room and did your nails, spreading your hands out on a dish towel to dry. I never smell nail polish, even today, without thinking of the enchantment those afternoons must have offered—you were always rushing to get ready, you were excited, looking forward to being with old friends. One day you were on your way out the door when you noticed a water stain on the pink shantung dress you had just finished making. You started to cry a little, and then you cried harder, and in the end you telephoned your regrets and went to bed.

This happened more often as you got older. It was your nerves, you said, or maybe someone else said it. You had bad nerves. Sometimes, when under stress, you broke out in hives. Once or twice you were hospitalized for reasons that were never revealed to me, but I think it must have been that old problem of nerves.

And I think, too, that you had an artist's side to you that was never fully expressed,[11] though everyone admired your flower arrangements. Your centrepieces—you lived in the great age of centrepieces, the '40s, the '50s—were cleverly concocted from whatever was at hand. You could slipcover a chair in an afternoon and always with an eye for texture and colour. I used to watch you canning peaches on hot August afternoons, how you would turn each peach-half with a fork so that the curve, round as a baby's cheek, gleamed lustrous through the blue glass. Now why would anyone go to all that bother? I didn't understand as a child, but now I do.

You would be surprised, and also baffled, to know that your birthday, March 8, is the official date for International Women's Day.[12] "International what day?" you would ask.

This event involves celebrations and also protests, all over the world. Women march in the streets on this day, picket porn shops, storm their various legislatures, hold candlelight vigils for women who have been murdered. Not everyone participates in this active and public way, though; some of us have found other means to focus our thoughts; as one of my colleagues says, we also serve who only sit and write.

You died when I was thirty-five. I was married then, and a mother myself, but I had not yet begun to publish.[13] I regret this terribly, not because I feel needy for your praise, but because you were uniquely enthusiastic about the awful poetry and stories I wrote as a child. One of those poems began

> Spring is here, horray, horray.
>
> Come on, boys, come out to play.
>
> Put away your scarves and hats.
>
> Grab your baseballs and your bats.

On and on it went through the four seasons, yards of it. Never mind. You carefully copied down these execrable words, validating them with the nib of your pen, and thereby demonstrating your belief in the act of creativity, and, by extension, the notion that your own child could be a writer. I would have told you how important this was to me, but—and this is what hurts my heart—it's only recently I've been able to articulate it to myself. I've only just begun, twenty-five years after your death, to know who you are and how much I need to reach out and touch your hand.

Your loving
Carol

At Home in Winnipeg[14]

Winnipeg means muddy waters in Cree, and by coincidence the city of my childhood, Chicago, is believed to be a translation of that same murky phrase. Is this mere coincidence—I put the question to myself—or evidence of some rare form of masochism? Might it suggest a predilection for swamp and muck and for flat secondary spaces, a perverse liking for geography that is modest, blunt, and untidy around the edges?[15]

I can't begin to unravel this conundrum. Who can explain why we end up in the place we do? I do know that, when I arrived here twelve years ago, I experienced a shock of instant recognition, the sweet, settled bliss of feeling at home.

"At home" is itself a teasing phrase and has to do, I think, with an instinctive sense of familiarity which is quickly refined until it becomes a form of entrenched intimacy. You are at home when you sense what's around the corner of a particular leafy street before you arrive at the turning. And in no time at all you know [where the good parking spaces are found in the downtown core,] how to locate the vast pre-retro Ladies Room at the Bay (second floor by the parking lot entrance), when to drop into De Luca's for your rolled leg of lamb (Monday mornings if you're in a hurry, Saturdays if you're in a convivial mood), and [you learn to work your way expertly through] where among the dozens of handicraft boutiques at the Forks to find the person (Mrs. Jessup) who makes charming toys in painted wood and will do a lovely little polished bison for your Christmas tree if you order a week ahead.

You learn to use certain Winnipeg locutions such as "social" or "dainty" without hoisting an ironic eyebrow. [You know the real names of places even if they're called something else, the Ledge being of course the Legislative Building, the WAG the Winnipeg Art Gallery (entrance free on Wednesdays).] You learn to identify people over forty because they refer to burgers and fries as nips and chips and those over sixty because they quaintly, nostalgically talk about the University of Manitoba as "the campus." And most importantly you learn the names of the city's neighbourhoods (Norwood, St. Vital, Fort Rouge, Transcona, Tuxedo, Charleswood, Wolseley), which are not just map names or extensions of a developer's pencil but places that breathe out their own ethos and come laden with social metaphors that are both comic and precise.

This isn't just information. This is the glorious indigenous shorthand of citizenship, and there's more. Instead of marking the seasons by the universals of solstice and equinox, you recognize in the Winnipeg you know that winter begins on the day Great-West Life puts up its trio of hokey camels, that spring starts officially—never mind the snow underfoot—when a couple of happy beer drinkers race through Osborne Village in shorts and *rien d'autre*.[16]

You may be rusty on Riel and the Red River Settlement,[17] but you're firmly embedded in a living folklore that includes the Winnipeg Strike (1919),[18] the Winnipeg Flood (1950),[19] and the Winnipeg Snowstorm (1966), when a crowd of exuberant late-day shoppers slept overnight at Eaton's downtown store, and what a party that was! (Or was it?—a measure of ambiguity attends all urban legends.) The ribs of an ongoing history are plainly visible in the railway tracks and bridges you are forever crossing and cursing. You know enough to be scornful of such epithets as "the 'peg" or "Winterpeg"—only outsiders use such handles—but you're not above bragging about the day it was colder here than at the North Pole.

And where would we be without the cold? Our cold is ours; we own it. It's communally held like a branch of mythology. It's the best and biggest and deepest cold there is, despite the indignity of having to wear a toque. Our cold transforms us into joyful martyrs, keeps us self-amused, drives us into the sympathetic spaces of theatres and concert halls, bars and restaurants, where we can huddle together and talk (heatedly) about the coldness of the cold, the persistence of the cold, the existential dimensions of the cold, and how—but this is a secret—how green and radiant and sudden are the summers in this strange city.

Feeling at home means being able to predict (more or less) how the people around you are going to behave. Still there are surprises. A few weeks ago I witnessed a collision between two cars on Osborne Street. The accident was minor, just a couple of crumpled fenders, but the two drivers were terribly shaken. They emerged, trembling, from their vehicles—a boy of perhaps seventeen and an elderly woman, her hat knocked askew. I expected the air to fill up with blame and bluster, but instead these two people reached out their arms and took each other in a spontaneous embrace, reaffirming what I have long believed—that there is something surpassingly gentle and open about this society.

Perhaps it's the fiercely rotating seasons that engender this spirit, or perhaps it is the isolation. I am always surprised, when returning after being away, to see how my adopted city looks from the air, a curious disk of population floating in all that immense undifferentiated space. It seems improbable, it seems *unreasonable*, and a question forms in my mind: Who on earth lives in this place? And then I remember: I do. And I'm coming home.[20]

Living at Home[21]

Children know how to live at home. Their world is microscopically comprehended and precisely knowable. Their sensory equipment takes in the contours of the crack on their bedroom ceiling,[22] the exact pattern of the linoleum in the kitchen, the shortcut to the garage through the prickly bushes, the mole on their mother's neck, the frayed end of clothesline hanging on its basement hook, the cup of bent nails on their father's workbench. In all probability, very young children feel that their homes and their bodies are continuous.

But a few years pass, and the map of home is never again as accurately possessed, for the larger world intrudes, blurring distinctions and demanding reduction. It's as though we suffer a diminution of our eyesight as we grow older. The clutter of home becomes generalized, without scent or inscribed touch, without particularity, and without the kind of worn and subtly lit spaces that constitute the essence of the familiar for most of us.

And without the same comfort. My second-grade teacher, Miss Sellers, must have known this. She established a reading corner in our classroom and furnished it with two small rugs she brought from home. On the scratched bookcase, she set a tiny shaded lamp, and if we finished our work quickly we were given the reward of turning on this lamp, bathing the dark corner with yellow light, then settling down on the floor with a book. Our refuge from homesickness.

Some of us really do suffer from this disease more than others, and I certainly was one of those children who longed for home even in the benign atmosphere of the neighbourhood school. The teachers were, somehow, too attentive, the surfaces too carefully maintained and assigned. At home, there were beguiling liberties. I could stretch out, kitten-like, on top of the living room radiator and listen to the radio serials in the late afternoon.[23] Warmth, familiarity. Jack Armstrong. Tom Mix. Here was my space. I had found it and claimed it as my own, and all this was allowed.

At five, I became homesick while visiting a favourite cousin in Wisconsin and had to be brought home several days early, to everyone's inconvenience, but to my grateful relief. Later I was homesick at Girl Guide Camp, and ended up in Healthy House with a strep throat, caused partly, I'm convinced, by away-from-home misery. At university, three hundred miles from home, I remember curious weepy episodes which would arrive in the midst of even the happiest occasion. My room in the women's residence with its matching curtains and bedspread was only a pathetic imitation of home. It had the wrong noise, the wrong dimensions. And, certainly, it was not a place where one could burrow. (Was it Auden[24] who said that life is mainly a question of burrows?)

The day comes, of course, when the need to stay home is at odds with the need to flee, and I can only suppose there is something Darwinian about this phenomenon. The cover of one of my books, *Various Miracles*,[25] illustrates this curious state beautifully. Jane Zednick,[26] the cover artist, has titled her piece *Trying to Fly*, and in it we see a small creature (an angel in training perhaps) lifting her frail wings and looking skyward, a look of perplexed hopefulness on her face. But she is securely tied to earth by a snake which is wrapped tightly around her ankle. The tension between rootedness and its opposite has, I think, characterized much of my adult life. At home, I yearn to travel; travelling, I hunger for home.

I have, of course, learned to make my own home—permanent and temporary—in such places as Toronto, Manchester, Ottawa, Brittany, Paris, Vancouver, and now Winnipeg, and to these homes I've brought the small attentions that Miss Sellers lavished on our second-grade classroom: softly lit corners, the comfort of our textured surfaces, permissions granted and accepted. These habitations, lovingly constructed, beckon to me whenever I'm away.

Some years ago, my husband and two younger daughters and I spent ten days in the Scottish town of Kirkcudbright, venturing out each day in search of ancient monuments. Our accommodation, a modest bed and breakfast, was comfortable enough, despite the fact that our landlady had plastered the house with small notices: Careful not to let the door slam, Please leave bathroom tidy, Kindly place empty teacups on hall table. We ate rather ordinary suppers at this woman's table and felt compelled for some reason to offer her extravagant compliments on her cooking. Our rooms were freezing; Scotland was experiencing a chilly

August. Our daily sightseeing trips, though, were full of marvellous adventures, and we remarked on how fortunate we were to have given ourselves such a leisurely block of time.

On our last evening in Kirkcudbright, my husband and I went to a local pub for a farewell drink and later found our way home down a dark, rainy street lined with narrow houses. The curtains to one of these modest houses had been left open, and I saw, seated on a deep red sofa, a young woman reading a book. A coal fire burned in the grate, and the light from this fire sent a warm glow across the room's surfaces, falling on the woman's hands and face, transforming the whole into a kind of golden stage setting. She never looked up from her book but turned the pages with a sense of absorption, almost of devotion.

It seemed to me that I had never seen a creature so rootedly "at home," nor had I ever before completely understood what that phrase, at home, meant. What I felt, watching her, was a pang of profound envy. The woman with her book was at home, and I was not at home.[27] But tomorrow—a mere twenty-four hours away—that's where I would be.

Sometimes, returning home by air, I look down at the immense width of prairie space, its fields and rivers and geological folds, and then I catch a glimpse, finally, of that strange, improbable disc of population at its centre. Why of all places is it there, and who is it that lives in this random spot?[28]

And then the thought comes to me: I do. This is my *home*, the place I come from.

Sunday Dinner, Sunday Supper[29]

In the Chicago suburb where I grew up, families sat down to midday Sunday dinners of roasts of beef or pork or chicken, mashed potatoes, jellied salads, homemade cloverleaf rolls, and pie. My father, at one end of the dining room table, carved the meat and distributed vegetables; my mother, at the opposite end, saw that the gravy got passed around and poured milk for the children, coffee for herself and my father.

I wish I could say that I appreciated those dinners, but in fact I found them, as a child, overwhelming and tedious. I ached to be outside or, when I was a little older, to be off to the movies with my friends. And I sensed an exhaustion on my parents' part: the sheer physical work, the hot disordered kitchen on the other side of the swinging door, and the heaviness of too much food.

But if Sunday dinner was an ordeal, Sunday supper was an enchantment. In my memory, Sunday supper seemed always to fall on winter nights. Darkness would have arrived, and outside the air was crisp, with a wafer-thin layer of snow covering the sidewalk. My mother would go from room to room turning on lamps. I knew—I could see plainly—that she took pleasure in this act, filling the darkened corners of the house with soft yellow light. Then she'd tidy the living room and ask my sister or me to set the supper table. On weeknights, we squabbled over who had to perform the task, but on Sunday evening we vied for it. For Sunday supper, we used the special dishes.

This set of china, a service for six, was kept on the top shelf of the china cabinet. It was, I thought, breathtakingly beautiful, with its deep tones of rose and dark blue and its fine gold band circling the edges. The hexagonal shape of the plates enormously expanded my love for them. The handles of the small cups were arched and whimsical and surprisingly light in the hand.

On Sunday nights, we children drank our milk from a set of pale-coloured tumblers of exceptional thinness. Milk served in these tumblers was cool, lustrous, exotic.

I can't remember, oddly enough, whether we switched on the chandelier as usual; I do remember a *sense* of candlelight, the luminous simplicity of the polished table, the strange china, the lovely look of milk through coloured glass. We ate roast beef hash, creamed eggs on toast, tuna salad on a lettuce leaf—accessible food, easy food. We lingered at the table, savouring the harmony of the family gathered together, readying ourselves for the busy week ahead.

Years later, when I was married and had a family of my own, I asked my mother what had become of the beautiful Sunday supper dishes. "Oh," she said, at last remembering, "that was just a cheap prewar set that I got from saving coffee coupons."

"And the coloured tumblers?"

"Dime-store junk," she said.

I had to smile, for by then I, too, knew that children are capable of finding richness in impossible places. But if the tableware was less precious than I remember, the priceless gift of inclusion and of ceremony was not. That was what we celebrated at our enchanted Sunday suppers and, I've come to see, at the long, heavy Sunday dinners, too. These rituals caught us at our very best, informing us of who we were and what we could be to one another.

My Favourite Place: At Home in Deepest France³⁰

Every summer, usually in the middle of June, we pack our bags and leave our urban North American existence behind for "*la France profonde*"—deep France, back-of-beyond France, the essential, irreducible France that lies at the end of a badly marked road.

Montjouvent, our tiny village in the Jura mountains, has thirty-nine residents, seventy cows, and one lazy rooster that doesn't get up before noon. A rather dusty, doll-like Virgin stares out from a niche at the centre of the village, next to a notice board announcing local fêtes and elections. Close by is an unremarkable public fountain, recently spruced up with fresh paint. In the distance can be seen the tower of a miniature château, briefly inhabited every August by a family from Paris. You won't find Montjouvent on most maps, though you might locate the nearest town, Orgelet, population two thousand, where we do our shopping.

Our three-hundred-year-old farmhouse, in a row of such houses, is rustic rather than luxurious. Vine geraniums, in brilliant reds and pinks, are blooming by the kitchen door when we arrive in June. Our neighbours see to that. Windows have been opened and the house aired. Our first night's sleep is always the best: the temperature cool and the sky filled with stars. Except for the distant ringing of cowbells, or perhaps a cat tap-dancing across the roof, all is silent. We sleep deeply, contentedly, knowing we've arrived at that other singular place in the world we're able to call home.

For the past twenty-five years, we've spent part of every summer in one or the other of France's regions, renting accommodations for ourselves and our children and settling, as well as we can, into a pattern of French domesticity. Only gradually have we come to understand something of the French character, the way things work, or don't work, in this society. It takes time to pick up the nuances of the language (when to use the formal *vous* or the familiar *tu*) and the strict, sometimes perverse priorities—why, for instance, the better wine must be served after, not before, the inferior one. We've lived aboard a houseboat on the Seine, in a Paris flat, on a Bresse farm, in an Alpine chalet, in a Burgundian château.

Our children grew up and left home, but still my husband and I came to France, and more and more we found ourselves wanting to possess our own little piece of the country. This longing rose out of an acknowledgement that we were incurable Francophiles and also from a yearning to make ourselves more comfortable. Our various rentals often lacked such amenities as armchairs or good reading lamps, important considerations for us. The kitchens tended to be minimally equipped and short on atmosphere. Furthermore, we were tired of dragging our bedsheets across the Atlantic. What we needed was a place of our own. But where?

Provence we eliminated as being too dry for our taste, too harsh. The weather in Brittany is wildly unpredictable; the Dordogne is overrun by English vacationers. We both love the undulating landscape and soft light of Burgundy, but real estate is prohibitively expensive. Friends in Paris suggested we look into the Jura, a part of France we'd missed along the way.

When North Americans ask where the Jura is, and they almost always do, we say, "Well, it's sort of in the middle, over on the right." Or else, "An hour's drive from Geneva." Or, for those who know France, "Straight north of Grenoble, east of Mâcon." The capital of the Jura is Lons-le-Saunier, a city not well known even to the French. Its claim to fame, according to the *Guide Michelin*, is the fact that the composer of the French national anthem once lived there, and thus, even today, the town carillon plays the opening bars of the "Marseillaise"[31] every hour on the hour. We occasionally shop at the Thursday morning market in Lons, seventeen miles from Montjouvent, then treat ourselves to coffee at the Café du Théâtre while we wait for those stirring notes to be struck.

The Jura is a region of villages, farms, forests, and rivers. Cows graze on sloping green meadows, and most of the larger towns have a *fromagerie*, where milk is turned into cheese, the distinctive Jura Comté. But the area has suffered from depopulation, and the locked-up churches and shuttered houses give an almost ghostly sense of a vanished past.[32] Today these houses are being bought and restored—by the Dutch, the Swiss, the residents of Lyons and Paris—and turned into vacation refuges. Whole towns are coming to life again; it is not the old agricultural life but a life that maintains, still, a kind of simplicity and ease.

We came upon Montjouvent by accident while taking a back-road shortcut between two towns. A cluster of red-roofed houses stood at the crown of a hill, and from there we glimpsed a magnificent unobstructed view across meadows and forests, dropping down to a narrow meandering river. We liked the way the name sounds, like Mont-jou-vent, which, syllable by syllable, translates to Mountain of the Playful Wind. To our ears, it had a lucky ring.

I had wanted a village with a bakery and a functioning church. Montjouvent has neither, though there is a small sawmill. My husband wanted a place out of range of the English language. We both wanted, though neither of us articulated it at the time, a place where we could go on doing the kind of work we do at home but deeper, better, with greater intensity yet more freely and with an expanded sense of possibility.

The house we bought had been empty for fifty years. Its two rooms—kitchen and bedroom—once housed whole families. (Two children who grew up there, a pair of white-haired sisters now in their eighties, live just down the road.) By the end of our first summer, basic electricity and plumbing were in place, and some of the old stone walls had been repointed. Then, gradually, the adjoining barn with its thirty-foot ceiling became our living room. For more light, we installed an east-facing window (the mayor, a local schoolteacher, came by on his bicycle to deliver our planning permit). Today the immense and ancient roof lets in splinters of light between its tiles, and sometimes rain as well, but we keep putting off the day for replacement. The cost is formidable, but beyond that is the sense that a roof is a house's most metaphorically charged element and its most authentic connection with the past. You can fall in love with the past. You can fall in love with the roughened, weathered, moss-choked surfaces of a roof, with its antique red richness, even while you're curing its personal failings.

Our days in Montjouvent begin early, with the sound of Monsieur Roger next door calling his cows for their morning milking. My husband runs his usual two and a half miles, and then we eat breakfast on the front terrace if it's warm enough, or else in our cozy kitchen, a lace curtain at the door, a red cloth on our long pine table. The bread is from our favourite *boulangerie*, made from a two-hundred-year-old recipe and shaped to order in the form of a wheat sheaf, a mermaid, or whatever you desire; the milk is direct from Monsieur Roger's herd, unpasteurized and often still warm.

Daily housekeeping is simple and oddly pleasurable, a rug shaken, a floor swept clean. It feels like playing house. Then I settle down to a morning of writing while my husband reads or putters—building a shelf or repointing a stone wall. In late morning, we drive into Orgelet to do errands and stop at the rather grandly named Café de Paris. Here half a dozen regulars will be gathered at the bar for their *petits rouges*, and the proprietor's daughter, a student on vacation, will bring us cups of bitter black coffee. We shake hands all around and exchange a few words about the weather. "*Ah, le soleil, le soleil! Pas si mal.*"[33]

After lunch, I often write letters home, and always I come up against the curious difficulty of trying to explain what we do with our long uninterrupted days. Our tiny improvements to the house, while absorbing to us, are hardly newsworthy. During our first years here, we made afternoon excursions to prehistoric sites in the area or to Lyons or to St. Claude near the Swiss border. But now we're less and less driven by tourist zeal. We live here, after all. We stay home. I work at my desk; my husband prepares articles or lectures for the coming year. We read through the drowsy afternoon or chat with passersby. We might take a walk into the woods, where an old grotto lies hidden, or discuss our next home improvement, or debate, in that singularly French manner, what we will have for dinner: fresh trout from the fish farm in the valley, the *haricots verts* that our neighbours are forever giving us, some good goat cheese, a plateful of pale green plums.

The simplest displacement brings refreshment, distorts time. A more radical shift of rhyme stirs in people new clarities, new raptures. Still, there are occasions, rainy afternoons, sitting in my French kitchen, the clock ticking, something steaming on the stove, when I realize that this paradise of mine is randomly selected and just as randomly embraced. History and context fall away at such moments. I could be anywhere on the face of the earth.

But I'm not. I'm here. At home, in the village of Montjouvent. *Contente.*

Travelwarp[34]

The bus between Buenos Aires and Rio took forty-eight hours, but it seemed there was no other way. Rail connections between Argentina and Brazil were non-existent, I was told, and travelling by air meant missing out on the great width of country in between. So, as the bus driver handed out blankets and pillows, I settled back in my seat and made myself as comfortable as possible.

That cramped seat became my home for two days and nights, and during that time I discovered a new truth: travel does not broaden the mind but instead narrows it. Narrows it to a [tight] haze of perception. To a numb opacity. To the soft-edged microchip of the present moment and the accompanying wish to escape or at least enlarge that moment.

My fellow bus travellers chattered away in Spanish and Portuguese, while I was sadly limited to English. Luckily, though, I'd a thick paperback for company, Jane Smiley's novel *The Greenlanders*, a book I'd had kicking around the house for months but hadn't found time to get into. This epic, with its huge cast of characters, is set in fourteenth-century Greenland and deals minutely, dramatically, with the life of the early Greenland settlers, their farms and villagers and seasonal rituals. Greenland in the Middle Ages was a society not only positioned at the edge of the world but poised on the cusp of decline, and Smiley writes of its final years with a beguiling mixture of erudition and empathy.

Frequently, during the forty-eight-hour journey through South America, I looked up to see banana trees flashing by, or villages with sunlit squares, and then I would return to my absorbing saga and its struggling men and women. The world of the novel was solidly created, furnished, and inhabited, a world I entered willingly, shutting the doors behind me or at least some of the doors. The pages felt curiously crisp and alive in my hands; there was an adulterous love affair, a murder of vengeance, a cruel banishment. Meanwhile, glancing up now and then, I took in the vast stretches of Argentina from the bus window, then a string of pollution-choked cities, and finally an astonishing glimpse of turquoise ocean. The printed images on my lap faded for a time, then rushed back in.

I read the final pages as the bus entered the suburbs of Rio, feeling by that time that I had one foot planted in twentieth-century Latin America and the other in fourteenth-century Greenland. It was impossible to say which was more securely rooted. The journey that I had expected to be linear, stern, and instructive had divided itself down the middle; its margins were blurred; real time had collapsed and also expanded.

I remembered how, some years earlier, well-meaning friends presented me with a biography of Bonnie Prince Charlie[35] to read during a coach tour of Scotland. I brought it home unread, having discovered that the last thing I wanted to do when I slipped into the hotel bed (freezing) under the reading lamp (dim) was to bone up for the next day's sightseeing. Far from desiring total immersion in Scottish culture, I looked for ways to blot it out for a few hours—first thumbing through copies of *The Spectator*[36] that some other vacationer had left behind, and then diving into an abandoned edition of *The Grapes of Wrath*,[37] a real find, coverless, underlined, the final chapter missing, but what did that matter so long as my icy Scottish hotel room was thronged with disenfranchised wanderers in search of California riches and sunshine? Another plane of reality was instantly available to me, an arm's reach away on the bedside table, offering a leavening of perception, balance, order, at the very least a backdrop against which I could define the dark, contradictory Scottish landscape, its tidy towns and wild purple hills and waterways.

For a good many of us, travelling is hard work. You would never guess from reading glossy holiday magazines that much of a traveller's time is spent being idle, bored, uncomfortable, hungry, sleepless, confused, lonely, and gravely concerned and frustrated by the rates of exchange. Cultural confrontation is often more exhausting than enlightening. The disturbing foreign currency—tissuey, vividly coloured—is constantly being handed back and forth in vague and disorienting commercial transactions, leaving the visitor—in the city of Fez, for instance— yearning to curl up with *Middlemarch* rather than venture out to taste Morocco's nightlife. After all, you've got yet another city *souk* to explore tomorrow, more traveller's cheques to cash, hearty postcards to write to the family back home—all this while you're still trembling with jet lag and reeling from a headache which you know perfectly well you can banish by applying a dozen pages of George Eliot, a journey back in time, a visit to gentle, suddenly familiar England with its landscape of hedge and yew and moss-coated church steeples, leagues away from Fez's sturdy palm trees and markets and mosques and the buzz of *here*. Switch on the reading light, if there is one, open to page 1, and an hour later you are no longer *here* but *there* and—with luck and readerly faith—soon lulled into a deep, dreamless slumber, that most cherished heaven for travellers.

But a good book, even a mediocre book, that reads *against* the journey offers far greater dividends than mere escape; the right book can enhance the experience, multiply the impact, increase your psychic travel points, enlarging book as well as voyage—an act of alchemy that turns both to gold.

You have, after all, left home and are primed for the exotic, for anything, in fact. (Isn't this what your travel agent promised?) Your antennae are up, your senses open. Otherness is what you're after. Difference. You've assigned yourself a suspense of time and structure simply by buying an airline ticket, by boarding a train, by filling up your car with maps and apples and bottled water. But don't forget your bag of books. Leaving home without a book is inviting a diminution of pleasure.

A book on Inca art, for instance, works nicely against a week in Boston. Or the endlessly enriching Jane Austen during a stopover in Hong Kong. Or Kafka at midnight after a day of scuba diving off the Mexican coast. One set of perceptions is brought edge to edge with another. These juxtapositions of life and print startle us awake and keep away the travel demons: fatigue, despair, aching bones, primal angst, simple homesickness. The benches of Hawaii can be brought into focus with a smart dose of Atwood; the Alps can be humanized by a chapter of Dickens or a story by Mavis Gallant.

I once experienced the vivid distortion of reading Paul Scott's *Raj Quartet*[38] when travelling through Ghana in the early '80s. And V.S. Naipaul's *A Bend in the River*[39] while on a tour of Japan. Such curious and random conjunctions of time and space can put a kind of torque on our comprehended vision of the world, doubling its power, tripling its dimensions, and confounding the traveller's careful itinerary.

A mere trip becomes a journey, a journey an odyssey. The sand beaches of Brazil, for me, will always lie in the path of a creeping glacier and the medieval austerities of Greenland enlivened by the blinding glare of South American heat and the faraway music of drums and castanets.

A Legacy of Stone[40]

For a writer, isles of the imagination
pale before the history and fascination
of the real thing.

I visited the Orkney Islands in my imagination before I made the actual journey. I was writing a novel, later published as *The Stone Diaries*, which begins with the story of a limestone quarry in the Canadian province of Manitoba, and a little elementary research at the Provincial Archives had informed me that our Manitoba stone workers originally came from the Orkney Islands around the beginning of the century. Suddenly, my novel was presented with another geographical leg but one that was unfamiliar to me.

I had, however, visited the Hebrides a few years earlier and remembered enough, I thought, to substitute that wild, wet landscape for the unknown Orkney archipelago, making the assumption that one northern island was much like the next.

But as I proofread the relevant chapters of the manuscript, I began to worry. Novelists may fantasize about their characters, but they like to get the terrain right. What if Orkney was an altogether different place, with its own ambience and distinctive culture? Perhaps I should go and see the place for myself.

It was June when my husband and I set off for our Orkney adventure, taking the ferry from Thurso,[41] on the north coast of Scotland, to Mainland, the largest of Orkney's sixty-seven islands. During our two-hour ferry ride, we passed the rugged cliffs of Hoy, but on Mainland, instead of the wild landscape of my imagination, we saw low-lying, cultivated, non-Hebridean hills covered with small white sheep. I saw at once that serious revisions in my novel would be called for.

Solidly built modern houses lay scattered in a dozen villages . . .[42] shoppers crowding narrow streets, the buzz of commerce and necessity. There were factories that made whiskey and others that produced delicious Orkney cakes and cheese. Nothing about this civilized place was quite as I had imagined.

The first night we stayed at a bed-and-breakfast a mile or two outside Kirkwall and were told by our apologetic landlady that we might be disturbed during the small hours of the morning. This happened to be the one night of the year when the young, unmarried women of the island hasten to the hillside where our B and B stood; there they bathe their faces in the first morning dew, seeking a legendary promise of beauty.

In the old days, our landlady said, the young women had walked to the hill: in later years, they came on bicycles or on special buses. Now they arrived by car or perhaps on their boyfriends' motorbikes.

Sure enough, shortly after midnight, we could hear shouting and merriment and the slamming of car doors. We crowded at the window, enchanted to find this old tradition preserved in so crisp and modern a context. Morning dew or the latest toiletry product? Perhaps it is all the same—a question of faith.

I had come to Orkney on a fact-checking expedition, not as a traveller, but the morning-dew observance became an unexpected metaphor for what the island offered, which was the overlapping presence of countless historical veins, each preserved in its own layer of time and contributing what seemed to my eyes a mythic Orcadian shimmer.

Behind and beneath contemporary Orkney lay prehistoric ruins—villages, standing stones, and burial chambers. There were remnants from Iron Age forts and Norse monuments[43] from the ninth century, a shifting palimpsest, rich with the mystery of time . . .[44] I had the thrilling sense of one era speaking to another. There on the beautiful five-thousand-year-old walls were more recent twelfth-century graffiti, the most endearing scribbled by an unknown, lovesick intruder: "Ingigerd is the most beautiful of women."

One fiercely rainy afternoon we visited an old farmhouse, now open to the public. This chimneyless dwelling's single room once sheltered a large family as well as provided space for chickens in a smoke-blackened corner. The crowding and discomfort must have been unbearable, and it was easy to understand why the Hudson's Bay Company[45] was welcomed when it arrived in 1702 to recruit servants and labourers from the local populace.

For the next two hundred years, the sons and daughters of Orkney families left the harshness of their islands, relieving the pressure at home, going out into the wider world to seek opportunity and wealth. Many, including the stone workers of Manitoba, never returned.

I was curious about how these quarrymen had learned their skills, since there was little evidence on Mainland of a limestone industry. In fact, I found that some farms possessed their own "home quarries," and many islanders grew up learning the secrets of cutting and freeing stone.

The stone was crucial as a building material, for the Orkney Islands are virtually without trees, though some believe woodlands flourished in the more modest climate around the year A.D. 1000, then perished between the fifteenth and eighteenth centuries, never again to establish themselves.

It was necessary, then, for the islanders to turn to their ubiquitous and easily worked beds of limestone. The heaviest stones were used for foundations and walls, the lightest for interior portions and roofing. Land-holdings were fenced by great upstanding stone slabs, joined end to end. Driving past farm houses, we were astonished to see limestone picnic tables ... much to the Norse as to the Scots—blunt, odd-sounding names like Ilysa, Fara, Florra, Switha, the Holm of Papa, and the Ring of Brodgar.[46] Surnames, too, are distinctive, and, after poking about in the graveyards and checking the local telephone book, I changed the family name in my novel from McAndrew to the very common Orcadian name of Flett.

The wind never stopped blowing the whole of our Orkney visit, and we blessed the travel agent who advised us, summer notwithstanding, to bring our warmest parkas and woollen gloves. Nevertheless, the Orkney weather in my novel is sunny and sublime. The owner of a hotel where we stayed in Stromness told me that she remembered just such a fine and rare summer years earlier.

Resurrecting this buried summer season seemed part of a writer's privilege and perhaps a way of saying "thank you" to the warm heart and storied history of the Orkney Islands.

Others[47]

There was a period in my early life when my friends and I, spurred by romantic yearnings, I suppose, spent great widths of time talking about the possibility and need of "truly knowing someone." This phrase chimed with half a dozen others in our vocabulary: the exposing of the soul, the opening of the head, the completion of one person by another, and so forth. We believed this kind of appropriative and intimate knowledge was possible and moreover that it was desirable.

Somewhere along the way I lost faith with the enterprise. What interested me instead was the unknowability of others, their very otherness in fact. It was apparent to me that members of close, loving families resisted the forces of coercive revelation and that even partners in long, happy marriages remained, ultimately, strangers, one to the other.[48]

Although we were living in the age of communication, the '60s, the '70s, it became clear that people who "spilled their guts" sacrificed a portion of their dignity in so doing and that, in any case, what they spilled was suspect, either self-pitying or self-aggrandizing or else projecting a single, touched-up version of who they were and how they preferred to be registered at a particular moment—for it was understood that a variant self could be brought forward the next day, or even the next day, or even the next hour.

It might be thought that I would be dismayed to discover the limited nature of human interaction, but instead I was heartened, in the same way I was heartened, and relieved too, when I realized that the Methodist God, with whom I'd grown up, did not necessarily observe every ripple of sensation that passed through my head. To be *known* was to be incapacitated and stripped bare; to be solitary, that is to be left in a state of privacy, was to hang on to the forces of originality and innocence.[49]

We are born alone, we die alone. Those two austere existential declaratives were a comfort to me as I grew to adulthood. But to be alone in the midst of life brought to the table a degree of solitude that required

a certain amount of philosophical accommodation. I found the prem-
ise, in fact, close to unbearable. Human activity with its random jets of
possibility and immobilization was the oxygen I sought. The hum of
human busyness engaged me at every level; it was what illuminated my
imagination and what found its way into my novels. My own life—what
a sorry admission, and yet it was true—was not quite enough. I desperately needed to know how other people lived, how they moved about
from room to room in their ordinary houses and gardens, what ordinary
or extraordinary things they said to each other and to themselves as
the clock struck midnight or 9 a.m. or noon—even though I saw my
curiosity about such things as lying side-by-side with the idleness of
gossip or in the wasteful longing of voyeurism.[50]

Judith Gill, the narrator of my first novel, *Small Ceremonies*, announces her need openly, that she requires for her survival the narratives
of other lives and that she is willing to suspend judgment and direction
and moral imperative in order to do nothing more than peer into the
windows of alternative human arrangements. Her need is so strong, in
fact, that she becomes a professional biographer, a vocation that allows
her to snoop, sniff, interview, eavesdrop, interpret, and bring to ripe
conclusion the motives and the figurative possibilities of her subjects.

When I first began writing novels, friends asked me what it was I
wrote about. At first, I didn't know what to say, for, in fact, I wasn't sure
what my subject was. I soon found out—by reading the reviews of my
books and listening to these same friends.

It seemed I wrote about ordinary people—whoever *they* are—and
their ordinary yet occluded lives. And I also wrote, more and more,
about that subjunctive branch of people (*mea culpa*) who were curious
about the details of *other* ordinary people, so curious, in fact, that they
became biographers or novelists, those beings who are allowed societal
permission to investigate—through the troughs of archival material,
through letters and diaries and blurred photographs, by way of offhand
conversations and reminiscences and abrupt literary interpolations and
fictional thrusts directed at the lives of the famous and the not-at-all
famous.

How do we arrive, then, at the lives of others, their assumed kernel of
authenticity? As a child, I did poorly at mathematics but enjoyed what
we called "story problems." Mary Brown is sent to the grocer's for two
pounds of cheese at a dollar and a half a pound. How much change will

she get back from a twenty-dollar bill? The answer came easily, or not so easily, but it was the tug of biographical curiosity I chiefly felt. Who was this Mary Brown, and what was she doing with all that cheese? Was she old enough to be trusted with a twenty-dollar bill? And what of her wider dreams and aspirations or even her immediate thoughts as she slipped home with her sack of groceries and her pocketful of coins?

I remember trying to "interview" my Canadian mother-in-law when she was in her eighties, wanting to access a portion of the childhood she had spent on a pioneer farm in Manitoba. The project was doomed from the beginning. I didn't know the right questions, and she didn't have any idea what I wanted to know. My line of inquiry, even to my own ears, felt intrusive and inappropriate, and her answers were, not surprisingly, vague and, for my purposes, not at all useful.

What I hoped for was the precise inch-by-inch texture of that early-twentieth-century Icelandic farmhouse located on a threadlike river sixty miles north of Winnipeg: the furniture, the floor coverings, the ceiling, the ornaments that rested on the rough kitchen shelves. What I got were generalities: "Well, it was homey. Well, we made our own cheese. The sheep, they were a bother. It was cold in the winter." In short, the experiment was a failure. I half expected it would be.

There is something oddly shaming about possessing too avid a sense of curiosity. I remember once seeing a young man seated in his front garden. Before him was an ironing board and a small manual typewriter. He was tapping away with such excitement that he didn't look up as I passed by. I wanted to stop on the spot and besiege him with questions: What are you writing? Why such concentration of energy? Let me see what you're working on.

Naturally, when I find myself on buses or trains, I feel a compulsion to know the titles of the books my fellow passengers are reading. And when I am being interviewed about one of my books, I often find myself interviewing back: How did you happen to become a journalist? What sort of articles are you usually assigned? Do you have any children? Tell me more.

More is what the indecently curious always want. They want the *details*, and no detail is too small to be of interest.

But we live in a society that forbids the intimate interrogating of strangers. Inquisitive people are discouraged and certainly disparaged. Journalists and biographers may be given special privileges, allowed to ask their Nosy Parker questions, but the rest of us are forced to deal imaginatively with the great gaps.

For novelists, this means observing, eavesdropping, gently probing, but, in the end, risking ourselves and our small truths, guessing at the way other people live and think, hoping to get it right at least part of the time.

And I long ago understood that the silences our society imposes give to the novelist a freshness of opportunity, a way to bring spaciousness and art into the smallest, most "ordinary" lives. Even so, I suffer, as many writers do, from a scavenger's guilt and always experience a desire to include on the title page of my books some small message of acknowledgement: "Forgive me." Or "I'm sorry."

What's in a Picture[51]

It's one of my pleasures to visit antique fairs and postcard markets in search of photos of unknown women.[52] They are easy enough to find since it used to be the fashion in the early decades of our century for people to have their photographs put on cards to send to friends; this has always seemed to me to be an exceptionally agreeable custom and one I would like to see revived. I suppose I buy my photographic images out of a muddled desire to redeem these forgotten women, just by taking notice of them and spending a dollar or so to bring them home.[53]

The picture of the woman in the fur-collared coat, though, was found not in a market but among my mother-in-law's things, so I can only suppose she was a friend or even relative of hers. The woman is probably of Icelandic origin because, almost without exception, everyone in my mother-in-law's circle belonged to Manitoba's large Icelandic community. The iron railing, the style of the awning, and the length of the woollen coat place this photo, for me, in the mid-'60s, but I could easily be out by ten years, either way. The total fashion statement here is quietly in conflict with itself and not easy to fix in time.

The scene speaks to me strongly of Winnipeg: the limestone foundation of the house, the board siding, and the bright prairie sunlight breaking through bare branches. It must be a relatively mild day in late October or November since the awning has not yet been taken down for the winter. Any minute now this awning will be weighed down with snow or torn to shreds by the ferocious winds that sweep in from the north. Manitoba is a place of climate extremes, with one season usurping the other and without warning.

The woman's face and body strike me as a brilliant mixture of vulnerability and strength. That sprightly hat, those thickly stockinged legs, that practical coat belted against the cold! The softness in her face is countered by a certain tension in the arms and the way in which her hands are clutched and drawn into her sleeves for warmth.

The lack of gloves and bag, scarf and overshoes, makes me wonder if she hasn't just this minute stepped outside her door in order to be photographed. She's clearly proud of her wings of fur but hasn't bothered to put on earrings, and it's possible that she doesn't own any.

My guess is that she is a widow, for otherwise those snowy steps would've been shovelled clean. Winter in our part of the world is hazardous for the elderly, and there are many who hibernate for the two or three iciest months. This woman, though, doesn't look like a hibernator. Her stance is tentative, yet at the same time rooted in her surroundings, ready to accommodate the weathers and vicissitudes of her world.

Rare Petals[54]

The strangest thing I ever ate was a chrysanthemum. This was during a holiday in Japan, at an expensive restaurant. I chopped the flower apart clumsily with my chopsticks and put a small portion in my mouth. It tasted like the oil it was fried in and also like the cakey bitterness of garden earth. There seemed no reason to eat it but no reason not.

I ate a lily once, too, or rather part of a lily. This was at Easter services in the Methodist church I attended as a child. Each of the children in the congregation had been handed a lily and told to reflect on its significance as we listened to the sermon. I was restless and hungry that Easter morning, the service seemed interminable, and I began, idly, secretively, to dismantle my flower and press the slightly contoured petals one by one onto my tongue, which they fitted perfectly. There was surprisingly little flavour to a lily petal but a good deal of satisfaction at my own cunning.

Dandelions were weeds. We knew that, and we knew our parents knew it too, and that they were only miming gratitude when we handed them our coarse, sour-smelling bouquets, and yet we performed this ritual over and over. People ate dandelion greens, it was said, and the blossoms could be made into a delicious wine. But if this were true, where was the flowing wine and where the tender salads? We suspected adult hypocrisy, special pleading for the lowly creature that fathers attacked with vicious chemicals on weekends.

It came as a surprise to learn that lilacs were weeds, too, or so my mother said. I wanted to take a lilac bouquet to my teacher, but instead my mother picked irises and tulips from the narrow bed by the porch. Real flowers, secured with precious foil and twine. Let other children bring lilacs, her look said.

There was a crabby old woman, Mrs. Dastas, who lived a few houses away from us. Her hair was dyed a depthless black and rose steeply above darkly rouged cheeks. A witch, we children thought. This vital information clearly was not known to our parents, for my mother sent me to her house one day to return a book. I went around the high-fenced back garden and cracked open the gate. There stood angular Mrs. Dastas in a garden utterly unlike my mother's, with its rectangular patch of lawn and straight perennial borders. Here oversized flower heads, dahlias I learned, leaned inward, exploded gloves, filling, it seemed, even the air over my head with an insistent vibrancy. Mrs. Dastas's dahlias were so large, my father's joke went, that the blooms had to be carried through her back door sideways.[55]

My mother had three sisters, each with a different kind of garden. Aunt Jenny in rural Illinois grew her flowers in straight rows, always with a wooden stake at the end of each row with the seed packet securely attached. Aunt Edna—"the difficult one"—lived in southern California, where she devised a crowded, exotic garden, crisscrossed by gravel paths which led to a central "lathe house" where she did her potting, out of reach of the coastal wind.

Trumpet vines grew against the side of the stout, sweet Aunt Olive's house in Wisconsin, and these flowers could be plucked and fitted over our fingers like tiny frilled puppets. A tangle of strange gourds thrived by the garage, ours for the asking, and raspberry canes filled in the waste space by the back lane. You could get lost in Aunt Olive's varied and perfumed kingdom, and getting lost was most of the pleasure. Scrambling, hiding, raiding, making twig houses with leaf dishes and cups—we spent long days in that garden, merging our bodies with its vegetal greenness and growing, I suppose, lushly flower-like ourselves.

A Purse of One's Own[56]

My mother's handbag, the one that I remember best, was big and black and aggressively pleated, with an enchanting amber clasp in the form of twin parrots. The bag's richly dark interior held the mingled fragrance of perfume and leather—calfskin, probably—and a cotton handkerchief dabbed with *Evening in Paris* wadded in one corner.

Her bag smelled, too, of coins and creased bills, of the finely composted silt of face powder (Coty), and of tobacco crumbs (Chesterfields) and the roll of butter-rum Life Savers that she always kept on hand to cancel out the smell of cigarettes on her breath. Her fountain pen would inevitably have leaked a stiff circular stain on the bag's taffeta lining. Her key ring—house, garage, car—bore the souvenir tag of the Wisconsin Dells,[57] and in my memory she is forever rummaging in the depth of her bag for those keys, mumbling a self-scolding imprecation against carelessness, against disaster—and then, finally, a rising gust of relief: "I knew they were in here somewhere!"

We children were not allowed to go into our mother's handbag. If we needed a quarter or so for an errand, we were instructed to fetch the bag from the hall table and bring it to her. I never questioned this privileged zone of privacy. It just seemed to me that it was a mother's natural right and not merely a means of protection against the small larcenies of children. A woman's handbag, I understood even then, was part of her being, an extension of her style and her soul, spiritual partner to her hat, her gloves, her everyday pumps. Later I came to suspect that the inside of a handbag is also the single inviolable space a woman possesses, other than the labyrinth of her own thoughts.

Why else would I have been so shaken by an unfortunate episode three years ago in Paris? I had entered a ticket gate in the Montparnasse[58] metro station. I was filled with a tourist zeal and a sense of well-being, yet a moment later my money and credit cards were gone. A stranger, someone without a face or form, had with great speed and cunning come up behind me, unzipped my handbag, and removed my wallet.

The shock lingered for days. I was grossly inconvenienced and embarrassed by the theft, not to say impoverished, but the emotional impact of the event outdistanced any sense of common robbery. At night in my Paris hotel room, I replayed the scene over and over in my head: I had inserted my ticket in the turnstile, pushed the security gate forward, and the next minute, aware only of a lightening of my shoulder bag and of a human shadow behind me, I was without my little cache of wealth, without my identity. For who was I without my portable clutch of documents and possessions? No one.

I must have been five or six when I was given my first "bag," a stiff little box, lightly padded and covered with tan Leatherette. At the time, I had no idea that Leatherette was a trademark for artificial leather, imagining instead that it was leather in its most rarefied and desirable form. A recently discovered family photo confirms that this small bag was carried on a thin strap, not over my shoulder, but around my neck so that it lay flat on my chest. The closure, two golden knobs that turned satisfyingly one on the other, would have opened to nothing but rattling space or perhaps a tiny ironed handkerchief and a Sunday school nickel. What else does a young child need to carry about? We might almost define childhood as that singular era in which there is no need to carry *things*.

But this possession-free period soon comes to an end. I was given, a few years later, a pencil case, a slim, zippered envelope of shiny green postwar plastic in which to carry my pencils and erasers, a few coins, and a compass-and-protractor set whose use would not be demonstrated for a number of years hence—but which I felt obliged to carry neverthe-less. At the school I attended, only the girls carried these pencil cases, which can be thought of, I suppose, as handbags in their embryonic form: training purses.[59]

Heidi's Conundrum[60]

Feminism sailed into the '60s like a dazzling ocean liner, powered by injustice and steaming with indignation. Its force for many of us was blinding, though like all authentic political revolutions it arrived amid a stream of attendant notions, some of them untested but most of them so beguiling that often it was difficult to separate solid possibilities from rhetorical fluff. The time had come. A woman had the power to choose. A woman was responsible for her own life. For the first time, a woman could have everything; she could have it all—meaningful work, love, respect, community.

Even then we could see that what the women's movement promised was utopian in nature, a perfected reality that might not be achievable overnight, if at all. Yet for some it seemed necessary to work through that truth rather than analyze what was feasible, what would set us free.

Not many foresaw the epidemic of exhaustion that would overtake women who "have it all." Not many guessed at the number and force of countermovements dedicated to keeping women from "having it all." Finally, hardly anyone realized in those heady days that "having it all" was perhaps as childish a notion as "living happily ever after."

In 1990, we find ourselves still dealing with the unfinished business of the '60s. Difficult choices were made during that time, and it's hard to live with difficult choices. You can end up alone or in bad company, or, like Heidi in Wendy Wasserstein's play,[61] you can end up stranded. That's the word Heidi uses—*stranded*. She's cornered, she's stalled, she feels, in fact, betrayed. Back in the '60s, she was told she could have everything, and now it seems she can't. She made her tough either/or decisions, but her chosen way of life, its purity and purpose, didn't work out. She understands this, and her understanding is punished by loneliness. Her sisters have jumped ship, and the men in her life, for all their sensitivity and intelligence, have proven to be more than a little substandard.

As a young art historian, she had a lot to be angry about. Wasserstein's play is a work of fiction, but the women artists she names are real: Sofonisba Anguisciola (the spelling varies), Clara Peeters, and Lily Martin Spencer.[62] These women lived vibrant creative lives, but their names are virtually unknown today. So, too, are such nineteenth-century Canadian writers as Susan Frances Harrison, Ethelwyn Wetherald, May Agnes Fleming.[63] How do works of art get "lost," and who is responsible for the loss? It seems futile to rage against history, and I find it hard to believe that any one man ever said to himself, "Now how can I go about systematically oppressing women artists and obliterating their art?"

Nevertheless, when we look ahead at this year's theatre season in Winnipeg,[64] it is troubling to see that the main stages are offering their subscribers a selection of fourteen plays, only four of which are written by women. (Ironically, there are those who will see these figures as evidence of progress, even of achieved parity.) And if we regard our local press as an index to our cultural attitudes (and perhaps it is unfair to do so), we observe that on Saturday, September 1st, the *Winnipeg Free Press* delegated its film reporting to Paul and John, its record column to Stephen, its visual arts space to Randal, its country music to Joe, its classical music to Don. David reported on the week's TV programming, and Scott, Ralph, and John spoke from the Book Page. There were four letters to the editor: from Fred, Bill, Ken, and Robert. Twenty-two individuals were mentioned by name on the front page—nineteen of them men. Of the nine films showing at Eaton Place on September 1st, *all* were directed by men. There is something deadening about this disproportion. It is not what we were promised, not at all.

So what is Heidi, and women like her, to do with the burdens of anger and abandonment? That is the Heidi conundrum, and it is a question many survivors of the '60s and '70s ask themselves. It is also the continuing dilemma for women artists in our society: how is it possible to live creative, productive, fulfilled lives when we so often feel exhausted, undervalued, obstructed, and *stranded*?

Happily, the central tenet of the women's movement, the permission to make choices, is still valid, even when that choice is to unmake earlier choices. Only a few women will come to the decision Heidi Holland does in the final scene of Wasserstein's play, but almost no one will deny her right to do so. "Either you shave your legs or you don't," Heidi was told back in the '60s, but most feminists today have moved beyond the tyranny of political correctness and its surface manifestations.

The women's movement has not been sleeping during the '80s; it has been adapting, growing up, becoming more tolerant, more open, more flexible, more resourceful. Distinctions have been drawn between useful anger and wasteful rage. Women's theatre groups are finding their feet. Women's presses are publishing books that might otherwise fall through the cracks: a women's book review sees that these books are noticed, and women's bookstores make them available to the public. Winnipeg women in the visual arts have found their own strategies and their own exhibition spaces. Canada's oldest feminist magazine has recently used the photograph of a bride on its cover, not (I think) ironically, but as an acknowledgement that women arrive at their potential in different ways.

Judy Chicago's *Dinner Party*,[65] by focusing on the female body, gestured toward the commonality of women, but charges of racism and classism in the women's movement have awakened us to the fact of diversity. The lives of women are infinitely varied and complex, and it is this complexity, in art and in life, that cries out for expression.

Parties Real and Otherwise[66]

Who doesn't love a party? All my life, it seems, I've been drawn to the idea of parties, of people gathering together in order to observe an occasion, to celebrate or simply rub up against each other.

Nevertheless, it came as a surprise to me to discover that all of my novels contain party scenes. It was a book reviewer who pointed out all these parties in my pages; I hadn't noticed, probably because parties seem so tightly woven into the fabric of the lives I write about—and my own life too—that it would be unthinkable to leave them out.

Even my first novel, *Small Ceremonies*, contains a party. Judith Gill, the main character, invites her friends and her husband's colleagues for a Saturday night gathering in the suburbs. I couldn't resist providing the invitation:

Buffet Supper

Where—62 Beaver Place

When—April 30, 8:00

Judith and Martin Gill

The time is 1975. Judith serves lasagna and a tossed salad, knowing full well that her party menu is ten years out of date—as are her décor, her hairstyle, and her skirt length. But she is a woman who understands the essence of hospitality, who refuses even to confess to the notion of datedness. The party hums along beautifully, just as we all hope our parties will. Judith's guests have a terrific time. Her simple supper for old friends is what I've come to think of as the "good-enough party," where the buzz of human interaction matters more than the quality of the flowers or the food. People, it seems, love any kind of party, and who can imagine a guest so churlish as to refuse an invitation because the occasion promises to be less than chic?

Judith Gill's party occurs about three-quarters of the way through the novel, and I suppose I felt it was time to show my heroine in her hostess role—a role almost all of us take on from time to time, planning parties and then seeing them through, even though we sometimes panic at the last minute and wish we'd never thought of the idea.

My own mother put on her entertainment hat four or five times a year, hosting a tea, a luncheon, a few tables of bridge on a Friday night, or, occasionally, as Christmas drew near, an "open house." But for all her skill at "entertaining," she remained a nervous hostess.

And so is Janey Carpenter, in my 1980 novel, *Happenstance*, who exhausts herself in her quest for the perfect party. Janey is careful to invite only those guests able to advertise themselves with a modicum of celebrity, and she introduces them to one another with their labels attached: "This is Jack Bowman, our local expert on Great Lakes Indians," or "Meet Hy Saltzer, he does bricks." The wine that is served is both expensive and rare, as Janey's husband, Larry, carefully points out to the assembled friends. An up-to-the-minute buffet is served: curried crab rolls, lobster roll, lobster salad with pecans, and a ghastly dip made of grated turnips, my own fictional invention. Sadly, the evening is one of those occasions that tries too hard, forcing the celebrants into various modes of false posturing. This chillingly artificial event dies of its own self-consciousness and leads, in the small hours of the morning, to a near-tragic conclusion.

This party, like Judith Gill's more successful party, gave me a chance to bring my characters together on stage, as it were, and draw the story to a dramatic turning point. But I also felt compelled to write about the ceremonial aspect of getting ready for a party, a set of rituals we can all recognize even when they differ from one household to the next.

I remember being baffled as a child by what adults actually did when they got together. It seemed they did nothing but talk. No pin-the-tail-on-the-donkey, no musical chairs, no competitive edge or excitement or wrapped prizes for the victor, only talk, talk, talk. It was worrying. Was this what the future held? Was this what a party was for?

Our human need to come together is primitive, and I suppose you could look all the way back to prehistoric feasts and ceremonies and see them as the world's earliest parties. If you set aside those parties that are merely obligatory and exist for the sake of reciprocating the hospitality of others, then there is something biblical and compelling about raining down a lot of food and drink on a group of people who have come together under a single roof at an appointed hour.[67] Parties can be cathartic, too, signalling a release of withheld generosity. The doors and windows are temporarily opened. Merriment is invited in, and we sometimes find that a different self emerges: our party self.

All this is useful material for a novelist who wants to show a book's characters from as many angles as possible. Judith Gill is a serene and competent hostess at her own buffet supper, but when she is invited to a friend's lunch party she slips into another role and becomes an exuberant storyteller, a vivacious and slightly out-of-control guest.

I can remember the mystery of seeing my mother and father transformed from dull parenthood into their other, and perhaps truer, party selves. I recall on bridge evenings—ribbon sandwiches or asparagus rolls would be served afterward, along with coffee—my astonishment at hearing their voices rise with social urgency, even breaking into unaccustomed laughter. They seemed younger on these occasions, stronger, lighter of heart, almost like someone else's parents. In the morning, we children would find the living room splendidly disordered, the card tables still in place, and, if we were lucky, there would be a few delectable salted cashews at the bottom of the glass candy dishes.

Our need for parties may be constant, but most of us can look back and see how different a '60s party was from a '70s party, how our expectations were subtly changed in the '80s and '90s, how our own chronological age and family conditions create new ways for us to come together. And new party menus! When my parents were newly married, they served their friends Welsh rarebit or scalloped oysters. Later, in the '40s, came chicken à la king with perhaps a Waldorf salad at the side. A company meal in my childhood was a good roast beef with browned potatoes and a lime gelatin pie for dessert or, if it were summer, my mother's homemade pineapple ice. In the '50s, my teenage years, we were served sloppy joes at parties and a curious new snack food called nuts 'n' bolts. Along the way, someone invented chips and dip, that revolution in casual party food, followed by such period offerings as mini-pizzas, wine and cheese, seafood crepes, beef fondues, and pasta salads in their various flavours and hues.

These shifting menus—familiar to all of us—make for fascinating social history and allow a novelist to set a scene in a precise period in history.

I love to read old newspapers, especially those from the early part of the century. We sometimes think of the old-fashioned society page as being rigidly formulaic, but it was also alive with sentiment and a warm effusiveness. Society editors knew what their readers hungered after: details, details, and more details. Readers of that time demanded the full gush and glow of other people's wedding parties, what exactly the bride wore, the style and material of her dress, the cut of her veil, a precise flower-by-flower description of her bridal bouquet. They wanted to know what was served at the prewedding shower, how the tables were decorated, and especially who was there.

Here is such a journalistic account from 1927 as it appears in my most recent novel, *The Stone Diaries*. My description is pure fiction, of course, but it follows very closely the format I found when doing my library research on the period, and I confess that I stole the name Grace Healy and her musical contribution—with its perfect '20s feel—from a real newspaper's society page. "*Mrs. Alfred Wylie entertained at a kitchen shower Thursday afternoon in honor of Daisy Goodwill, a June Bride-to-be. The rooms were prettily decorated with wisteria, bells, and streamers. Guests included Mrs. Hoad, Mrs. Stanton Merrill, Mrs. A. Caputo, Mrs. B. Grindle, Mrs. Fred Anthony, Miss Labina Anthony, Miss Elfreda Hoyt, and the Misses Merry Anne and Susan Colchester. During the afternoon, Miss Grace Healy contributed several delightful vocal and piano selections.*"

I also found, while reading my reel of microfilmed newspapers from the '20s, a number of mysterious references to something called a White Dinner, an event hosted by parents of the bride in the week or so before the wedding. What on earth was a White Dinner? My first thought was the guests would be expected to come to dinner wearing white, but a friend of mine set me straight: A White Dinner is a meal in which all the food is white or at least off-white.

This type of meal may not strike us today as being particularly attractive, but in the interest of authenticity I decided to give my heroine Daisy Goodwill a White Dinner before her marriage. The menu included bay scallops, fillet of Dover sole, supreme chicken served with an accompaniment of creamed onions, and a dessert of vanilla Chantilly ice, moulded in the form of twin doves. I set the table with a profusion of white flowers and lit it with ivory tapers.

Finishing my White Dinner description, I felt suddenly sated. It was almost as though I had actually attended or even hosted such a celebration. And herein, of course, lies one of the unlooked-for pleasures of writing fiction. Picking up our pens or sitting before a word processor, we writers can happily attend the kind of parties to which I for one will never be invited. As a novelist, I have the freedom to dream up eccentric parties-on-paper, elaborate formal parties, crazy impromptu parties, parties that sing or else go slightly out of whack. Just moving a pen down a page, I can do the planning, the shopping, the cooking, the greeting at the door. I can set the table any way I like, I can decide on background music, define the mood, introduce a charming invention or two, and, most important, I can create my own guest list.

In my 1992 novel, *The Republic of Love*, I hosted (that is, I wrote about) a house party celebrating a fortieth wedding anniversary. Being fond of round numbers, I invited one hundred people exactly, and the invitations were extraordinarily beautiful, tiny handmade leather folders—one of the daughters of the family is a cobbler by profession—holding two photographs, one of the couple as they looked on their wedding day forty years earlier and another, more recent likeness. The hundred guests are specifically instructed not to bring a gift, but only a single, long-stemmed flower, and these flowers are placed in an immense pottery gift vase, the centrepiece of the party. There is recorded music, dancing, generous pourings of wine, and then—because this is a novel with a story to tell—an intimation of trouble ahead for the celebrating husband and wife. This, in fact, is why the party is planted in the novel, although I like to think it's there for its own pleasures as well.

An entirely different party—my favourite fictional party for some reason—takes place in my novel *Swann*, set in 1987. It is Christmas Day in a small Ontario town. Rose, the town's unmarried librarian, has invited her friends in for eggnog and a snack, as she does every Christmas Day and as her mother had done before her. Rose is too modest to call the occasion a party; instead, she calls it asking people in. She makes better eggnog than her mother did, adding more rum, for one thing. And invariably she serves something called a cheese log. This offering from the '50s, or perhaps earlier, was made by combining cubed processed cheese, crumbled soda crackers, pieces of green pepper, and a dash of Worcestershire sauce. The mixture was shaped into a log (or a Christmas tree if you wanted to go fancy), decorated with strips of pimento and sliced stuffed olives, then placed on a platter and surrounded by crackers.

Every writer has a favourite fictional character, and mine is Rose. I wanted her to have a successful Christmas party because she is at a point in her life when she is deeply frightened by the thought of the future. I wanted her friends to appreciate the effort she's gone to, and they do. There is ease in the little room, merriment, a stirring of hope. The eggnog goes down, the cheese log is nibbled away, time slips by. Rose is seized with optimism, and from nowhere comes the sudden shine of happiness and faith in the future.

I am an invisible presence at this gathering, an authorly mouse under a fictional chair, watching Rose's friends come together to share holiday warmth and hospitality, saying to one another as they at last put on their coats and scarves and head for home: "Thanks so much. It was a wonderful party."

The Best Teacher I Ever Had . . . [68]

The best teacher I ever had was Miss Pelsue, who taught me in Grades 3 and 4 at Ralph Waldo Emerson Grammar School in Oak Park, Illinois. The time was 1943–45, the war years. It was one of the beliefs of our school district that a teacher should remain with a class for two consecutive years; this could be a nightmare if you didn't like your teacher but pure joy if you did. Miss Pelsue created in our classroom a refuge, a haven.

Like all the teachers I knew in the early years, she was an unmarried woman in middle age with a body that suggested motherliness and comfort. (There seemed to be some vague universal rule that decreed these arrangements, though I never penetrated it.) The school district was wealthy; classes were no larger than fifteen or sixteen; there was always enough chalk and construction paper and a wide range of books on the classroom shelf.

I was a child who grew homesick even in the benign atmosphere of the neighbourhood school, but Miss Pelsue had the knack of allowing just enough individual freedom so that we ceased to feel confined. She was soft-voiced and gentle; she was patient. She chuckled in a deep, relaxed way that made me feel safe. She monitored our interactions so that there was no bullying or exclusions. It's only now I see that her attitude toward each of us was one of respect, *respect* for her eight- and nine-year-old charges. It seems astonishing. She didn't scold. She didn't line us up like little soldiers and march us out to recess. Was she up on the latest teaching methods? I have no idea. Her gift was to create a climate for happy children.

School began at nine, but if we came in at eight-thirty—and everyone did—she read aloud to us for half an hour: *Mary Poppins. Alice in Wonderland. Winnie the Pooh.*[69] On Friday afternoon, if we wanted to stay for an extra hour—and we all did—she taught us a few words and phrases of Spanish. She had visited Hawaii, common enough today, but in those days extraordinarily exotic, and she taught us how to make Hawaiian leis out of crepe paper.

I had a schoolteacher mother, and so I knew enough about the discipline of teaching to understand what Miss Pelsue offered her pupils went beyond the required. I valued her, then and now, for those unasked-for gifts of herself, but I cherish even more what she taught me about work.

I love work. I love writing about work as well as doing it. But when I was growing up in Oak Park in the '40s and '50s, it was mostly men who worked. They put on their suits and ties every morning and took the El down to the Loop,[70] leaving their wives at home to look after the children and keep house. I didn't understand that that, too, was work. I did believe, absolutely, that it was my destiny.

It seemed to me when I was a child that work was a hardship, something people endured, and that they lived for their Sundays and for their two weeks of vacation in the summer—at a rented cabin on a shallow lake—and the rest of the time felt thwarted. The only working women I knew were schoolteachers, poor souls, and when I went away to college to study English literature my parents insisted that I also pursue a teaching licence so that I would have "something to fall back on." This curious phrase was never explained, but I knew what it meant. If I should fail to find a husband, if I were widowed or, God forbid, divorced, I would be able to earn my bread and somehow survive.

But I had observed that my teacher, Miss Pelsue, loved her job. The signs were unmistakable. She sailed into the classroom in the morning and unpinned her hat and prepared *joyously* for the day: for all that we would do together, the problems we would solve, for the small exchanges between us that arrived like an embrace.

Later I read about the Amish, who, when they do their bookkeeping, place their labour on the credit rather than the debit side. I began to see that my two passions, reading and writing, might become my work. And that my work would ground me in the world.

The Visual Arts[71]

It is an honour—and somewhat of a surprise—to find myself, a non-painting, non-sculpting, non-visual consciousness, in the midst of such an accomplished assembly, those whose view of the world and interpretation of it are manifested by something other than words. Or, rather, the same words exist between writers and visual artists, but, for you, they take expanded meanings: form, line, colour, composition, space, shadow, edge, depth, and idea—these variables and their mastery have brought you together, the members of the Royal Canadian Academy of Arts.[72]

I congratulate you, Morley Blankstein,[73] and your committee for all your efforts to bring this celebration into existence. And I congratulate all members of the Royal Academy for your long history and for your very active and innovative revitalization plan, now under way. And as a member of the Canada Council, I would like to remark on the coincidence that we have arrived together at an elegant and vibrant middle age, you celebrating, if my figures are correct, your 117th anniversary and the Canada Council, which is this year observing its slightly more youthful but still substantial fortieth.

It was in 1957 that, with the stimulus of a generous private gift, a group of farseeing citizens decided that our country, Canada, could afford its own culture. An Act of Parliament brought the Canada Council into being, and since then we have seen an astonishing flowering of the arts, our own arts, from sea to sea to sea. Theatre, film, music, dance, literature, and the visual arts. Along the way, there have undoubtedly been misdirections, mistakes made, and probably funds misspent, but I think we can all understand, and appreciate, the difference it makes to artists to know that they live in a nation that values what they do.

And I think, too, that, if we define culture as the sum of our shared experience, we can say that the making of art and our ability to respond to works of art form part of the glue that keeps the various communities of our country together.

Artists of all kinds require three basic conditions; they need, in fact, what everyone needs. To feel that the kind of work they do is respected. To know that they belong to a community of others who pursue similar kinds of work. And occasionally—not often but occasionally—to celebrate their work and to celebrate themselves. For this last reason, I want to salute you and the exhilarating RCA show that opened last night at the Winnipeg Art Gallery.[74] That enormous and deeply appreciative crowd. That excitement. That gratitude. And the quality of what we were offered.

I have always been fascinated with the problem of how art gets made. Who gets to name and contribute to the culture? Who gets to say what art really is? How is it that ordinary human beings are capable, occasionally, of making sublime art? How is great art made from the common clay that most of us, whether we admit it or not, are?

Years ago, at an archaeological museum at St-Germain-en-Laye[75] in France, I found myself staring into a display case at a row of stone hammer heads shaped in prehistoric times, each one very like the other, though some—two or three—were, oddly, more graceful in their configuration than the others—somehow, though I couldn't have said how, more achieved. And then I glimpsed, at the far end of the row, a hammer head shaped—it was unmistakable—in the form of a crouched human body and above it the exuberant and rather grand label *Commencement d'art*—the Beginning of Art.

Who, I wondered, was the person who one day decided that a hammer head could do more than be a hammer? Of course, it must perform that task, too, and effectively, but it could also delight, amuse, and satisfy the sense. It could unmistakably be—itself. A thing, an artifact, valued in its society, probably passed from generation to generation (for here it was preserved in all its completeness), and maybe, eventually, given a name and awarded a ceremonial rather than a practical function and perhaps thought to possess that ineffable substance we call, for want of a better word, spirit. Human spirit. Transcendence.

Early societies also made stone arrowheads, and you've seen them, I'm sure, everywhere in our large and local Canadian museums. Apparently, arrowheads are quite easily flaked into existence; they were objects that almost anyone with a little experience could make. But I strongly suspect that some of these arrowheads, a rare few, possessed a finer balance than the others, a greater elegance of curve, or proportions that surprise and tease our aesthetic sense, so that they lie in the human hand like the perfect little sculptures they are, works of art that transcend their definition and their usefulness.

I remember once going to an exhibition of the work of Édouard Manet.[76] All his great paintings were there, but what I loved the most was a tiny drawing, almost lost among the others, of a solitary spear of asparagus.

I can't now recall the medium, watercolour or simple crayon, but I do remember being struck with wonder: why should anyone want to draw a stalk of asparagus, and why did I find it a pleasure to look upon? I can only suppose that Manet chose it as a subject because it was lying around, asking to be noticed, and because of the subtlety of its greenish-white colouring—this was European asparagus, not our greener version—and the slender organic line of its stem, and, finally, the curiously textured, almost quilted-looking, busyness of its head.

Like everyone else, I was familiar with asparagus, bunched and rubber-banded and carried home from Safeway and later steamed and arranged on a plate, but this asparagus spear was floating on its side, in orbit as it were, thrillingly strange and all alone—without any of its fellows, without a napping of hollandaise sauce or even a lemon slice to keep it company, and it was posed against a flat white background as if to say "Please pay attention to the real me." Its asparagusness gave it a curious and pure power, and its appeal was not to my appetite at all, for it seemed to have no scent or taste or promise to the palate but only the beauty and newness of its form. To my mind, it performed a double trick, being both the essence of asparagus and announcing, at the same time, detachment from its vegetable personality and asking me to put my previous asparagus narratives in the vault. I realized, too, that I had never really seen asparagus before, not like this anyway, that I had never experienced it in its wholeness or newness or appreciated its organic and transcendent perfection.

And, of course, there is the apocryphal story of the artist who, with paint and brush and with desire and great talent and persistence and perhaps with a bit of luck, transformed a thick, dumb limestone block into the sheerness and splendour of glass.

It happened that, in the last years of the eighteenth century, a revolutionary new social idea came into being in England: that the nobility, instead of being protected and enriched by the crown, should instead pay a proportional share of their wealth in the form of taxes. But how was this proportional share to be determined since wealth in those days was so easily concealed? There were no official receipts, no numbered Swiss bank accounts, of course, but extravagant ball gowns or embroidered silk could be exchanged, at least in public, for austere muslin and the gold and silver plate hidden in the walls when the tax inspector came calling. No one, even then it seems, liked very much to pay taxes, and who could blame them?

Someone then struck upon another brilliant notion—and this someone has no name, though surely he (it must have been a he since he was listened to) was a bureaucrat of rare intelligence. He saw that a family's level of wealth could be determined rather easily, in fact, by counting the number of windows in their dwelling. Glass windows were only just becoming common in the late seventeenth and early eighteenth century; one of the reasons we call the dark ages dark, in fact, is that people lived most of their indoor lives without natural light, and even at this time in England there still lived a remnant of the old feudal society so poor that they huddled in blackened one-room hovels that possessed not a single window or even a chimney.

Their slightly better-off neighbours had advanced to the point of having one or two windows in their cottages, windows fitted, to be sure, with rather cloudy inferior glass but glass that allowed, at least, the entrance of a little light into the household.

Down the road, in the rising new villages and industrial towns, were houses incorporating all the latest architectural notions, and these houses wore their windows—ten or even twenty of them—like shining jewels. The families in these houses took light for granted: their rooms, even on rather dark days, were closed to the elements but open to light.

And yet they were nothing compared to the great mansions of the rich, the palaces and castles with their hundreds of marvelous, newly contrived windows. Windows running floor to ceiling. Bay windows, circular windows. Windows of brilliantly coloured glass. Prismatic windows. Dazzling sheets of light-inviting glass that changed the lives of those who lived within.

But suddenly, with the announcement of the new tax laws, the windows had become an index to wealth, and thus a liability and threat to solvency, and so the earliest form of tax evasion became, as you can imagine, a retreat to the old darkness. One by one, and then hundreds by hundreds, these wonderful apertures to the world were walled in with bricks or with blocks of solid stone. Inside, once again, was darkness; outside, the hurriedly filled-in windows gave houses the blank, stunned look of abandonment.

Today we understand how one economic shift inevitably creates secondary or tertiary shifts, and what happened in England was the creation of a band of wandering artists whose highly specific task and skill was to paint over the newly installed exterior stones so that they looked like windows. Thus, the architectural integrity of the houses was at least superficially respected, though the problem of interior darkness and ventilation and a view onto the world remained.

The new window artists became extraordinarily adept at their work. The mullions, those non-structural bars dividing the lights or panes of the windows, proved relatively easy to master, being simple wood, sometimes grooved, sometimes carved, but always maintaining cousinage to stone. What was harder was to paint stone so that it looked like glass. Window glass, as you will have observed, is a curious half-silvered substance, a sort of gleaming liquid that has been frozen into a solid pane. Then, too, glass possesses different colours at different hours of the day. Sometimes it pretends it's a mirror. Other times it gathers checks and streaks and bubbles of brilliance and elegant flexes of mood. Its transparency winks back at you, yet it withholds, in certain weathers, what is on the other side, revealing only a flash of swept-back drapery, a shadow of a room leading to another room, a pattern of infinite regress, or perhaps a human figure moving across its width. It is green like water or blue like sky or a rectangle of pure gold when the setting sun strikes it or else a midnight black starred with lamplight, candlelight, or the shy and courteous reflection of the moon.

Each of the travelling artists in those days developed a particular style. Many were content with a sort of primitive suggestiveness—window as architectural detail, window as gesturing toward windowness, but falling short of verisimilitude. Other artists worked hard on their mouldings, their shadows, and the *tromp d'oeil*[7] effects. There were window artists so cunning they made you believe that, if you reached out, you could open a casement on its very hinges. A few artists—and these had been in the business for some years—managed to articulate the spark and glance and surprise of real glass without, of course, stretching toward the achievement of air.

But there was one artist—and we have no way of knowing his or her name, or how old this person was, or what part of the kingdom he/she sprang from, or how his/her skills had been acquired—but one artist who broke through the frame of painting itself.[78] He/she had inherited an elaborate convention, elaborately respected. Nevertheless, a decision was made on the part of this artist to work the window in a new way that was not imitative but creative. Paint was mixed and layered, rubbed out, then reapplied—this is hindsight, of course, the opinion of contemporary art historians who agree and also agree to disagree. How does one make light dance on a flat surface, and how does an artist bring transparency to what is rigid, solid, opaque, and unyielding? Were these questions buzzing in the head of the artist on the morning—or perhaps afternoon—when the small miracle came into being? No one knows.

All we know is that a certain blocked-in window was freed in such a way that light flowed with a burst through it. Not a real light, of course, but the idea of light, which is infinitely more powerful than light itself. Illusion, accident, meticulous skill all played a role, and those who gathered to pay tribute were happy to set aside, for the moment, scientific proofs and to stand in awe of the power of creative achievement—a window that had become more than a window, better than a window, greater than a window, the window that would rest in the mind as all that was ideal and desirable and transparent in the world of windows. . . .[79]

Now, whether this became a taxable window I can't tell you since some of the history surrounding this event has been lost, and the story itself has softened into a kind of fable. Every fable, of course, has its moral tag, and I think this fable tells us that art is part of our everyday lives, as common as, well, as chairs and tables and walls and floors and, well, windows. It sustains us. It makes our world new and also possible. It obeys no laws, and it has no limits.

A Delicate Balancing Act[80]

The best book reviews, I think, are given orally. A friend, for instance, might phone to tell you about a book he has been up all night reading. There's a young man who works in the department where I teach who, last summer, bought up two dozen copies of Anne Tyler's book *Dinner at the Homesick Restaurant* and distributed them to friends who promised to read it. I remember that my young daughter once said to me about a book she was reading, "I love this book because when I look up fast I think I'm going to see the two people in the story standing next to me."

Written book reviews, on the other hand, often show a great deal of conjecture and judgment and very little lively response, a phenomenon which I think arises from reviewers' misconception about their roles. Anatole Broyard[81] has it wrong about reviewers when he asks us to picture a scales of justice with the author on one side, the reader on the other, and the critic as fulcrum in the middle. Not only is this presumptuous, but it leads to a distortion in which reading becomes an act of judgment, a mechanical process of evaluation which ends up with explanation points in the margin where you approve and vigorous underlinings wherever you've managed to catch the writer out. Instead of being open to the sensations of delight and instruction,[82] there is a narrowing down to a checklist fulfilled or unfulfilled. It was Sartre[83] who once said, "to read a book is to write it," and I think this is a perceptive remark since, in a sense, the attentive, open-hearted reader—the reader we all dream of—retraces the steps of the creative process and becomes engaged in the book as total experience.

The actual writing of the review is clearly an absurd reduction. The complex has to be made simple. A reviewer must, in a column or two of print, convey to the reader the essence of a book which took its author three years or six years or twenty years to write. Furthermore, this review is often written to a tight deadline and for little or no pay, for it's a sad fact that considerable reviewing is treated as a kind of sideline journalism, hack work for the hungry, or ego fodder for those eager to see their names in print, or "good works" for those whose conscience has been prodded. It's a wonder really that books *are* occasionally reviewed with wit, wonder, balance, erudition, and grace.

Because reviewing is absurdly difficult, it seems to me unwise to formulate too strict a body of guidelines. Different books demand different approaches. Nevertheless, there are some decencies which a reviewer owes a writer, beginning by asking the question "Do I *like* books?" This question may seem superfluous, but reviews are fairly frequently written by people who take an adversarial position when it comes to literature, putting themselves in the finger-wagging pose of approval or disapproval, and finger-wagging is not criticism.

A second question might be "Am I a good person to review this book?" Not the best person—for the best person doesn't exist, except in the fantasy of the nervous writer—but am I, for example, predisposed to dislike this book because I detest the genre, despise the writer, am bored by his previous books, am deeply unsympathetic to his belief, for instance, that literature is a linguistic game or a mirror of reality or whatever? Will reviewing this book turn me into an outraged defender of standards or a moral policeman? Or should I abstain from book reviewing because I myself am a writer, perhaps of the same form? Consider who the other *possible* reviewers might be. Local journalists or academics? I don't think it matters greatly as long as a love of books exists and is seen to exist. We like to *think* that in England and in New York there is a corps of professional reviewers—the fact is novelists in these places routinely review each other, though they may not have our special problem—which is that we tend in this country [that is, Canada] to know each other.

Which leads to another question in the same area: am I committed by friendship to like this book? This is a difficult and not unusual dilemma, and so is the problem of future self-insurance. Noel Perrin,[84] writing in the *New York Times*, says he finds it both funny and repellent to read the reviews poets write of each other's books and to note the special heightened language they have evolved to dignify one another's modest achievements.

Once the difficult questions of suitability have been answered satisfactorily, it seems to me a good idea to write a first draft at once while still wrapped in that cocoon of heightened pleasure or disgust which immediately follows an enjoyable or execrable experience. Certain sections of the book under review will, of course, have to be reread and reflected upon and then revised, but the primary impression, which the reviewer is committed to trust, should be preserved.

After the review is drafted, and after generous quotations have been provided, it is a good idea to give oneself a sort of self-administered test, asking a battery of questions, some trivial, some basic. First, a few words to avoid. One is the word *indescribable*, the one word that those who describe themselves as describers should never use. The expression "a good read" is soft as well as meaningless, a fast-food phrase, cheap and lazy. Joan Barfoot, the author of two novels, says she is tired of the word *promising*. Evenness, unevenness—we are often told about the sin of unevenness, but was *Shakespeare* even? Are we sure we *want* evenness? I am personally cranky about the word *rendered*, which I think is better saved for the making of lard. The expression *tour de force* is a perfectly good term, or was, until it started getting pasted on any short and brutish[85] work which defied categorization. Then there are the words *protagonist* and *denouement*; both carry the aroma of the academy. *I* strenuously avoid that critical term "unity of vision,"[86] also "unity of consciousness," for who on this earth ever possessed such a thing or for that matter wanted to? The expression "flawed" or "seriously flawed" is one to watch out for, for it seems to suggest that *un*flawed works of art have actually been produced from time to time. Distinction between major and minor works is tricky. Mary Gordon pointed out in a recent essay that Hemingway writing about boys in the woods is considered major while Mansfield writing about girls in the house is minor. The words *exquisite* and *delicate* and *microcosmic* are often used pejoratively in reviews, meaning insignificant and unsubstantial and fluffy.[87] "Austenesque"[88] (Jane, that is) is meant to be flattering, but it is applied fairly indiscriminately to writing which happens to be exquisite or delicate or microcosmic, hence insignificant, unsubstantial, et cetera.

Another question to ask yourself after you've written a review is "Have I been guilty of playing the rating game?" Have I dropped the suggestion that such-and-such a writer is perhaps the third best woman writer in southern Saskatchewan to have emerged in the last seventeen years? Have I placed a writer as being somewhere between Grace Metalious[89] and Hortense Calisher,[90] and, if I have, then I haven't been thinking about the writer I am considering but about Grace Metalious and Hortense Calisher. The same goes for comparing a book with pre-vious books by the same writer. True, one book can illuminate another, but each book is a separate endeavour and not a signpost to growth. In other words, it's unfair to a writer to imply that each new book must top the last; creative evolution doesn't work that neatly. Thank God.

Another question to ask yourself: "Have I directed my remarks to possible readers, or have I been praising or lacerating the writer?" My own thought is that, if you wish to communicate or offer advice to a writer, you can phone or send a letter but that reviews are for readers. Some disagree with this view, and I hope the subject will be discussed today.

Another question: "Have I reviewed the writer or the book?" This is a question that for some reason seems to come up more often with the reviewing of women's books. Cynthia Ozick[91] said recently—and this is a quote—"I think I can say in good conscience that I have never—repeat never—read a review of a novel or especially a collection of poetry by a woman that did not include somewhere in its columns a gratuitous allusion to the writer's sex and its supposed effects." The quote ends here. We are told, for instance, that such and such a book of poems was written by so-and-so, who is a soft-voiced mother of three—as though this information would strain our credulity or reflect on the poetry. Sometimes reviewers assume all women write autobiographically and mistake the clichés and prejudices of the characters for the supposed clichés and prejudices of the writers.[92]

Another question to ask yourself: "Have I been too timid, too equivocal?" Reading American reviews, one is stunned to see that critics will start off with such phrases as "this is a wonderful book" or "this is a dreadful book." A Canadian review might begin "This writer, considering her youth and the fact that this is her first extended prose work, can perhaps be seen, by those willing to overlook occasional, though not entirely damaging, lapses, to have, more or less, partially succeeded." Why do we do it? Out of fear? Or fairness? It takes a lot of energy to write even a bad book. True, but sadly, in writing, as in all art, there can be no A's for effort.

Here's another stern question but a necessary one: "Have I tried to guess the author's intention and respected it?" In other words, this may not be the great panoramic book I want to be reading at this moment; it may not touch on certain issues which are presently occupying me;

it may not soar in my expectation in terms of lyricism, but it is, never-theless, the book I am reading at this moment and which is under my consideration.

One last question: "Has the gender of the author altered my judg-ment in any way?" We can't, of course, be unaware of gender; it exists. But has the consciousness of gender narrowed my appreciation or cramped my response, or has it—and this is most important—limited my ideas about what one has permission to write about? Virginia Woolf says in her essay on "Women Novelists,"[93] "there rises always for consideration the very difficult question of the difference between man's and woman's point of view of what constitutes the importance of any subject." Is, for example, the mothering experience, which in-volves roughly one-third of the human race, to be banished from fiction because reviewers find it trivial or unsavoury? Mary Gordon says this: "It was all right for young men to write about the hymens they had broken, the diner waitresses they had seduced. These experiences were significant. But we were not to write about our broken hearts, about the married men we loved disastrously, about our mothers or our children. Men write about their fears of dying by exposure in the forest; we could not write about our fears of being suffocated in the kitchen. Our desire to write about these experiences only revealed our shallowness; it was suggested we would, in time, get over it."

Is there such a thing as *geographical* discrimination? The question is sometimes asked: "Do writers in the Toronto, Ontario, area have an advantage when it comes to receiving coverage through reviews?" I have to say I haven't noticed this to be true, though I sometimes suspect that we non-Ontario writers are regarded as bare-footed children, exotics who require special handling and patient understanding and allowances made for prairie dust in our lungs or salt spray in our faces. In Winnipeg, writers complain because the *Free Press* book page editor does *not* feel he has an obligation to review Manitoba books—but if the alternative is provincial boosterism, then I prefer things as they are. When I lived in Vancouver, I noticed a preponderance of sailing books under review and in Ottawa a surfeit of political books. And I have never, in eight years as a novelist, been reviewed in the Maritimes or in Saskatchewan. I don't know what this means—perhaps someone here can enlighten me.

Reviewers *do* have power, particularly if they persuade writers (women) that their experiences are without value. Book reviewing is a delicate balancing act requiring not obsequiousness or scorn but respect. And if in doubt, a little humility never goes amiss. Remember, nobody ever reviewed *Hamlet*. No one ever reviewed *Paradise Lost*.[94] God knows, we all write the best books we are capable of. All we ask is a listening ear and a careful, caring eye.

Divorce[95]

When I was a young child back in Illinois, my Aunt Marjorie and Uncle Fred came over for supper on Wednesday evenings. My mother made meatloaf on those nights, with lemon pudding for dessert; this was Uncle Fred's favourite meal. Once in a while Aunt Marjorie came alone. After a while she *always* came alone. The ghost of Uncle Fred grew thinner and thinner, though his name oddly persisted. "When's Uncle Fred going to come?" I asked Aunt Marjorie one night. "Hmmmmm," she said, and looked down at her hands, frightened.

Later my mother explained about the divorce. Sometimes married people didn't stay married. You could change your mind, it was allowed. Uncle Fred had turned out to be a "rolling stone." He'd rather be on the road than be married to Aunt Marjorie, who, naturally, was very, very sad about the way things had worked out. She didn't want to be reminded of it; it hurt her feelings. It would be better if I didn't mention Uncle Fred to her again. And I mustn't tell anyone else either—the neighbours, my school friends—they didn't need to know.

This was in 1942. The word *divorce* felt hard, ugly, full of suffering and secrecy. Some people at that time associated divorce with movie stars, with glamour, but I didn't. My aunt, a woman in her late thirties, went to night school to learn typing and shorthand and later found an office job with Magnavox.[96] She lived alone in a small Cleveland apartment; she sent her nieces and nephews birthday cards with dollar bills enclosed; she grew old, developed severe osteoporosis, moved to a Florida trailer park, and died in her bathtub. In all those years, the only contact she had with Uncle Fred was a valentine he mailed from California—no return address—in the mid-'50s. The thought of this whimsical greeting fills me with horror: Uncle Fred's careless act of sentimentality rattling down on my aunt's smashed heart. She bore that as she had borne her other injuries, and the divorce, *her* divorce, seemed almost to disfigure her with time, its molecules joined to her fragile bone structure, her powdery skin, her humility, her lack of ease in the world.

Of course, divorce in those days was rare, and its scattered victims were stamped with failure. Today's high divorce rate dilutes blame, some believe, invoking the old raspberry jam analogy: the farther you spread it, the thinner it gets. It's no one's fault. The stresses of contemporary life are cited. People's expectations are too high. Or too low. There's too much intervention or not enough. Power struggle. Communication problems. Cost of living. Sexual dysfunction. Co-dependence. Inability to establish intimacy. Victim, victimizer. A subtle inversion has taken place in our thinking, and we remark what a wonder it is, really, considering all the pungently labelled enemies of conjugality, that marriages sometimes survive.

And yet they do. Despite the fact that the divorce rate in North America stands near the fifty percent mark, almost all of the people I know are married. Not only married but involved in long, established, ongoing marriages—thirty years, forty years. Is it by accident that theirs are the faces I find most often around our dining room table, conversing, reminiscing, toasting each other's anniversaries, and giving an altogether convincing performance of people who are at ease with one another? And news comes from the wider world, too, as year after year Christmas greetings arrive from Tom and Marvie in Toronto, Judy and Sam in London, Dot and Al in California. Our married friends. Still together. Still breathing the old trusted oxygen of matrimony.

I understand the textures of these particular seasoned marriages; after all, they're very like my own. I apprehend the compromises, the unspoken bargains, the rituals, and the jokes too—the biggest joke being that a good many of us are astonished to find ourselves citizens of the undivorced world, part of a robust kicking chorus, the fortunate few who have fallen through a rent in today's statistical charts. We've had a lucky escape—and we know it—from the tug of social evolution and can't help feeling that there's something just a little bit ludicrous about our situation.

There's something worrying about this, too, for what draws us toward those whose domestic arrangements mirror our own. Surely, we don't consciously, or unconsciously either, reject the company of the single and the divorced. What could be more unpardonably smug? And yet there does seem, when I sit down to review my various tiers of friendship, a preponderance of those like ourselves, the marriage survivors, our comrades in a baffling demographic warp. Why?

Might our flocking together suggest egregious self-congratulations? Did we "try harder"? Did we unwind with greater care the skeins of consequence, or were we simply fortunate enough to marry at a time when there were fewer guarantees for parts and services? Are we less sexually imaginative? Or too complacent to countenance disruption—putting the house on the market, breaking the news to the children? Is it a question of temperament that draws us together, a willingness to shrug and put up with things while *they* had the courage to cry *halt*?

Or is it the thought of the emotional gulf that divides us from the divorced? The divorced and separated know, as we can't possibly know, that dark zone that surrounds the cessation of love. We've never had our life cleft by a moment of decision, that particular morning—I always imagine *it* happening on a Monday morning in November, wind, sleet, the window rattling in its frame—when it is understood, finally, that the shared life, that which has been pledged, sealed, and witnessed, is about to be withdrawn.

But if there exists a negative statistical deformation among my own circle of friends, there is an inverse bulge in the world of fiction. Here the divorce curve runs wildly out of range. In literary novels, in works of popular romance, in mysteries, in science fiction, from genre to genre and sparing none—the line on the graph climbs straight up, leaving America's fifty percent divorce figures in the shadows of an impossibly innocent time.

Ask yourself when you last read a novel about a happily married couple. For one reason or another, enduring marriages find little space on the printed page. How is a novelist to pump the necessary tension into the lives of the happily committed? Even the suggestion of a sound marital relationship posits the suspicion of what is being hidden and about to be revealed in a forthcoming chapter. Couples who have good sex, who discuss and resolve their differences and care deeply about their bonds of loyalty, are clearly as simple-minded and unimaginative as their creator. There they sit with their hobbies and their wallpaper and their cups of decaffeinated coffee, finishing each other's sentences and nodding agreement. She sends his winter coat to the cleaners and frets about his asthma. He continues to find her aging body erotic, and he's also extremely fond of her way with grilled peppers. This is all very well, but what can be *done* with folks so narratively uncompromising?

It might be thought that novelists would come running forward to pick up the gauntlet. Six hundred fast-turning pages without a single marital breakdown; now there is a challenge. Man and woman meet, fall in love, and integrate their unspotted histories. Crises of all sorts arrive, but their marriage holds firm. Really? You expect readers to believe that kind of fairy-tale stuff?

As a marriage survivor—thirty-eight years—I would like to write that book. I've tried to write it. The modern novel may not be a glass reflecting life back to us, but shouldn't we at least be able to find a measure of congruity between what we experience and what we imagine? We depend on contemporary literature to bring us bulletins from the frontier, just as we looked to the literature of previous centuries for an outline of societal patterns. Why, then, do today's novelists distort the state of marriage by concentrating on connubial disarray? To this I can only cry *mea culpa*, for, despite my long, happy marriage, my novels and short stories are as filled with divorce as any other writer's.

My early novel *Happenstance* is as close as I've come to presenting a picture of married contentment.[97] In this book, Jack and Brenda Bowman have been married for twenty years. They speak to each other kindly, they honour their vows of fidelity, and they still have fulfilling sex; it's right there in Chapter 3. A number of their friends, though, have gone through divorce, and this casts a shadow over their own happiness. Brenda wonders how the divorced cope with the detritus of all those married years. Like all couples, she and Jack have built up a hoard of shared anecdotes, their private stock, exquisitely flavoured by the retelling. The timing and phrasing of these accounts have reached a state of near perfection. Brenda wonders what happens to such stories when couples separate. Do they cease to exist? How do people bear such a loss?

As the novel opens, both Brenda and Jack are experiencing undefined feelings of restlessness, and, during a week spent apart, they toy with images of temptation. The two of them are as close as people can be after twenty years, and yet they remain, ultimately, strangers, one to the other. The distance between them is as wide as a football field; it is also delicately gauged. Anything could knock them off course. This novel about a happy marriage, then, is fuelled by the fear of its loss and the possibility of a diminished life.

Tom Avery, the hero of my 1992 novel *The Republic of Love*, has been divorced not once but three times. His marriages lie strewn about him. Quickies. He tells himself he's been unlucky but only half believes it. He lives in a small city where at any moment he's likely to run into his ex-wives or one of his six ex-parents-in-law. There isn't a day when he doesn't feel his three failed marriages pressing down on him. He lives in fear of meeting his old drinking mates, who like to kid him about rice coming out of his ears, about going for *The Guinness Book of Records*, about buying the Wedding March on compact disc. Friday nights are spent, dismally, in a community centre with the members of the Newly Singles Club, companion divorcees who long to repair their lives and perhaps meet someone new. The program rotates every six months, and by now Tom has heard a variety of lectures on such subjects as "The Ghettoization of the Single in Contemporary Urban Society," introducing three key coping strategies: bonding, rebonding, and disbonding. He is beginning to weary of these talks and has grown skeptical of the way in which human behaviour divides itself into categories of three. Nevertheless, at forty years old, he's out looking, once again, perhaps foolishly, for the kind of married love that lasts.

Luckily, he has a few married friends, but he's noticed that he's seldom included anymore in their dinner parties. Instead, he's more likely to be asked for brunch, joining the family around the table for waffles or to participate, perhaps, in a backyard project. He feels obliged now to earn his invitations with gifts of fresh flowers or bottles of expensive wine. He admires his friends' babies and dutifully bounces them on his knee in hearty faux-uncle fashion. In return, these married friends dispense well-meaning advice and occasionally fix him up with single women. Blind dates, though, have become a nightmare since they lead straight to the agonizing moment when he must confess the details of his splattered history and brace himself for the inevitable response: "Three! You were married three times!" The novel is a love story, employing a classic pattern of enchantment, rupture, and reconciliation, but in the end it is driven less by love than by the failure of love.

An early novel, *The Box Garden*, should have been a warning to me of the danger of writing about unlived experience. Charleen and Watson, the divorced couple in the book, meet after twelve years of separation, but the encounter felt flat on the page, so flat, in fact, that my two editors, both divorced themselves, asked me if I would rethink the scene. They urged me to show greater *intensity* and *strangeness* and the *bittersweet resonance* such a meeting would arouse. I took their advice, setting the scene up more carefully and turning the emotional thermostat to high. But today, rereading the section, I find Charleen's reaction forced.

A twisting breathlessness like a rising funnel-shaped cloud of anguish pressed on my lungs, robbing me of speech and, for a moment, of coherence.

Oh, my. More like a purple-shaped cloud of incomprehension!

Still, the fact is that I *would* like to see more marital equity in the pages of our fiction. And I'd be willing to honour the principle of mimesis and settle for a straight fifty percent success/failure right. Coupledom, especially when seen in an unsparing light, should not necessarily equal boredom, should it? It might be interesting to see novelists look inside their own specific human packaging and admit that a long marriage—the union of two souls, the merging of contraries, whatever—can be as complex, as potentially dynamic, and as open to catharsis as the most shattering divorce. "It takes more courage to stay together," a friend once said to me, "than to go our separate ways."

We all know that a steadfast marriage can be dismantled in an afternoon, but how much is understood about the aesthetic light that such a revealed arrangement can produce? Long-term marriages do accrue a kind of compacted understanding, and there seems every reason to believe this material can be shaped to form a useful and novel dramatic arc, the prickly, conflicted spine of narrative fiction.

Perhaps it is this notion of conflict that needs revisiting; we may find that conflict is centred not in the fibre of human arrangements but in the intricacies of human thought. What exactly are we owed? What can we aspire to? How well can we know another human being? I'd like to begin over again—a project for the late '90s—asking why the rub of disunity strikes larger sparks than the rewards of accommodation and how we've come to privilege what separates us above that which brings us together.

Introduction to *Duet*[98]

I've always thought of my first two books as "companion novels," a term I seem to have invented. *Small Ceremonies* was published in 1976, and, a year later, in 1977, came *The Box Garden*. There is no sense of this second book being a sequel to the first, but a number of threads connect them. Above all, they are about two women, Judith and Charleen, who happen to be sisters.

The mother of the two women also appears in both novels. Mrs. McNinn is a sour, disenfranchised housewife whose only relief is found in the manic redecorating of her small suburban house. Judith, a biographer, is scarcely touched by her narrowness; Charleen, on the other hand, a poet, has been thwarted by her bitter mother.

These are both short novels, and the idea of publishing them together makes sense to me. Each enriches the other and fills out the other, and together they lead to the sisters' discovery of what their mother really is; an artist who, like themselves, stumbles toward that recognition.

Carol Shields's Booker Prize Report[99]

Now follows a brief Booker [Prize] Report. Brief because it seems so far away, dreamlike, though it was only a few weeks ago. It was both dazzling and awful. Extraordinarily sophisticated and curiously boorish. The Guildhall, where the awards dinner was held, is utterly beautiful—and the people, men in black tie, women sparkling with jewellery, and wearing mostly black too, were also rather beautiful. (I bought new earrings for the event, my only investment in beautiful peopledom.) We sat at round tables for the dinner, trying to ignore the TV cameras which seemed to be everywhere. Cigars were passed around after dinner. Now that's pretty boorish. The speeches had little cynical edges on them, past grievances trotted out, not quite "nice." (The head of Booker Inc.—an immense, red-faced man—informed me that Winnipeg was a very, very dull place, and I was quite lost for a reply. "Is it?" I said. Lamely.) Our table was Fourth Estate (English publisher of *The Stone Diaries*) people with some *Guardian* people too—they are a major investor in the firm. I thought the head of Fourth Estate, Victoria Barnsley,[100] would burst into tears when Roddy Doyle's name was announced, but I have to admit—ever the pessimist—I'd expected it. By the way, Roddy Doyle[101] and I both forgot to bring our invitations to the dinner and had to go into a little anteroom to be "interviewed" before they'd let us in. Security at the dinner was extremely tight since Salman Rushdie[102] was there—looking, I might say, exactly like Salman Rushdie. Someone whispered into my ear after dinner, "Mr. Rushdie would like to meet you," and then led me through what I thought was a crowd of friends but was, in fact, a crowd of bodyguards, four men deep. We had a nice chat about the Future of the Novel, and he said he was in the middle of mine. I didn't know whether to believe this or not but decided I might as well. I also met Stephen Spender,[103] eighty-four, erect and handsome still, and his wife, who looks like an El Greco[104] ghost, very old, very stately—they both told me they were rooting for me, though I think they put it more elegantly. After dinner, I met Margaret Drabble; we had a pleasant chat, very polite and friendly, though I don't think we said anything memorable to each other. All quite marvellous, so that I almost forgot I'd lost. I also met all the other nominees briefly, including Caryl Phillips,[105] who gave me a stiff hug and whispered something about the tyranny of colonialism in my ear. A sort of roller coaster night, and suddenly it was over, and I was on the way to California. Then back to Toronto. Then back to normal, whatever that means.

Foreword to *The Stone Diaries*[106]

I have never written with such happiness as during the two-year period when I was working on *The Stone Diaries*. The book seemed to be about something that mattered (though I didn't know what it was), and it went along willingly enough once I'd discovered a framework, which was the borrowed design of an old-fashioned nineteenth-century biography with its title sequences of "Birth," "Childhood," "Love," and onward to "Death."[107]

When I first began the novel, I thought I was writing a family saga or, rather, a subversion of the family saga as we know it. Before long, I realized I was, instead, writing about the subject of autobiography, about the central question of whether or not we can know the story of our own lives. How much of our existence is actually recorded, how much invented, how much imagined, how much revised or erased? The most substantial parts of a human narrative, it seemed to me, were borrowed from the impressions that other people—friends and family and passing acquaintances—had of us, and I wanted these imagined voices to enter the novel and to inform Daisy Goodwill Flett, born in rural Manitoba in 1905. What do people think of us? These received thoughts, sometimes tragically, make a life. Daisy survived into her nineties, and her life corresponds, more or less, with the span of the century, posing the question of where these last hundred years have delivered women, especially those women who failed to make the public record.

My plan was to cut into Daisy's life every ten years or so, just to see what she was doing. I realized that my writer's scalpel, with its autocratic and methodical slicing, would miss some major moments: Daisy's sexual initiation, her education, her childbirths. But such arbitrariness might gather into its grasp something other: perhaps those less exclamatory and genuinely revealing events.

Each day as I sat down to write, I conjured up an image of a series of nesting boxes. I was making the outside box, Daisy was making the inside box—and inside her box was nothing. She was thinking—not writing—her own life story, but it was a life from which she, the subject, had been subtracted. This was the truth, I felt at that time, of most women's lives.[108]

Musing about autobiography made me think about the photographs that always accompany such books. I asked my publisher, Christopher Potter,[109] if we could have a clutch of such photos in the middle of the book. I explained that I wanted, somehow, to gesture toward another form. I expected him to say no, that the photos would be too expensive, and, furthermore, one didn't offer photographs with a novel. But he said yes, we can do that. Immediately, I thought about what else I might ask for. What about a family tree? Yes, he said, we can do that too. And an epigraph from the family archives? Yes. His handful of permissions kept me steady as I finished the book.

Writers, famously, resist talking about their work in progress, but I talked and talked and talked about this book to everyone. I asked my friend Jennifer Graham about her elderly father, Alf, and she told me where she suspected his thoughts drifted to and what they were made of. I asked my colleagues at the University of Manitoba—over lunch, meeting in the hallways of the Arts Building—about certain period phrases I wanted to use. Professor Lew Layman managed to track down the expression "See you in the movies" to a novel published in 1929. (That was good news—I could use it!) *The Stone Diaries* only *seems* like a private book, almost, in fact, a woman's intimate journal; I am astonished, looking back, how public the writing of it was. I loved this collective *assemblage*, this gathering of verbal cues and scattered anecdotes. This process was a large part of the joy I felt at that time.

I did believe, as I wrote the final chapter, that I had written a sad book. From its inception, I found myself writing toward the phrase "I am not at peace." When I got there, finally, on the second-to-last page, I was reluctant to register those words. My wont had always been to find the harmony and reconciliation, but the phrase pressed on my consciousness—and my conscience. Finally, I committed it to print. I've learned to live with that hard choice.

Carol Shields
December 2001

Afterword to *Life in the Clearings*[110]

As readers, we like to think that books are prompted into print through a sense of authorial urgency and that a writer picks up a pen out of the heat of intense conviction. We imagine that the resulting manuscript goes on to forge a mystical bond with an editor—wise, principled—who instantly grasps the historical significance of the work and foresees how its pertinent observations and narrative leaps will fuse with the consciousness of a contemporary audience, speaking with its authentic voice and awakening its best instincts.

This romantic notion holds little truth today, as we all know; nor did it in the summer of 1852 when the English publisher, Richard Bentley,[111] wrote to Susanna Moodie of Belleville asking if she would consider writing a second book on the subject of life in Canada. His terms of reference were genial but specific: "If you could render your picture of the state of society in the large towns and cities of Canada, interesting to the idle reader, at the same time you make it informing to those who are looking for facts it would be acceptable. Present them to the reader's eye as they were years ago and as they are now, and are still every year I imagine rapidly prospering it might form a good work as a pendant to *Roughing It in the Bush*."

In November, she replied. She was eager to begin, so eager that she enclosed a partial manuscript. She was, she explained to Bentley, recovering from a life-threatening illness and at the urging of her doctors had recently undertaken a restorative boat trip to Niagara Falls. "My idea was," she wrote, "to describe as much of the country, as I could in my trip to Niagara, beginning with Belleville, and going through our lovely Bay, sketching the little villages along its shores, and introducing as many incidents and anecdotes illustrative of the *present state of Canada*, as I could collect or remember, to form a sort of appendix [*sic*] to *Roughing It in the Bush*."[112]

Considering the differences of geography and privilege, gender and sensibility that lay between Bentley and Moodie, it is impossible to say whether his "pendant" bore any resemblance to her "appendix." Bentley's intentions can be imagined; he was a gentleman but also a businessman with an eye to capitalizing on the romance of immigration and on the widespread need for practical information.

Moodie's expectations were more complex. She was understandably anxious to profit from the success of her previous book and ever in need of money for "bread, butter and tea," and she also hoped to correct what she perceived to be the public's grave misunderstanding of *Roughing It in the Bush*. She had never, she maintained, discouraged immigration to Canada; she had only warned that life on an uncleared farm offered hardship, isolation, and ruin for those of the middle or higher classes who were unfit for hard labour. Far more suitable for such settlers were farms already under cultivation or positions in Canada's progressive and prosperous towns.

It seems likely that Bentley anticipated a new manuscript, freshly conceived and composed, but Moodie, ever practical and always re-sourceful, saw the book as a chance to reissue old work, both published and unpublished. Thrifty housewife that she was, she emptied her drawers, added a few new chapters and a thin tissue of connecting material, and quickly arrived at a complete manuscript.

It is little wonder that the book she wrote was not the book that she promised. Once settled in Canada, Moodie scarcely ever travelled more than a few miles from Belleville, and so she was far from being a knowledgeable and objective witness to the state of contemporary society. Her sensibility, too, was firmly rooted in pre-Victorian England, and her syntax was shaped—decorously, protectively—for a readership she had long since lost touch with. The "facts" specified by Bentley in his letter of contract for *Life in the Clearings versus the Bush* either sink beneath the weight of Moodie's didactic commentary or are annihilated by her indefatigable enthusiasm. Also fragmented along the way is her proposed structural device, the journey to Niagara Falls in search of health.

The idea of such a pilgrimage is an ancient one, and so, particularly, is the idea that water possesses restorative properties: the pure spring, the enchanted fountain, the sacred river, the calm lake, the bracing seaside. A change of air, a change of scene—these held out the promise of a renewal of the body and spirit, and what more abundant source of refreshment could there be than the waters of Niagara? Here the power of purity of nature merged, and here too was a tourist attraction that Moodie shrewdly judged would interest her English readers.

But she seems unable to decide whether this is a literary or historical journey. Again and again in the early chapters, she pleads for postponement—"My dear reader, before we proceed further on our journey . . ."—and imposes her own agenda. From time to time, she catches herself, briefly relocating the reader on the map and painting in a few landmarks. Only the final chapters accommodate themselves to the journey scheme, but these suggest an anecdotal travelogue rather than an Odyssean voyage. The vision soon deteriorates, and the vigour with which she devours information, consumes scenery, and thirsts after vignettes refutes her claims to physical frailty.

Life in the Clearings, then, succeeds by default. Moodie was ill-equipped to write the kind of book Bentley commissioned, and she quickly loses control of her organizing framework. Her voice is discursive, euphemistic, overblown, and sometimes oppressive—in the way that all storytellers are oppressive—but it is unmistakably authentic.

When we speak of the voice of a period, we most often mean a voice of authority and munificence, the far-ranging voice of the lavishly gifted or the arbitrarily powerful. In the past, that voice frequently was both aristocratic and male, securely located, rich with certitude and learning, a voice either self-anointed or baptized by the circumstantial unfolding of a literary tradition.

An *authentic* voice is something else. We know it when we hear it. The texture of the quotidian is in it, and every cultural moment secured suggests a thousand others. Even its self-consciousness, even its silences, can make a statement. It whines and falters but manages to catch enough thieving narrative to reveal the configuration of a society and how it invests itself with meaning.

Susanna Moodie's life spanned the greater part of the nineteenth century. Her lifetime coincided with enormous shifts in political dominion and, more important, with dramatic new concepts of personal power. To these phenomena, she is a perplexed but never disinterested witness. She immigrated to Canada when she was close to thirty years old, and so her consciousness was stretched across two cultures, two continents, and two political philosophies. Her adopted culture exposed her to the new radical democracy but failed to erase her conflicting instincts of privilege. "That all men, morally speaking, are equal in the eyes of their Maker, appears to me to be a self-evident fact," Moodie says in one chapter, but goes on in the next breath to say that "equality of station is a dream." Her fixed view of society was shaken, finally, by her growing suspicion that many of the grievances of the lower classes were justified and that immigration and education offered at least a measure of class mobility.

Happily, Moodie's comments are never deformed by that critical straitjacket; unity of vision, and her struggle to maintain her idealistic vision in a harsh landscape, provide *Life in the Clearings* with much of its tension. Romanticism and realism, those competing forces, not only reflect the turbulence of the period but also that element in her nature that urged her toward decency and fairness. She examines, she vacillates, she contradicts herself.

Her contradictions are her chief delight. She is one minute praising the natural beauties of the land and the next minute smarting under the bad manners of her fellow tourists. She enjoys local folk customs while longing for those at home. Always a woman to relish irony in human behaviour, she was perhaps unaware of the way in which her own bewilderment and indecisiveness gave weight to her account. Writing for Moodie was both a financial opportunity and a personal outlet; she is forever trying to reconcile the two and never realizing that she has succeeded. To her work she brings a kind of fortuitous innocence, mingling the historical and the sentimental with results that are sometimes earnestly clumsy, at other times vividly dramatic.

The experience of her life is so long and varied, so splintered and buffeted by social upheavals, that she is obliged to create a new form. *Roughing It in the Bush* and *Life in the Clearings* are both books that generously and disconcertingly embrace elements of travel writing, the literary sketch, narrative fiction, meditation, factual material, and poetry. The tone varies widely, from injured and defensive to astringent and bright, and the theme of dislocation and adaptation is anchored to the seemingly random ceremonies and stories with which she shapes her sense of the world. *Life in the Clearings* is the kind of patchwork, unofficial document that allows us to "read" a slice of our national history, and a rather large slice at that.

Trying to place such a text in a governing tradition is to miss the book itself. The form is Susanna Moodie's invention; it fits like a comfortable and hand-knitted sweater. She is at home with her divagations, liberated by them, in fact. "Allow me a woman's privilege," she begs us, "of talking of all sorts of things by the way." Her digressions are only superficially intrusive, however, since they carry us into unmapped territory and provide us with an interlinear gloss, giving her voice not just authenticity but particularity.

For today's reader, the ringing subtext reveals even more. Beneath Moodie's "enthusiasm" (a favourite word of hers and also the title of her 1831 volume of poems) is a sense of a woman making the best of things, of bitter longing transcended by fervour and commitment. Moodie is a Crusoe[113] baffled by her own heated imagination, the dislocated immigrant who never fully accepts or rejects her adopted country. When her methodology wobbles, her reflexes can be counted on. Her acts of reimagination rise from an unconscious strategy of survival; she states her belief in male dominance, for instance, but reserves for women characters like Jeanie Burns qualities of courage and endurance. She struggles with the image of a beautiful lake disfigured by a new saw mill—natural harmony confronted by necessary progress—and is unable to resolve her feelings.

It is precisely this human ambivalence of Moodie's, as well as her shifting focus and telling silences, that defines her for the modern reader and places *Life in the Clearings versus the Bush* near the heart of our developing literature.

Introduction to *Mansfield Park*¹¹⁴

Jane Austen welcomed her author's copy of *Pride and Prejudice* in 1813, claiming it as her "own darling child." "But now," she announced, "I will try to write something else, & it will be a complete change of subject—ordination."

The subject of church ordination sounds lumpish and unpromising, as though Jane Austen, delighting in her recent success, felt, suddenly, a compensatory duty to assign herself a stern moral task. Now that she had a readership, she would be responsible and earnest, paying an act of redress for the "sparkle" and the lack of "shade" that characterized her earlier books.[115] With *Mansfield Park*, she would mute her frivolous irony, even her natural inclinations, and plunge into the philosophical subject of virtue and depravity. Her mockery of clergymen,[116] for which she had been gently reproved, would be reshaped into admiration, and she would demonstrate, through the character of Fanny Price, the ascendancy of goodness.[117]

Luckily for us, *Mansfield Park* pauses for only brief glances at the matter of ordination and gives far more notice to the subject of moral conduct. For many readers, this novel is the most spacious and complex of Austen's fictions. Certainly, it involves more pieces of the world, a wider range of social classes, and a more nuanced commentary on decency and social behaviour. Its overriding theme is difficult to isolate since the novel is about everything it touches upon: nurturing, steadfastness, belonging and not belonging, about fine gradations of moral persuasion, about human noise and silence, and about action and stillness. And it is, like all narratives that carry weight in our culture, about the search for home, that enabling place, real or metaphorical, where we can be most truly ourselves.

Austen may have intended to blunt her ironic voice with *Mansfield Park*, but a deep dichotomy rumbles beneath the surface, for Mansfield Park, the Northamptonshire home of the Bertram family, is the making of Fanny Price, but Fanny Price, at the same time, is the saviour of Mansfield Park. This paradox rests on the belief that the human sensibility can be refined and educated and that virtue itself cannot be confined by the narrowness of class.

None of Jane Austen's heroines begins life as radically disentitled as Fanny Price of Portsmouth, and in the reading and understanding of her character some of our contemporary psychological insights can be called upon. A sensitive child, Fanny spends the first decade of her life with a rough drinker of a father and a slatternly mother who prefers her sons to her daughters. But neglect and abuse, instead of coarsening the young Fanny, make her submissive, obedient, and self-denying. Where Fanny's finely attuned moral sense comes from is something of a mystery, a triumph over both genetics and environment, but today's readers, at least those who are familiar with the self-protective strategies of the victim, will understand exactly why Fanny is Fanny, a child of almost saintly qualities.

"A benevolent scheme," as Jane Austen terms it, is launched by Fanny's relations at Mansfield Park. In order to relieve the pressure on the Price family in Portsmouth, ten-year-old Fanny is plucked from her disorderly home and placed in elegant Mansfield Park, where she is quartered in "the little white attic" and educated along with her four cousins, who have every advantage over her. We see immediately that it is impossible for her to win family favour; homesick at first for her miserable parents, she is thought unappreciative of her new circumstances; on the other hand, not missing her home would have signalled lack of feeling.

The Bertram family, clinging to tradition and isolated in the deep countryside, are not much changed by Fanny's presence, but they are wildly awakened by the arrival in the neighbourhood of Henry and Mary Crawford. The Crawfords, brother and sister, come from London. They are young, vigorous, and consecrated to the future, to change, and to movement. Jane Austen is sometimes thought of as a writer who neglected the world she was born into, but the confrontation between the Crawfords and the Bertrams—standing in for the much larger social revolution that waged in England between traditionalists and modernists—proves that she registered, and with great accuracy, the social and economic rhythms of her times. The Crawfords are attractive and compelling but morally empty. Crawford "toys" with the idea of falling in love with Fanny Price, who has grown to womanhood, and then finds that he really *has* fallen in love. Her rejection of this match brings upon her the wrath of the Bertram family and a punishing banishment back to her own family in Portsmouth, where she is powerless, virtually without funds, and kept ignorant of her future.

The question is can readers sympathize with Fanny; can they love her as Jane Austen clearly does? ("My Fanny," she calls her in the novel's remarkable final chapter, in which all the narrative lines are brought to conclusion and the whole cast of characters summed up.)

Fanny succeeds in the end partly because Austen has cleverly cleared the field for her. The two Bertram daughters are in disgrace. Aunt Norris has been sent packing. Mary Crawford has been exposed in her moral shallowness. Fanny's uncle, Sir Thomas, humiliated and lost, requires the consolation of a daughter he can trust, and the ever-faithful Fanny stands ready to assume that responsibility. Furthermore, Austen has put the reader in a near-impossible situation, for, if we underrate Fanny's essential value, we put ourselves in the same camp as the Bertrams.

But Fanny does have real claims on our attention despite her joylessness. She shows growing signs of independent thought—her little discourse on memory, for instance, in volume II, chapter 4. "There seems something more speakingly incomprehensible in the powers, the failures, the inequalities of memory, than in any other of our intelligences." She bursts into a promising articulation in the second half of the novel—in volume III, chapter 2, when the obdurate Henry Crawford refuses to believe that she cannot love him. "Now she was angry," Austen says plainly.

And, most particularly, we can esteem Fanny's resourcefulness when she is returned to her awful Portsmouth family. There she brings order where she can, assisting one of her brothers in his departure and introducing a sister, Susan, to the joys of literature. She saves Susan by bringing her to Mansfield Park, where her life will be greatly improved. It is this instance of the helpless coming to the rescue of the even more tragically helpless that wins our hearts and convinces us once again that Jane Austen has read all the signs and correctly apportioned the rewards.

Afterword to *Dropped Threads:*
What We Aren't Told[118]

I was twenty-one years old and standing in line to receive my Bachelor of Arts diploma from Hanover College. Major in English, minor in history. It was June, and the temperature was ninety-seven degrees Fahrenheit. Under our black academic gowns, my girlfriends and I wore, by previous agreement, nothing. Nothing at all. This was considered high daring in those days, 1957. The night before, seven or eight of us had gathered in the woods above the campus and conducted a ritual burning of our saddle shoes. We were utterly ignorant of what lay ahead of us but imbued, for some reason, with a nose-thumbing rejection of the suffocating shell of convention that enclosed us.

And yet most of us were prepared to inhabit that safe place our parents had defined for us. We married the same summer we graduated, joined our lives with men no older than we were, and within a year we were buying houses, having babies, and planting petunias. Hardly any of us thought of a career other than wife and mother. No one had suggested such a notion to us.

The 1957 graduation address was given by a very popular math professor at the college. He began his talk by telling us that we would remember nothing of what he would say that hot June morning. This was true; I sat dreaming of my wedding, which was just six weeks away, and of the apartment where I would live with my new husband. The charm of domesticity, its sweetness and self-containment, pulled at all my passions. But suddenly he broke through my daydreams. "I ask you to remember only two things," he said. "Remember the date, 1957, and remember the words *tempus fugit.*"

I had studied Latin, but even if I hadn't I would have known what that phrase meant: *time flies*. Our convocation speaker was reminding us that our lives would speed by before we had grasped them. It was our responsibility to seize each moment and fill it with accomplishment.

Otherwise, our life would be wasted, worn away with the turning years, and we would grow old and disappointed in what we had made of it.

The phrase haunted me in the ensuing years. I was occupied with babies and with the hard physical work that babies involve. We moved several times, and so there were always new domestic arrangements to carve out. Cleaning, cooking, coping, running errands—my days were filled with such minutiae. It was in the calmer, cooler evenings that the phrase *tempus fugit* would return to me, beating at the back of my brain and reminding me that the time was rushing by. I was spooked, frightened by what this meant.

And then, quite suddenly, I realized it meant nothing. *Tempus* did not *fugit*. In a long and healthy life, which is what most of us have, there is plenty of time. There is time to learn another language. There is travel time, and there is stay-at-home time. Shallow time and fallow time. There is time in which we are politically involved and other times when we are wilfully unengaged. We will have good years and bad years, and there will be time for both. Every moment will not be filled with accomplishment; we would explode if we tied ourselves to such a regimen. Time was not our enemy if we kept it on a loose string, allowing for rest, emptiness, reassessment, art, and love. This was not a mountain we were climbing; it was closer to being a novel with a series of chapters.

My mother-of-small-children chapter seemed to go on forever, but, in fact, it didn't. It was a mere twelve years, over in a flash. Suddenly, I was at a place where I had a little more time to reflect. I could think, for instance, about writing a real novel, and I did. And then another novel and then another. I had a desk in this new chapter of my life, a typewriter, and a pile of paper that belonged just to me. For the first time, I needed a file cabinet and a wrist watch, something I'd done without for a decade. I remember I spent the whole of an October afternoon working on a single sentence; I was not by nature a patient person, but for this kind of work and at this time in my life I was able to be endlessly, foolishly, patient.

In 1985, I looked up from my desk and realized that the children had gone, all five of them. The house was quieter now. The days were mine to arrange any way I wished. I wrote a novel in which, for the first time, there were no children. It was a different kind of novel than I'd written before, with a more inventive structure. The publisher was worried about this innovation, but I was insistent.[119] The insistence was something new, and it coloured the chapter I was living in, my early-middle-age chapter. The woman I saw in the mirror looked like someone else, but I knew it was really me, relocated in time and breathing another grade of oxygen. I was given an office and a key to that office. I loaded it down with plants and pictures, a soft lamp, a carpet. It felt like a tiny apartment, offering solitude and giving new permission, another space in which to live my ever-altering life.

Friendship took time, but luckily I had time as I entered yet another phase. My women friends provided support, amusement, ideas, pleasure, wisdom. The two-hour lunch was a luxury I could afford during this period; moreover, it was a kind of necessary music. The more words we tossed into the air the closer we felt to the tune of our own lives. We talked about what we knew and what we didn't know. Our conversations were punctuated with the joyous discovery of commonalities, the recognition that the narratives of our lives bumped along differently but with the same changing rhythms.

But one day, over a long lunch with my friend Marjorie Anderson, we spoke for the first time of all that went unspoken, even in an age of intense and open communication. There were the things our mothers hadn't voiced, the subject our teachers had neglected, the false prophetic warnings (*tempus fugit*, for example) we had been given, and the fatal silence surrounding particular areas of anxiety or happiness. Why weren't we told? Why weren't we warned? What contributed to the reticence between generations, between one woman and another?

We decided to ask some of our women friends to talk about the skipped discourses in their lives and how they had managed, at last, to cope with the surprise of self-discovery, stumbling on that which had been missing: an insight, a truth, an admission, a dark hole. The proposals poured in. This was an exciting time; Marjorie and I were exhilarated by the ideas that were suggested and astonished that so few overlapped. The areas where women had been surprised by lack of knowledge ranged from childbirth to working with men, to illness, loss, friendship, and secrecy, to the power of sexual feelings, the frustrations of inherited responsibility, and the recurrent patterns that haunt us.

The finished essays, which arrived like dispatches from the frontier, described these varied experiences and reported on how they were confronted or accepted. Each voice was separate, and yet each connected subtly with others, as though informed by an underground stream. The essays expressed perplexity at life's offerings: injury and outrage that could not be voiced (*Woman, hold thy tongue*), expectations that could not be met, fulfillment arriving in unexpected places, the need for toughness, the beginning of understanding, the beginning of being able to say what had once been unsayable. Or, in my case, the apprehension of a structure that gave fluidity and ease to a long life, the gradually (or suddenly) shifting scenes, each furnished with its own noise and movement, its particular rewards and postures.

We move through our chapters mostly with gratitude. Who isn't renewed by startling scenery or refreshed by undreamed-of freedoms? Surprise keeps us alive, liberates our senses. I thought for a while that a serious illness had interrupted my chaptered life, but no, it is a chapter on its own. Living with illness requires new balancing skills. It changes everything, and I need to listen to it, attend to it, and bring to it a stern new sense of housekeeping.

But I have time for this last exercise. All the time in the world.

Afterword to *Dropped Threads 2:*
More of What We Aren't Told[120]

A dozen or so years ago, a senior colleague treated me with great disrespect and insensitivity. The incident struck me like a blow to the head, though you might think I had been fortunate indeed to have arrived in my mid-fifties without suffering a social injury of this kind.

I registered a protest to the head of the department but was told nothing could be done. I felt invalidated, baffled, powerless, and even became ill for some months, suffering seizures to my neck and shoulder muscles. I could have gone to the dean, who would have set the situation right, but for some reason this didn't occur to me.

Instead, I began to talk about the conflict: to my family, then to my friends. I confess I made rather a drama of it. I told the story some twenty times, thirty times, probably fifty times. Each time I told it the pain lessened slightly. A noticeable dilution took place, and my tale of humiliation developed wavy side curls of absurdity. My tongue became more and more eager to exploit my shame, and I caught myself, oddly, relishing my own anger. Imagine!—I possessed a colleague with whom I was not on speaking terms. Now, that was interesting. Eventually, I collapsed the narrative and inserted it into a novel, *The Stone Diaries*, and there it rests, enervated now, incapable of hurting me further.

When I consider the essays in this anthology and those published in its predecessor, I feel the heat rising from the words and the human relief of having shared a story and thereby mitigating its power. By getting such stories "off our chests," we are lightened and enabled. Frequently, we discover that what we believe to be singular is, in fact, universally experienced. No wonder Holocaust survivors seek each other out. No wonder those who have lost a child turn to others who have endured the same loss. We need these conversations desperately.

I remember once sitting in a circle of women who had undergone mastectomies. One of the women was eager to show us her new, light prosthesis, which had replaced one that was heavy and misshapen. She reached inside her shirt and removed it and handed it to the woman next to her. We passed this very private cone of plastic and foam around the circle, each of us admiring it in turn, weighing it in our hands, comprehending it, and understanding that this ad hoc ritual linked us together and eased the shared loss of our bodily integrity.

I want to thank each of the women who have brought their stories so bravely in this book. Many of the contributors to the first volume suggested further stories that needed to be told and writers who might be called upon. Susan Roxborough of Random House has encouraged us. Marjorie Anderson has shaped this book lovingly and with great intelligence and tact. Catherine Shields has brought her critical attention to all the manuscripts. Readers across Canada have responded with their own narratives and the knowledge of how women can help each other.

I am honoured to be a part of this ongoing project, which locates itself at the juncture of my two favourite things: language and the company of women. There we can find courage to go forward in our lives.

Carol Shields
May 2002

CONCLUSION

While she found a home in Canada, Shields never neglected the land of her birth. While she applied for and received Canadian citizenship, she never relinquished her American citizenship.

She found in the 49th parallel not "the world's longest . . . one-way mirror," as Margaret Atwood labelled it, but a permeable two-way margin.[1] Shields proved that the border is a two-way crossing, as she criss-crossed the 49th parallel frequently to visit her American family and friends—including spending a sabbatical year in Berkeley with her engineering professor husband in 1993–94.

Shields also portrays two of her most beloved protagonists as border-crossers: Daisy Goodwill travels to the United States and marries there in *The Stone Diaries*, and Larry Weller moves to the United States to become a "maze maestro" in *Larry's Party*. She portrays Daisy and Larry as crossing the border, but viewing Canada as home: Daisy views her travel back to Canada as "a mythic journey" returning "home" to Canada (*SD* 132). Larry "finally chooses to settle in Toronto and be a Canadian," as Georgiana Colvile notes: "back to the womb also means back to Canada" (90). Because Canadians are considered "nice"—"the sweet Canadians," as Atwood labels them in her 1981 novel *Bodily Harm*—Shields notes that Larry's "seasoned goodwill is attributed to Larry's Canadian background" (*LP* 206).

In her essay "Coming to Canada," Shields concludes, as a Canadian Colossus with one foot on either side of the border: "Do I consider myself a Canadian after thirty-six years in the country? . . . The equivocal and very Canadian answer is yes and no. I still carry two passports and have friends and family on both sides of the border. My novels are published in New York but also in Toronto, and these novels are set in Chicago, Ottawa, Vancouver, Philadelphia, Toronto, Manitoba, Indiana, and Florida. It feels natural and also fortunate to have one foot planted in each country and to be able to say, definitively, noisily: here is where I live."[2]

Having "one foot planted in each country" enabled Shields to do what no writer had done before: namely, to enjoy the unique distinction of being the only writer ever to be awarded both the Governor General's Award for Fiction in Canada and the Pulitzer Prize in the United States, *and* for the same novel. She accomplished this feat with *The Stone Diaries*, reissued by Vintage Canada in 2023 with an audiobook version, on the thirtieth anniversary of its initial publication.

These two awards, enabled by her dual citizenship, were a testament to her critical acclaim, as well as popular success, on both sides of the border, as well as in Britain. *Unless* was the only novel written in the last forty years to make the top ten in a 2003 poll of favourite books by women writers.[3] These awards catapulted Shields into the stratosphere. Publishers welcomed and even invited her contributions. Her first four novels were reissued in pairs—her two sister novels, *Small Ceremonies* (1976) and *The Box Garden* (1977), were republished as *Duet* in 2003 and her husband-and-wife pair of novels, *Happenstance* (1980) and *A Fairly Conventional Woman* (1982), were republished as *Happenstance*, "The Husband's Story" and "The Wife's Story."

At the outset of "Writing from the Edge," Shields, as an established Canadian author, declares, "Now I am going to contribute to the nexus of Canadian identity" (*SI* 131). And she did—by writing about Canada, setting her novels in Canada, and continuing to support her fellow Canadian writers, especially women writers, by recommending them for Canada Council grants. She wrote approximately fifty book reviews, never allowing herself to reveal a "glint of the fang," as she put it in her essay "The Writing Life" (139). She understood how sensitive newly-published authors are to unkind comments, as she had been hurt by brutal reviews that she nick-named "cruelies" (*MF* 4). She also honoured her community of Canadian women writers in more personal ways, such as preparing the menu described in *Larry's Party* for the fiftieth birthday of one of her friends.

Celebrity did not disturb her modest manner or generous spirit, as Lorraine York has documented so well in "Arriving Late as Always': The Literary Celebrity of Carol Shields." As Shields supported her fellow writers generously, they, in turn, honoured her.

Like Margaret Laurence before her, who, as President of the Writers' Union of Canada, was den mother to what she called her "tribe" of fellow Canadian writers, Carol Shields was also viewed as a maternal figure by Canadian authors. In "Remembering Carol," Isabel Huggan calls her "maternal, as well as sisterly and collegial" (53–54) while, in "Readers are an Unruly Lot," Elizabeth Hay calls her "motherly and knowing and fierce" (52). Finally, in "Carol's Kindness," Martin Levin affirms, "she was a unique blend of the matronly and the mischievous" (132).

I had been reading Shields's novels since the 1970s. When I began to see the light at the end of the tunnel of my monograph, *Divining Margaret Laurence: A Study of Her Complete Writings*, I resolved to work on Carol Shields's writing. When my grant proposal was accepted, I screwed up my courage to contact her through colleagues and mutual friends.

When I emailed her to ask if I might visit, she replied simply, "When can you come?" I telephoned (they were listed in the phone book as "Carol and Don Shields," just like regular—that is, not yet famous—people) to arrange a date. She said, "You realize that I'm at the end of a long illness. So sooner is better than later." Although she had been diagnosed with terminal breast cancer in December 1998, she had survived long beyond the two years that her oncologists had predicted.

When I arrived at their spacious, light-filled house in the exclusive Rocklands district of Victoria—which she, ever modest, said she did not deserve—on a beautiful day in early May 2003, I could hear children's footsteps running through the house. A child opened the door, saying, "Grandma's in the kitchen." Carol Shields emerged from the kitchen and took my hand warmly. She invited me into her sunroom, where we chatted over tea. A celebrated domestic goddess, she apologized for the lunch crumbs on the table.

Then the author of many books, and the recipient of many awards and accolades, Carol Shields had reason to be proud. But she was as friendly and down-to-earth as she had been a decade earlier when I had first met her when she read from *The Stone Diaries* at a 1993 ACCUTE AGM, long before her fame. Where she had been sunny ten years earlier, she was now luminous.

We talked about many issues of common interest over the three days of my visit, among them family. Shields had five children and eventually twelve grandchildren, and still managed to write all those books. We compared parenthood and authorship, producing babies and books. She agreed that there were many "commonalities": "I remember the birth dates of my books," she said. She talked about the pleasure of assembling a book, which she compared to forming the character of children. "Character building" was her forte in more ways than one. She said she needed motherhood to grow up, because being responsible for "that tiny body" demanded maturity. "I do means I am," she said, varying Descartes's rational proof of existence with a practical one. "Children offer you a wonderful window on the world of the young."[4]

Despite her illness and manifest weakness, Shields was as enthusiastic as ever about discussing literature in general and her own writing in particular. Accordingly, she invited me to come the next morning at eleven o'clock, following an interview for Shelagh Rogers's CBC radio show, *The Next Chapter*. Since she had retired to bed, she invited me to pull up a white wicker chair beside her bed to chat with her. She said a CBC TV crew had set up an interview in her bedroom just two weeks before.

She mentioned that Margaret Atwood had visited her the previous week. She had a basket overflowing with books on the floor by her bed, and Atwood's 2003 novel *Oryx and Crake* teetered on the top of the pile. Margaret had brought it as a gift. Shields said she was a great admirer of Atwood's work.

I had brought her a luxuriant African violet from a floral shop on my way to her house because I thought she might enjoy its literary associations. She had her youngest daughter Sara place it on a little white wicker table by her bed while we conversed. Later still, her eldest daughter Anne wrote me a thank-you note, explaining that her mother was becoming too weak to write.

Years later, while researching her archives at the National Library in Ottawa, I was astonished to discover that she had woven the violet into her short story "Segue"—the story that introduces her posthumously-published *Collected Stories* (2004), which was to be the opening chapter of her unfinished novel, *Moment's Moment*[5]—and employed it as a symbol of nurturing. It illustrates the creative writer's ability to interweave external with internal realities. In the draft novel, Jane Sexton, President of the Sonnet Society of America, presents her colleague Victor with a violet. I had suggested to Shields that, instead of watering a flowering plant from above, the blooms flourish better if watered from below by being placed in a bowl of lukewarm water so that the roots can drink. Shields managed to work this into her story, giving it moral significance. Shields writes that Jane Sexton views the violet as "symbolically useful, though I'm not sure the others understood the subtleties [as] African violets must be watered from the bottom, not the top, and this, I believe, is analogous to the writing of sonnets in the twenty-first century" (15). These comments demonstrate Shields's writerly ability to amalgamate reality into her fiction and to employ the most mundane details of daily life metaphorically.

As we talked, she faded out occasionally, as if listening to inner voices, but rallied and continued the conversation. We had such an absorbing discussion that I lost track of time. To my surprise, Don entered bearing a tray with French bread, cheeses, and wine and said, "Let's pretend we're in France." Don recalled that, when they were on sabbatical in France, they had a small apartment. Shields needed the place to herself to write in the morning while the children were at school, so Don absented himself. Because it rained every day, he sat and read in the car, where he had plenty of time to plan lunch, he reminisced.

When I left on the second day, I gave her my proposal for my monograph on her work, *"Sparkling Subversion": Carol Shields's Vision and Voice.* The next morning, when I pulled up the white wicker chair beside her bed, she told me that she approved of my project. That has meant a great deal to me throughout the years I have been editing her collected poetry, editing a collection of essays on her work, editing this collection of her own writings, and writing my monograph about her work. She remarked that she liked my phrase, "sparkling subversion." I explained that it was her own phrase. She was surprised. I told her it was from *The Stone Diaries* and that I thought it represented her work very well. I explained that the "Vision and Voice" part was a reversal of the title of her study of Susanna Moodie: "'Voice and Vision.'" She responded, "I always thought I should have reversed those words. After all, vision comes before voice." Fortunately, we still have her voice, which conveys her vision.

Shields invited me to return the next day, my last, at nine o'clock. When I suggested that we talk about morality, Don responded, "Oh, *morality*. I thought you said *mortality*. *Morality* is all right. We don't talk about *mortality* in this house." Shields laughed. *Mortality* is, in fact, the title of a play to which she contributed, and it is one of the last pieces that she composed before her death. So, the next day we discussed narrative method and the question of ethics and the novel.

We also discussed her teaching career—including her years as Professor of English at the University of Manitoba and Chancellor at the University of Winnipeg—plus writers she admired, including Jane Austen and Margaret Laurence. She remarked, "It was when I read *The Stone Angel* when I was an MA student at the University of Ottawa that I decided to enrol in the Ph.D. program in Canadian literature." She and Don planned to visit Lorraine McMullen, who had supervised Shields's master's thesis on Susanna Moodie, in Victoria, as she was also dying of cancer.

On my last day, as I was leaving, Carol asked Don to fetch her copy of the British edition of *Jane Austen* from their basement, which she then inscribed to me. When I reached out my hand to shake hands and say goodbye at the end of my third and last day, Shields grasped my hand and pulled me to her, kissing me on the cheek and saying, "Thank you for coming, Nora, dear. Good luck with your project." I did not expect to see her again. As Jane Urquhart wrote in "A Generous Spirit" after Shields's death, "She leaves an empty chair at all our tables" (138).

When Carol Shields died in July 2003, tributes poured in from writers around the world, including the eulogy by Atwood that provides the foreword to this collection. Her death inspired "a thanatology of loss," as Aritha van Herk wrote in "Debris" (4). Jane Urquhart declared, "Carol Shields was the most beloved of Canadian writers, beloved by her family, her friends, her colleagues and her readers" (138). Isabel Huggan affirms "Carol's generosity of spirit" (56), and Elizabeth Hay confirms, "she was a lovely and generous woman" (51). Shields's co-author Blanche Howard affirmed, in "Collaborating with Carol," "Carol is generous and she is loyal" (48).

Shields's former student, Martin Levin, praised "her personal kindness" (131), "her talent for friendship" (132), her "gift for intimacy"

(137), and "the bounteousness of her spirit" (136). Aritha van Herk asserted, "she illuminated; and she inspired" (3). Numerous collections of essays honouring Shields, in addition to the plethora of articles in scholarly journals, poured forth: *Carol Shields, Narrative Hunger, and the Possibilities of Fiction* in 2003; *Carol Shields and the Extra-Ordinary* in 2007; *Carol Shields: Evocation and Echo* in 2009; *The Worlds of Carol Shields* in 2014; and *Relating Carol Shields Essays and Fiction: Crossing Borders* in 2023.

Although she died much too soon in June 2003, shortly after her sixty-fifth birthday, with her next novel in draft and many other novels in mind, she left us the legacy of her oeuvre. "We are bereft," her daughter Anne lamented, because "She had many novels left to write."

We are left with her distinctive voice, as recorded in her writing, which expresses her unique vision. Atwood declares, "And live she did, and live she does; for, as John Keats remarked, every writer has two souls, an earthly one and one that lives on in the world of writing as a voice in the writing itself. It's this voice—astute, compassionate, observant, and deeply human—that will continue to speak to her readers everywhere." Lorna Crozier also celebrates "the warm glow of her voice, the flavour of her speaking" in her afterword to this volume, titled "Carol's Haunting Voice."

Shields is famous for her fiction, and rightly so, but few readers are aware that she was also an accomplished poet, playwright, short story writer, biographer, and literary critic. Her list of works includes ten novels, three collections of short stories, four collections of poetry, four plays published and produced, and two collections of essays. It is my hope that the fifty short stories and essays in *The Canadian Shields: Stories and Essays* will contribute to that oeuvre.

"Carol's Haunting Voice"

by Lorna Crozier[1]

When Carol died in 2003, a year after her novel *Unless* was published, she was a decade younger than Patrick [Lane][2] is now. I hadn't seen her for a few weeks and heard about her death while I was at a writers' retreat at a Benedictine monastery about seventy-five miles north and east of Saskatoon. It's a working farm with cattle and chickens, a big vegetable garden, an orchard, and fields of wheat, hay, and canola. One of the monks approached our group of eight writers at the breakfast table and told us that he had heard the news of a famous writer's death on CBC Radio earlier that morning. He wondered if any of us had known her.

Even though you know that something is inevitable, when it happens, it still comes as a surprise. Part of you feels stunned and looks around for meaning and significance, for some kind of sign to match your sadness and mark the change that's taken place. The night Carol died, a fierce wind had blown through the monastery grounds, had awakened me and kept me tossing in bed until sunrise. In the morning, in the huge old cottonwood outside my window, the wind continued to roil and thrash as if the tree wouldn't let it go, its big-leafed branches whipping with the effort. I couldn't help but see the frenzied motion as a powerful spirit trying to leave the world. Though it was early, before eight a.m., I poured myself a glass of wine and stood under the green roar. I toasted Carol, then threw the rest of the wine against the runnelled trunk, wishing her an unimpeded journey when she broke free from all that wanted to hold her and, heading east, rolled across the prairies all the way to Winnipeg, then south to Chicago and home.

Later the same day, one of the other writers who'd been at the breakfast table when we heard of Carol's death, a young poet about to publish her first book, was walking the dirt road that ran between a group of barns and sheds. She had never met Carol, but she'd read her books and, over the years, listened to her on CBC. Daydreaming her way into a poem, gazing at the clouds that scudded past, she suddenly heard Carol's voice. Eerily distinct and clear, it wafted through the air above the sound of the wind. It seemed to be coming from the long, narrow shed a few yards ahead of her and to the left.

Hesitant and slightly scared, she walked towards it. The door of the shed was missing, though a grid of wire was nailed across the opening so nothing could go in or out. Carol's voice was louder now. She was reading from *Larry's Party*. The young woman recognized the passage about Larry leading his small son through the maze he had built in his back yard. She peered through the door into the darkness, not knowing what she'd see.

From inside the shed came the clucking of hens. Dozens of them walked the floor near the back, placing their feet with precision as if they knew ahead of time where each foot should fall, as if they woke up every morning with maps glued to the bottom of their toes. Dozens more roosted in the rafters, and at the very back of the shed, on a white plastic pail turned upside down, sat a big transistor radio. Although the woman couldn't see the dial, she knew it had to be set on CBC, Carol reading, "It may be that Larry has romanticized this particular memory. The soft kiss of the evening sun, the dizzy, unalarming purr of mosquitoes in his ear, his little boy's hand in his. . . ."

The smell of the coop drifted through the wire as she stood and listened: a whiff of wet feathers though they were dry, dust shuffled by the chickens' feet, an acrid pungency from the soft white droppings that streaked the rafters and spotted the floor. With the smell, Carol's mellifluous voice floated in the air above the glottal sound of hens. It is common knowledge that many farmers play tapes of Beethoven and Mozart in dairy barns to settle the cows and make them give more milk. The CBC voices and music that came from the radio must have been there to relax the hens and encourage them to lay.

During that day of tributes and Carol's elegantly turned, considered sentences winding to the end of thought, in the long dark shed in the monastery yard, the hens were laying eggs. Inside each shell would be the warm glow of her voice, the flavour of her speaking. I wish I could tell Carol this story. She would have loved knowing that her reading and writing had been put to good use, that her voice had gone to such a place. For the next few mornings at breakfast, I paused for a moment after I'd lopped off the top of my soft-boiled eggs as if there were a sound caught inside and about to be released. If I listened hard enough, perhaps I'd hear a word as tasty and numinous as *unless*.

NOTES

Notes to Foreword

1   Atwood's tribute to Shields was first published in *The Virginia Quarterly Review* 81, no. 1 (2005): 139–42, http://www.jstor.org/stable/26441736.

2   Carol Shields's daughter Anne Giardini explained that *Unless* was composed mainly in Victoria, British Columbia, during a few months of relatively good health after being diagnosed with breast cancer in December 1998.

Notes to Introduction

1   Shields recalls, "In 1957, I crossed the border with my young husband, all our belongings, including an ironing board, packed into our six-cylinder Ford" (*SI* 138).

2   After an evening in May 1991 in New York City celebrating Canadian literature, Shields wrote to Blanche Howard, "The theme of the night was Canadian humour, surely an oxymoron.... Susan Swan ... told a few Canadian jokes, of which I can only remember one: Why did the Canadian cross the road? To get to the middle" (qtd. in Howard 238). Shields repeats this distinctively Canadian joke in her essay "The Unity of Our Country," included in this collection.

3   Shields had an indirect connection to Hemingway because her mother, Inez Sellgren Warner, boarded, with a couple of friends, in the Hemingway home while they attended Normal School to train as schoolteachers. Shields recalls in "Writers Are Readers First" her mother reporting that Ernest's father, Dr. Clarence Edmonds Hemingway, dismissed his son, then living in Europe, as "a time waster" (*SI* 3).

4   For further discussion of this topic, see Stovel, "American or Canadian.'"

5   I wish to thank Guy Vanderhaeghe for confirming the accuracy of this recollection, although neither he nor I can remember where it was published.

6   The delegates at the Carol Shields conference at the University of Winnipeg in 2009, led by her husband, Don Shields, walked the hedge maze, which was no challenge since the hedges were only a few inches high at that time.

7   Emphasis in original. See this volume, 60–61.

8   Catherine was born in England while the Shields family was spending the year in Manchester.

9   Shields writes, "Anne of Green Gables captured the love of her adoptive parents, won the heart of Gilbert Blythe, and transformed the society she was born into, but Lucy Maud Montgomery was obliged to remake her world through the nib of her pen." She adds, "It may be that this is what all writers do, and why we can't stop writing about it" (qtd. in Levin 133).

10 Novelist Marian Engel (1933–85) was best known for her controversial 1976 novel *Bear*, which portrays a female archivist's erotic relationship with a bear and which won the Governor General's Literary Award.

11 This speech is in the Carol Shields Fonds, Accession LMS-0212, 1994-13, vol. 63, file 5.

12 In Shields's 1987 novel *Swann*, the character Sarah Maloney declares, "Some days the only person I can tolerate is Virginia Woolf" (6).

13 This speech is in the Carol Shields Fonds, Accession LMS-0212, 1994-13, vol. 63, file 5.

14 Shields had been disappointed not to find interesting women in recent fiction. She recalled, "I was conscious that the women in the fiction I read were nothing like the women I knew. They weren't as intelligent" ("Interview" 20). She resolved to fill that gap.

15 Shields, "The Unity of Our Country," 130, in this volume.

16 Shields adds, "The MA took 5 years, 1969–75 The graduate advisor was not encouraging."

17 The title of Lowther's posthumously published collection of poetry, *The Stone Diary* (1977), inspired the title of Shields's 1993 novel *The Stone Diaries*, and her murder by her husband, Roy Lowther, a failed poet and teacher, in 1975, inspired Shields's portrayal of the murder of poet Mary Swann by her husband, Angus Swann, in her 1987 novel *Swann*.

18 McMullen, "Carol Shields" 41–42. Shields's term papers from her graduate student period at the University of Ottawa are housed in Library and Archives Canada.

19 Sandy Frances Duncan, born 1942, is a Canadian writer of novels, mysteries, and short stories.

20 "Writing from the Edge" includes part of "A View from the Edge of the Edge."

21 The referendum on Quebec sovereignty on 30 October 1995 was defeated by a narrow margin.

22 "A View from the Edge" was delivered as an address at Harvard University in 1997 and published in 2007 in *Carol Shields and the Extra-Ordinary*, edited by Marta Dvořák and Manina Jones. It is partially included in "Writers Are Readers First" (*SI* 1–14).

23 Shields served on a panel on the short story in Canada with Robert Weaver, John Metcalf, and Norman Levine. She recalls, "I was, of course, asked to speak on women writers in Canada. Hmmmm" (*MF* 126). Diane Turbide reports Shields observing that "Every time I'm in Europe interviewers ask me to explain my theory on the explosion of writing in Canada."

24 Christl Verduyn has written about Canadian Women Writers as Essayists in *Her Own Thinker: Canadian Women Writers as Essayists*.

Notes to Part 1: Carol Shields's Previously Unpublished Stories and Essays

1 Connie Steenman-Marcusse defines Shields as "a writer who crossed global boundaries" (10).

2 Another recovered story text, "Four Fictional Letters," which recalls Shields's *Snow*, an undated sequence of twenty-nine poems composed of the correspondence between two sisters (one, not yet twenty, who has married and emigrated to the New World, probably Canada, possibly Ontario, and another who has remained,

unmarried, at home in Suffolk [*CP* 201–31]), was not included in this collection because it is incomplete. These "Four Fictional Letters" might have formed the beginning of a projected manuscript. The letters alternate between 1882 and 1929: that is, between generations, a grandmother and a granddaughter, like Margaret Laurence's children's book *The Olden Days Coat* (1979) or her draft novel "Dance on the Earth,"which alternates between 1985 and the Battle of Batoche in 1885 in a manner employed by John Fowles in his 1969 novel *The French Lieutenant's Woman*.

3   Regarding Reynolds Price's article "Men, Creating Women"in *The New York Times Book Review*, 9 Nov. 1986, urging "men to write about women and vice versa," Shields notes, "He says so exactly what I didn't quite know I believed. His belief is that we're born with a full range of sympathies, but that these become narrowed and throttled by gender and that this is currently poisoning our fiction" (Howard and Howard 145).

4   Carol Shields Fonds, box 129, file 9.

5   "Protein Dust" is from a clean typescript in the Carol Shields Fonds, Accession 11805, volume 129, file 9, nine pages, with the date "Oct 9/98" handwritten in pencil at the top of the first page. There are no notes or emendations on the typescript. The Carol Shields Literary Trust published in 2021 a limited edition of 211 copies of the story in chapbook form printed by Colophon Press.

6   Shields's novel *A Fairly Conventional Woman* (1982), republished as *Happenstance: The Wife's Story* (1991), includes a similar scene (35–41), in which the heroine, Brenda Bowman, flying from Chicago to Philadelphia for a quilting conference, is irritated by a young man who insists that she is in his seat and requires her to move and then confides in her, leading her to ask herself, "What had she expected? Not this, not this" (41).

7   "A Message from Beyond"is an unpublished story submitted to a *Chatelaine* fiction contest by Carol Shields, age forty-seven, of 191 Harvard Avenue, Winnipeg. The typescript is housed in the Carol Shields Fonds, Accession 1994-15, box 51, file 9, fifteen pages.

8   "The Golden Boy, or Some Things Only Happen Once" is an unpublished story found in the Carol Shields Fonds, Accession 1994-13, box 51, file 4, fifteen pages. This might be one of her earlier short stories.

9   The Hardy Boys books, written by Franklin W. Dixon and David L. Robbins, were mystery novels featuring brothers Frank and Joe Hardy as amateur detectives, similar to the Nancy Drew mysteries, published from 1927 to 2005. Shields recalls reading the books for young readers, such as *Anne of Green Gables*, on her parents' bookshelves. Since several of her own books can be described as mystery novels, as Wendy Roy demonstrates in "Misreading the Literary Evidence in Carol Shields's Mystery Plots," it is possible that these books influenced the nascent writer.

10   The Shields family moved with their two youngest children to Winnipeg in 1980, where Don was a professor of engineering and later dean of engineering at the University of Manitoba, and Carol was a professor of English at the University of Manitoba and later the chancellor of the University of Winnipeg.

11   Shields recalls in *The Staircase Letters: An Extraordinary Friendship at the End of Life* how she would put herself to sleep by descending a staircase in her imagination (Motyer et al. 38).

12   "Gifts"is a typescript in the Carol Shields Fonds, Accession LMS-0212, volume 62, file 25, with "24 Feb 92" handwritten in pencil at the top of the first of two pages. The several brief handwritten insertions in the typescript are included here.

13 "Christmas Interruptus" is a typescript in the Carol Shields Fonds, Accession LMS-0212, 1997-04, volume 40, file 30, with the note "DRAFT—11/7/1998" handwritten on the first of seven pages that display only a few minor corrections, all included here.

14 "Coming to Canada" is a three-page typescript in the Carol Shields Fonds, Accession LMS-0212, 1994-13, volume 62, file 53, dated 13 May 1994, with no annotations. "Coming to Canada" is also the title of a poem by Shields that provides the title of her third collection of poems, *Coming to Canada* (1992). The poem can also be found in *The Collected Poetry of Carol Shields* (178).

15 "Did Anything Much Happen to You in the Fifties?" is a four-page typescript in the Carol Shields Fonds, Accession LMS-0212, 1994-13, volume 63, file 23, with the note "draft 1" handwritten at the top of the second page.

16 Shields frequently mentions Margaret Laurence in her essays and reminiscences, and one of her few critical essays focuses on Laurence's Canadian short-story collection, *A Bird in the House*: "Leaving the Brick House Behind: Margaret Laurence and the Loop of Memory." Shields emailed Blanche Howard on 8 January 1997, claiming that "Margaret Laurence led the way for us to a large extent" (Howard and Howard 349). After reading Laurence's *The Stone Angel*, Shields entered the doctoral program at the University of Ottawa in 1975.

17 In 2013, Alice Munro was the first Canadian author to be awarded the Nobel Prize for Literature.

18 Shields submitted early writings under the pen name Ian McAllister (with the initials I M), just as Laurence submitted poems to the University of Manitoba literary magazine under the pen name Steve Lancaster, and Atwood submitted poems using her initials, M.E., for Margaret Eleanor, leading Louis Dudek, editor of *Delta* poetry magazine, to send her a letter of rejection addressed to "Dear Mr. Atwood."

19 Shields originally wrote "with scarcely a single woman's voice" and replaced it with the phrase "with ten poets in its pages, only three of them women," inserted by hand.

20 Adele Wiseman (1928–62), a Winnipeg-born Canadian author and close friend of Margaret Laurence, is best known for her Governor General's Literary Award–winning novel *The Sacrifice* (1956).

21 In Shields's novel *Unless* (2002), Reta Winters, the protagonist, writes, but does not send, angry letters to male authors of lists of the world's greatest thinkers and writers that do not include women.

22 "Writers Are Readers First" is an untitled, undated, three-page typescript in the Carol Shields Fonds, Accession LMS-0212, 1994-13, volume 6, file 6, that corresponds to the essay of that title in *Startle and Illuminate*. The first paragraph is crossed out but included here, and there are several excisions and handwritten insertions. The legible insertions are quoted in the text.

23 *Small Ceremonies*, Shields's first published novel, although not her first written novel, was first published by McGraw-Hill Ryerson in 1977 and won the Canadian Authors Association Award for the best novel of 1977. The speaker quoted is the protagonist/narrator Judith Gill, a biographer occupied in writing a biography of Susanna Moodie, about whose novels Shields composed a master's thesis at the University of Ottawa in 1975. Revised and published in 1977 as *Susanna Moodie: Voice and Vision*.

24 Shields has pencilled in "Name them." She has also pencilled in the statement "The fact that I was never given a book for Christmas or for my birthday did not seem at all odd."

25 Fraternal twins Nan and Bert were the principal characters of the Bobbsey Twins books, the Stratemeyer Syndicate's longest-running series of American children's novels, written under the pseudonym Laura Lee Hope, from 1904 to the 1980s (*Encyclopaedia Britannica*). These books, found on Shields's parents' bookshelves, might also have influenced the budding novelist.

26 Dick and Jane are the two main characters created by Zerna Sharp for a series of basal readers written by William S. Gray to teach children to read. The characters first appeared in the Elson-Gray Readers in 1930 and continued in a subsequent series of books through the final version in 1965 (*Encyclopaedia Britannica*). Shields's poem "Learning to Read" begins thus: "Grass grows on the graves of Dick Jane Sally and Spot / They were boring and middleclass and, worse, / they were stereotypes—there's nothing worse than that" (*CP* 162).

27 "Books that Meant" is a four-page typescript in the Carol Shields Fonds, Accession LMS-0212, 1997-04, volume 45, file 40, dated "09/15/06" with the date "17/11/97" handwritten at the top of the first page. It partly parallels Shields's essay "Writers Are Readers First" (*SI* 1–13).

28 Horatio Alger Jr. (1832–99) was an American author who wrote young adult novels about impoverished boys who rise from humble backgrounds to middle-class security through good works. He published almost one hundred books between 1864 and 1896 (*Encyclopaedia Britannica*). These books, also found on Shields's parents' bookshelves, might have influenced the young writer.

29 To the typescript of this essay is appended the following note: "Carol Shields is a reader, novelist and playwright living in Winnipeg, Canada. Her novel *The Stone Diaries* won the Pulitzer Prize for fiction in 1995. Her most recent novel is *Larry's Party*."

30 "The Reader-Writer Arc" is an untitled, undated, six-page typescript in the Carol Shields Fonds, Accession LMS-0212, 1997-04, volume 45, file 45, with the word *DRAFT* handwritten across the first page.

31 Poetry was the first form in which Shields published. She published over 160 poems in three collections—*Others* (1972), *Intersect* (1974), and *Coming to Canada* (1992). *The Collected Poetry of Carol Shields* (2021) includes 240 poems. Poetry contributed to making her a successful writer, as I argue in my introduction to that edition of her collected poems.

32 Shields was deeply involved in theatre during her two decades in Winnipeg in the 1980s and 1990s, both as a spectator and as a playwright. She published four plays in the latter decade: *Departures and Arrivals* (1990), *Thirteen Hands* (1993), *Fashion Power Guilt and the Charity of Families* (1999) with Catherine Shields, and *Anniversary* (1998) with David Williamson—all republished in the collection *Thirteen Hands and Other Plays* in 2002.

33 Alan Bennett (1934–2022) was an English actor, author, playwright, and screenwriter.

34 *A Doll's House*, written by Norwegian playwright Henrik Ibsen (1828–1906) in 1879, is often viewed as the first feminist drama since the heroine, Nora Helmer, leaves her husband's home at the conclusion of the drama in order to educate herself and become a true adult.

35   *Death of a Salesman*, written by American playwright Arthur Miller (1915–2005) in 1949, is an early and influential example of a play that focuses on an ordinary person. Critics often observe that Shields's own writing focuses on ordinary people.

36   Samuel Richardson's *Pamela, or Virtue Rewarded*, published in 1740, is regarded as the first novel in English. The epistolary form of his novels is reflected in *A Celibate Season*, the novel published in 1991 that Shields co-authored with Blanche Howard.

37   "The Reader-Writer Arc" reads like a talk or live presentation. The phrase "narrative hunger" suggests Shields's talk "Narrative Hunger and the Overflowing Cupboard."

38   "The Writer's Second Self" is an untitled, undated, three-page typescript in the Carol Shields Fonds, Accession LMS-0212, 1994-13, volume 60, file 7.

39   Ernest Hemingway (1899–1961), born in Oak Park, Illinois, the birthplace of Shields, was a famous and influential American novelist, short-story writer, and journalist. *A Moveable Feast* (1964) is a memoir recalling his life as a struggling writer and journalist in Paris in the 1920s. Shields refers to Hemingway in "Making Words/Finding Stories," included in this collection.

40   Shields's mention of a "second self" recalls Sarah Maloney's assertion in *Swann*— "Pick up a pen and a second self squirms out" (22)—and reflects Shields's addiction to dualities. Shields is often indignant with critics who wish to read an author's fiction as autobiography. In *Small Ceremonies*, heroine Judith Gill, a biographer who has a fling with fiction, discusses the similarities and differences between (auto)biography and fiction. Shields is also impatient with academics who wish to categorize works of literature into arbitrary genres.

41   Shields told me in 2003 that her favourite Laurence text was *A Bird in the House*.

42   Atwood's *The Journals of Susanna Moodie* (1970) might have helped to persuade Shields to compose her master's thesis at the University of Ottawa on Moodie (1975).

43   "The Writing Life" is an undated, two-page typescript in the Carol Shields Fonds, Accession LMS-0212, 1994-13, volume 110, file 9, titled "Bio and the Writing Life." The typescript has no annotations, but has the name Carol Shields at the end, plus the note "A longer version of this essay has been previously published in the *Washington Post*." This essay was first published in that newspaper on 13 August 2000 and reprinted in *Carol Shields: Evocation and Echo*, edited by Aritha van Herk and Connie Steenman-Marcusse (2009), on pages 139–43.

44   "Making Words/Finding Stories" is a seven-page typescript in the Carol Shields Fonds, in the file "Speeches, Essays and Articles," with the number R-11805, volume 112, file 1. The following information is appended to the title: "Shields C. Making Words/Finding Stories. *Journal of Business Administration & Policy Analysis* [serial on the internet]. 1996, Jan, [cited 15 May 2011]; 24-2636."

45   The name of Nathaniel Hawthorne Public School has been changed to Percy Julian Middle School, after the African American chemist.

46   The name of Ralph Waldo Emerson Public School has been changed to Gwendolyn Brooks Middle School, after the African American poet.

47   In her final novel, *Unless* (2002), Shields introduces a pet, a dog named simply Pet.

48   Susanna Moodie (1803–85) was a British-born writer who immigrated to Ontario in the nineteenth century and wrote about her experience as a settler in *Roughing It in the Bush* (1852) and its sequel, *Life in the Clearings* (1853).

49   *The Republic of Love*, Shields's novel about Tom Avery, a disc jockey, and Faye McLeod, a folklorist, who live in Winnipeg and fall in love, was published by Viking in 1992.

50 *Swann*, Shields's novel published by Viking in 1989, is her most postmodernist novel to date, structured in five sections, featuring four main characters, and concluding with a screenplay.

51 "Chemistry" is included in the 1989 collection *The Orange Fish* (11–33).

52 "Hinterland" is also included in *The Orange Fish* (68–89); it portrays a couple, Meg and Roy Sloan of Milwaukee, visiting the Cluny Museum in Paris in 1986, where they discover a *vierge ouvrante*, an image of the Virgin Mary that opens to reveal images of the life of Christ.

53 "Fuel for the Fire" is also included in *The Orange Fish* (170–85); it portrays a family burning bowling pins during their New Year's Day (not Christmas Eve) celebration.

54 "Hazel," also included in *The Orange Fish* (34–60), portrays a woman finding her niche in society following the death of her husband.

55 *The Stone Diaries*, first published by Random House Canada in 1993 and by Viking in 1994, won the Governor General's Literary Award for Fiction in Canada in 1993 and the Pulitzer Prize in America in 1995, catapulting Shields to instant fame. *Larry's Party*, published in 1997, was very successful, especially among male readers, and explores the male persona in the person of protagonist Larry Weller.

56 The typescript of "My Back Pages" is headed by the statement "Carol Shields has written a number of novels about novelists, poets and biographers." The typescript is addressed "To: David Meghan, Assistant book Editor, the Boston Globe, Boston USA. From: Carol Shields, U. of Manitoba." It concludes with a note: "Dear David, I hope this is okay. Let me know if I'm on the wrong track. I'm going to be in Boston on the 12th—to do a reading with Elinor Lipman—and I'll give you a call." It concludes with "Good wishes from Winnipeg, where it's snowing snow at the moment, not cherry blossoms." The essay is in the Carol Shields Fonds, Accession 1997-04, box 45, file 47.

57 Shields published several novels featuring writers, from her first published novel, *Small Ceremonies*, to her last, *Unless*, including *The Box Garden* and, most famously, *Swann*.

58 V.S. Naipaul (1932–2018), a Trinidadian-born British writer of works of fiction and non-fiction in English, was awarded the Booker Prize and the Nobel Prize for his publications.

59 John Updike (1932–2009), an American novelist, poet, short-story writer, art critic, and literary critic, is best known for his Rabbit novels. Shields often mentions him with admiration and cites his visit to Gloverville to research the glove industry.

60 Michael Frayne (1933–), an English playwright and novelist, is known for his 1982 play *Noises Off*. Carol and Don Shields were frequent theatregoers.

61 A.S. Byatt (1936–2023), the sister of English writer Margaret Drabble, was an English novelist, critic, and academic. Her 1990 novel *Possession* won the Booker Prize. Shields told me in May 2003 that she admired Drabble's fiction, and doubtless she was familiar with Byatt's novels.

62 "Women's Voices in Literature" is an undated, eight-page typescript in the Carol Shields Fonds, Accession LMS-0212, 1994-13, volume 112, file 1, titled "Drafts of Speeches." The typescript partially parallels the essay "The Short Story (and Women Writers)" in *Startle and Illuminate* (97–108). References to awards in the essay date it as composed in 1996 or 1997.

63 *Loitering with Intent* was published in 1981.

64 Shields was an admirer of Munro's fiction.

65 Mavis Gallant was born in Montreal in 1922 and died in Paris, where she lived for much of her adult life, in 2014. Best known for her short stories, many of them published in *The New Yorker*, she also published novels, plays, and essays.

66 Robertson Davies (1919–95), a novelist and playwright, focused on Canadian attitudes.

67 Timothy Findley (1930–2002) wrote short stories, novels, and plays from the 1950s to the 1990s and twice won the Governor General's Literary Award. He was best known for his 1977 novel *The Wars*.

68 Guy Vanderhaeghe (1951–), a writer and playwright, is best known for his 1982 short-story collection *Man Descending* and his western novel trilogy, *The Englishman's Boy*, *The Last Crossing*, and *A Good Man*, set in the nineteenth-century American and Canadian west.

69 Michael Ondaatje, a poet, novelist, and filmmaker, born in Sri Lanka in 1943, is best known for his 1992 novel *The English Patient*, adapted as a film in 1996.

70 Simone de Beauvoir (1908–86), a French feminist existentialist writer, was best known for her work *The Second Sex* (1949) and her relationship with French existentialist philosopher Jean-Paul Sartre (1905–80), who was best known for his 1944 wartime drama *No Exit*.

71 Betty Friedan (1921–2006), an American feminist writer, was best known for her 1963 book *The Feminine Mystique*, which influenced Shields profoundly.

72 Kate Millet (1934–2017), an American feminist writer, was best known for her first book, *Sexual Politics*, published in 1970, which views English novelist D.H. Lawrence (1885–1930) as a male chauvinist.

73 Virginia Woolf (1882–1941) was a British writer and essayist whose non-linear approach to narrative and stream-of-consciousness technique were major influences on modernist fiction. Most famous as the author of novels, such as *Mrs. Dalloway* (1925) and *To the Lighthouse* (1927), she was also the author of influential feminist essays, such as *A Room of One's Own* (1929).

74 Margaret Atwood (1939–) is a celebrated Canadian poet, novelist, short-story writer, playwright, and essayist known for her feminist writings. Her books, especially her 1985 dystopia *The Handmaid's Tale*, have been adapted as plays, movies, operas, ballets, and television series. Shields writes of Atwood's work with great admiration. Atwood visited Shields in May 2003, shortly before Shields's death in July.

75 Kennedy Fraser (1948–), an English essayist and fashion writer, wrote for *Vogue* and the *New Yorker*.

76 Bonnie Burnard (1945–2017) was the author of the short-story collection *Women of Influence* (1988), which focuses on the lives of women and their ordinary challenges.

77 William French (1926–2012), as literary editor of the *Globe and Mail* for over forty years, influenced Canadian literature through his book reviews.

78 Judith Gill is the heroine and narrator of *Small Ceremonies* (1976); Charlene Forrest is the protagonist and narrator of *The Box Garden* (1977); Brenda Bowman is the protagonist and narrator of *A Fairly Conventional Woman* (1982); Sarah Maloney and Rose Hindmarch are characters in *Swann* (1987); Maloney is the first-person narrator of the first section of the novel.

79 "Women and the Short Story," the typescript of an untitled panel discussion that took place in Ottawa in 1986, with "Panel Discussion" typed at the top of the typescript, is in the Carol Shields Fonds, 2000-04, volume 94, file 7. "The Short

Story (and Women Writers)" is a related essay in *Startle and Illuminate* (97–108).

80 J.M. Ludlow (1821–1911) was the founder and editor of *The Christian Socialist* newspaper.

81 The *Norton Anthology of Short Fiction*, edited by R.V. Cassill, likely refers to the third edition, published in 1986 (the same year as the panel discussion).

82 The *Reader's Guide to the Canadian Novel* likely refers to the first edition, published in 1982; the second edition was published in 1987.

83 The *World Classic Edition of Australian Short Stories* likely refers to the edition published in 1951.

84 *TLS* is the *Times Literary Supplement*, a weekly literary journal established in 1902, originally published as a supplement to *The Sunday Times*, in London.

85 *The New Press Anthology #2: Best Stories* was published in 1985.

86 This anthology likely refers to *Canadian Short Stories, Fourth Series*, published in 1985.

87 Edgar Allan Poe (1809–49), a notable American poet and short-story writer, was known for his poem "The Raven" (1845), among others.

88 Nathaniel Hawthorne (1804–64), a notable American fiction writer, was known for his novel *The Scarlet Letter* (1850), among others.

89 Isak Dinesen is the pseudonym of Karen Blixen (1885–1962), a Danish writer known for her use of supernaturalism and her memoir *Out of Africa* (1937).

90 Katherine Mansfield is the pseudonym of Kathleen Mansfield Beauchamp (1888–1923), an English writer whose work, notably *The Garden Party* (1922), influenced the short-story form.

91 John Middleton Murry (1889–1957) was an English writer and critic who wrote prolifically as a journalist. Murry was the husband of Kathleen Mansfield.

92 "The Feminine Line" is an undated, eleven-page typescript in the Carol Shields Fonds, Accession LMS-0212, 1994-13, volume 63, file 8. The typescript of this speech includes some handwritten insertions that are included in this text.

93 Smaro Kamboureli is the Avie Bennett Chair in Canadian Literature at the University of Toronto. She has published extensively on Canadian literature.

94 Samuel Johnson (1709–84) was a widely known eighteenth-century English writer, famous for composing the first great English dictionary (1755).

95 Daphne Marlatt (1942–) is known for her use of biography, environment, and feminism. Notable work includes *Vancouver Poems* (1972).

96 Betsy Warland (1946–), an author, poet, and activist, is known for her use of genre mixing and feminism, including *Two Women in a Birth* (1994), written with Daphne Marlatt.

97 Shields's reference to "that terrible tyrant *unity of sensibility*" recalls her railing against all the unities, especially "the unity of vision," in her essays.

98 The legends that Laurence uses to enrich *The Diviners* are detailed in https://www.thecanadianencyclopedia.ca/en/article/the-diviners.

99 *Dancing in the Dark* was published in 1982.

100 Pamela Banting, who now teaches at the University of Calgary, focuses on eco-criticism and environmental and Canadian literature.

101 Linda Hutcheon (1947–), a Canadian literary and art critic and professor, served as president of the Modern Language Association of America. Her work, notably *A Poetics of Postmodernism* (1988), focuses on contemporary and postmodern studies.

102 *Canadian Forum*, established in 1920, is the oldest continually published political periodical in Canada and publishes poetry, fiction, and art.

103 Audrey Thomas (1935–) focuses in *Intertidal Life* (1984) on themes of family and mother-daughter relationships.

104 Kristjana Gunnars (1948–) is an Iceland-born Canadian writer, poet, and professor, best known for *The Prowler* (1989).

105 Some of the poems in Shields's sequence of twenty-nine *Snow* poems (*CP* 201–31) could be considered "frost pieces."

106 Marilynne Robinson (1943–), an American novelist and essayist, is best known for her 2004 novel *Gilead*.

107 Merna Summers (1933–) is a journalist and fiction writer best known for *North of the Battle* (1988). Edna Alford (1947–) is a short-story author whose work features realism and mundane circumstances. Aritha van Herk (1954–) is a professor, novelist, and essayist known for her critique of gender roles through her protagonists, notably in *Judith* (1978), and for her studies of western Canada, notably her 2001 exhibition and book *Mavericks*. Joan Clark (1935–) is a novelist and short-story writer whose early work consisted largely of children's literature. Notable adult work includes *The Victory of Geraldine Gull* (1988). Margaret Clarke is the name under which Helen Buss (1941–2023), known for her engagement with women's issues, including *Healing Song* (1988) and *Mapping Our Selves* (1993), published popular novels, short stories, and poetry. Sandra Birdsell (1942–) is known for her portrayal of women in small towns, notably in her novel *The Chrome Suite* (1992). Joan Barfoot (1946–) focuses in her work, such as *Dancing in the Dark*, on the domestic lives of Canadian women. Joy Kogawa (1935–) is a Canadian of Japanese descent best known for her novel *Obasan* (1981). Susan Kerslake (1943–) is known for her first novel, *Middlewatch* (1976).

108 Jane Rule (1931–2007) was known for her writing about lesbians, including her novel *Desert of the Heart* (1964), prior to the decriminalization of homosexuality.

109 "The New Canadian Fiction" is an undated, eleven-page typescript in the Carol Shields Fonds, Accession LMS-0212, 1994-13, volume 112, file 1, titled "Speeches and Essays and Articles." The typescript includes a few brief handwritten insertions that are included in this text.

110 Donald Barthelme (1931–89) was an American short-story writer known for his modernist experimentation and his children's book *The Slightly Irregular Fire Engine or the Hithering Thithering Djinn* (1971).

111 William H. Gass (1924–2017) was an American author known for his experimentation with style and construction, notably in his critical work *Habitations of the Word* (1985).

112 Italo Calvino (1923–85) was an Italian author known for his fables and use of fantasy and whimsy, notably in his novel *The Baron in the Tress* (1957).

113 Don DeLillo (1936–) is an American novelist known for his work with postmodernism, as demonstrated in his novel *White Noise* (1985).

114 Ann Beattie (1947–) is an American author known for her unemotional style of writing, notably in her novel *Chilly Scenes of Winter* (1976).

115 *Lost in the Funhouse* (1968) is a short-story collection by American author John Barth (1930–) characterized by elements of biography, performance, and experimental style.

116 Don Coles (1927–2017) also wrote novels.

117 William Styron (1925–2006) was an American novelist known for his use of tragic themes, including *Sophie's Choice* (1979), adapted as a film.

118 The word *Holocaust* means "sacrifice," the title of Adele Wiseman's 1956 novel. Because the Holocaust did not constitute a willing sacrifice, however, some Jewish people prefer the Hebrew word *Shoah*, meaning "the horror."

119 American writer Annie Dillard, born in 1945, is known for her memoir *An American Childhood* (1987). She taught for twenty-one years in the Department of English at Wesleyan University in Connecticut.

120 The essay appeared in November 1989. Tom Wolfe (1930–2018) is best known for his 1987 novel *Bonfire of the Vanities*.

121 Gabriel García Márquez (1927–2014), a Colombian novelist who won the Nobel Prize for Literature in 1982, is best known for his 1967 novel *One Hundred Years of Solitude*. Robert Coover (1932–) is an American author known for surreal and experimental work, including his 1976 novel *The Public Burning*. John Hawkes (1925–98) was an American author whose novels used dreamlike intensity and suspense through their structure, notably in his 1961 novel *The Lime Twig*.

122 Samuel Richardson (1689–1761) was an English novelist credited as one of the founders of the English novel and the inventor of the epistolary novel, which uses letters as form, whose notable works include *Pamela* (1740) and *Clarissa* (1747); Henry Fielding (1707–54), an English author also credited as one of the founders of the English novel, composed *Joseph Andrews* (1742) and *Tom Jones*, published as *The History of Tom Jones, a Foundling* (1749); Tobias Smollett (1721–71) was a Scottish satirical novelist known for *The Adventures of Peregrine Pickle* (1751), among others.

123 Émile Zola (1840–1902) was a French author known for his naturalist approach and twenty-novel series *Les Rougon-Macquart* (1871–93), which includes his 1880 novel *Nana*.

124 Sinclair Lewis (1885–1951), an American author who won the Nobel Prize for Literature in 1930, is known for his satirical novels, including *Main Street* (1920).

125 Alison Lurie (1926–2020) was an American novelist and academic best known for her 1984 Pulitzer Prize–winning novel *Foreign Affairs*.

126 Mary Gordon (1949–), an American author from New York, a professor of English at Barnard College, and the author of novels and literary criticism, is best known for her first novel, *Final Payments* (1978), her novel *The Company of Women* (1981), and her latest novel, *Payback* (2020).

127 Scott Russell Sanders (1945–) is an American novelist and essayist awarded the Mark Twain Prize and a Guggenheim Fellowship.

128 Russell Banks (1940–2023) was an American novelist known for his portrayals of contrast between characters' interior and exterior lives, as demonstrated in his novel *Hamilton Stark* (1978). Nicholas Delbanco (1942–) is an American author of fiction and non-fiction, including *Why Writing Matters* (2020). Don DeLillo has already been noted. Louise Erdrich (1954–) is an American author known for her writing about Ojibwa people in the American Midwest, notably in *The Round House* (2012), which won the National Book Award, and *Love Medicine* (1984). Ursula K. Le Guin (1929–2018) was an American author known for her science fiction and fantasy works, including *The Left Hand of Darkness* (1969). Chloe Anthony Wofford Morrison (1931–2019), who published under the name Toni Morrison, was an American author awarded the Nobel Prize for Literature in 1993 and the Pulitzer Prize in 1987 for her novel *Beloved*. Morrison is best known for her examination of the black female experience in her work.

129 *The Mezzanine* is a stream-of-consciousness narrative conveyed principally through extensive footnotes which delve deeply into the fleeting thoughts of the protagonist.

130 Kazuo Ishiguro is a British Nobel Prize–winning author whose 1989 novel *The Remains of the Day*, focusing on Stevens, a butler at Darlington Hall in Oxford, England, won the Booker Prize and was adapted as a film with the same title in 1993.

131 Mary Grimm (1949–) is an American writer known for her fiction, including her 2001 novel *The Power of the Dog*, adapted as a film with the same title by Jane Campion in 2021.

132 Shirley Jackson (1930–65), an American novelist and short-story writer, was the author of the famous story "The Lottery," first published in *The New Yorker* in 1948.

133 Mona Simpson's first novel, *Anywhere but Here* (1987), portraying a mother's and daughter's conflicting ambitions, won the Whiting Prize and was adapted as a film in 1999.

134 Jane Smiley (1949–), an American novelist and winner of the Pulitzer Prize, published *The Greenlanders* (1988) in the epic tradition of the Old Norse sagas.

135 *The Trick of It* (1989) is an epistolary novel following a professor who marries the writer whom he has spent his career studying.

136 *Cat's Eye* (1988) features fictional painter Elaine Risley's recollection of her youth in Toronto in what might be a partially autobiographical memoir.

137 Cynthia Ozick (1928–) is an American writer whose novels, short stories, and essays focus on Jewish American life.

138 The short-story collection *A Friend of My Youth* was published in 1990 and won the Trillium Book Award for that year.

139 Bharati Mukherjee (1940–2017) was an Indian American author whose fiction, including her novels *The Tiger's Daughter* (1972) and *Wife* (1975), centres on the cultural alienation that immigrants experience.

140 "Crossing Over" is a seven-page typescript in the Carol Shields Fonds, Accession LMS-0212, 1994-13, volume 94, file 7, with the notes "(panel paper: Carol Shields)" and the date "September 1990" at the top of the first page. It parallels "To Write Is to Raid" in *Startle and Illuminate* (31–36).

141 Some of the stories in Shields's 2000 collection *Dressing Up for the Carnival* could be defined as "What if—" stories. See Stovel, "'Be a Little Crazy,'" for a discussion of these stories.

142 Russell Hoban (1925–2011) was an American author whose work focused on myth and identity, as demonstrated in *The Mouse and His Child* (1967).

143 Oonah McFee, née Brown (1916–2006), was a Canadian novelist and short-story writer who won the *Books in Canada* First Novel Award for her 1977 novel *Sandbars*.

144 Shields's phrase "To write is to raid" links this essay to her essay of that title in *Startle and Illuminate* (31–36).

145 Sandy Duncan (1942–), based in Vancouver, is the author of novels and stories.

146 Barbara Kingsolver (1955–), an American novelist, poet, and essayist, is best known for her 1998 novel *The Poisonwood Bible*.

147 Kennedy Fraser, an American essayist and journalist born in England in 1948, won the Whiting Award for Non-Fiction and a Guggenheim Fellowship. Fourteen of her essays, many of which were first published in *The New Yorker*, were collected in her book *Ornament and Silence: Essays on Women's Lives from Edith Wharton to Germaine Greer* in 1998.

148 Peter Ward, a professor emeritus of history at the University of British Columbia, argues in that book that people were constrained in nineteenth-century Canada with regard to love and marriage.

149 Theodore Zeldin (1933–) is a British scholar at Oxford University whose writing investigates practical issues of human life. His book *The French* (1973) might be the text to which Shields refers here.

150 English novelist Margaret Drabble (1939–) was referred to as "the chronicler of our times" after the publication of her novel *The Ice Age* in 1977. Recalling that quotation, Shields told me in May 2003 that she had thought, "I can do that." Drabble is best known for her 1987 novel *The Radiant Way*.

151 This untitled, undated, ten-page typescript from the Carol Shields Fonds, Accession LMS-0212, 1994-13, volume 62, file 5, has a few minor handwritten emendations that are included in this text.

152 Victor Sawdon Pritchett (1900–97), known as V.S. Pritchett, was a British author and literary critic best known for his short stories.

153 Oscar Wilde (1854–1900), an Irish poet and playwright, best known for his play *The Importance of Being Earnest*, which premiered in London on 14 February 1895, was arrested and sentenced to two years of hard labour for homosexuality. He died shortly after being released.

154 Anne Robinson Taylor's book was published in 1981.

155 Irish Canadian novelist Brian Moore (1921–99) is best known for his 1987 novel *The Lonely Passion of Miss Judith Hearne*, which portrays an alcoholic spinster's search for love in Belfast.

156 French author Gustave Flaubert (1821–80) was best known for his 1856 novel *Madame Bovary*, considered his masterpiece, in which he both sympathizes with and satirizes his female protagonist.

157 Barbara Pym (1930–80) was an English novelist best known for that 1961 novel.

158 "Writing the Male Character" was Atwood's Hagey lecture delivered at the University of Waterloo in 1982. A revised version is included in her 1983 collection *Second Words: Selected Critical Prose, 1960–1982*.

159 Daniel Defoe (d. 1713) was an English writer, journalist, pamphleteer, trader, and spy who was most famous for his 1719 novel *Robinson Crusoe*.

160 Moll Flanders is the eponymous heroine of Defoe's novel *Moll Flanders* (1722).

161 Clarissa is the eponymous heroine of the 1748 novel *Clarissa: Or, The History of a Young Lady*, by English author Samuel Richardson (1689–1761).

162 Esther Summerson is a central character in the 1853 novel *Bleak House*, by English author Charles Dickens (1812–70).

163 Fanny Burney (1752–1840) was an English novelist best known for her 1778 novel *Evelina: Or, The History of a Young Lady's Entrance into the World*.

164 English author Charlotte Brontë (1816–55) was most famous for her 1847 novel *Jane Eyre*, which portrays an orphaned girl's quest for independence, respect, and love; Brontë published her novel *The Professor* ten years later.

165 Joyce Carol Oates (1938–) is an American author of short stories, novels, plays, and essays.

166 English author Mary Shelley (1797–1851) is best known for her early science fiction novel *Frankenstein: Or, The Modern Prometheus* (1818), which depicts a young scientist, Victor Frankenstein, who creates a sapient monster.

167 French author Charles Baudelaire (1821–67) belonged to the "Decadent" or Symbolist or Modernist movement and was most famous for his 1857 poetry collection *Les fleurs du mal*.

168 Leon Rooke, who was born in North Carolina in 1934 and moved to Canada in 1969, is best known for his 1980 novel *The Fat Woman*, about an obese but charming wife and mother named Ella Mae Hopkins.

169 Hugh Garner (1913–79), a British-born Canadian novelist, was best known for his 1950 novel *Cabbagetown* and won the Governor General's Literary Award for *Hugh Garner's Best Stories* in 1963.

170 Elizabeth Hardwick (1916–2007), an American novelist, short-story writer, and literary critic, is best known for her 1979 novel *Sleepless Nights*.

171 Marie-Henri Beyl (1783–1842), known by the pen name Henri Stendhal, a French realist novelist, was best known for his 1830 novel *Le rouge et le noir* (*The Red and the Black*); Count Lev Nikolayevich Tolstoy (1828–1910), known as Leo Tolstoy, was a Russian writer best known for his novels *War and Peace* (1869) and *Anna Karenina* (1878); Fyodor Mikhailovich Dostoevsky (1821–81) was a Russian novelist, short-story writer, essayist, and journalist best known for his novels *Crime and Punishment*, *The Idiot*, *The Possessed*, and *The Brothers Karamazov*; Marcel Proust (1871–1922) was a French author best known for his novel *A la recherche du temps perdu* (*Remembrance of Times Past*), which, published in French in seven volumes between 1914 and 1927, influenced the development of the modernist novel; Joseph Conrad (1857–1924), born in Ukraine, a Polish British novelist and short-story writer for whom English was a third language, was best known for his 1899 novella *Heart of Darkness*; Ben Jonson (1572–1637), an English Jacobean poet and playwright based in London and a contemporary of William Shakespeare, was best known for his 1610 play *The Alchemist*.

172 Doris May Lessing (1919–2013) was best known for her 1962 feminist novel *The Golden Notebook* and her science fiction; she was awarded the Nobel Prize for Literature in 2007.

173 Anne Tyler (1941–) considers her ninth novel, *Dinner at the Homesick Restaurant* (1982), shortlisted for several awards, her best novel. Her eleventh novel, *Breathing Lessons*, was awarded the Pulitzer Prize for Fiction in 1988. Alice Malsenior Tallulah-Kate Walker (1944–) is an American novelist, poet, and social activist who became the first African American woman to win the Pulitzer Prize for Fiction for her 1982 novel *The Color Purple*, later adapted as a film and musical. Gail Godwin, born in 1937, is an American author of short stories and novels. *The Finishing School* (1985) might be the best known of her fourteen novels. Shields acknowledged being influenced by Drabble's fiction (see Stovel, "'Excursions'"). Muriel Spark (1918–2006) was a Scottish novelist best known for her 1961 novel *The Prime of Miss Jean Brodie*, depicting a teacher at a girls' school in 1930s Edinburgh and her influence on her students.

174 "The Angel in the House" is the title of an 1854 narrative poem by English author Coventry Patmore (1823–96) portraying the Victorian ideal of woman as wife.

175 Tillie Olsen (1912–2007) was a Jewish American author, professor, feminist, and political activist best known for her 1961 short-story collection *Tell Me a Riddle*, which includes the story "I Stand Here Ironing."

176 George Eliot (1819–80) was the pen name of author Mary Anne Evans, a notable Victorian poet, novelist, and journalist. *Middlemarch, a Study of Provincial Life* (1871–72), set in the Midlands, is the most famous of her seven novels.

177 Jane Austen (1775–1817), the author of six Regency novels, was one of Shields's favourite authors and exerted considerable influence on her writing (see Stovel, "'Moral Seriousness'"). Shields composed the biography *Jane Austen: A Life* (2001).

178 Marilyn French (1929–2009) was a radical American feminist author best known for her 1977 novel *The Woman's Room*, which portrays a group of female friends in 1950s and 1960s America.

179 This essay is located in Accession 2000-04, volume 94, file 7. Shields pencilled in the sentence "Rotary, its structure and rituals, is, of course, part of the fabric that holds the country together," suggesting that the speech was given to a Rotary Club.

180 *The Stone Angel*, published in 1964, is the first of Laurence's Manawaka cycle of novels. It won the Governor General's Award for Fiction in 1964 and presents the retrospective narration of an octogenarian matriarch, Hagar Currie Shipley.

181 Juliette Augustina Cavazzi, née Sysak (1926–2017), known simply as Juliet, or Your Pet, Juliet, was a Canadian singer and television host featured on CBC Television on Saturday nights from the 1950s through the 1970s (*Canadian Encyclopedia*).

182 The Happy Gang was a CBC Radio lunchtime variety show hosted by Bert Pearl that ran from 1937 to 1959 during the Golden Age of Radio. Shields, who immigrated to Canada in 1957, would have heard their show (*Canadian Encyclopedia*).

183 Author, journalist, and broadcaster Pierre Berton (1920–2004) published fifty best-selling books, primarily about Canadian history and popular culture.

184 Morley Callaghan (1903–90) was a Canadian author of short stories and novels, best known for his 1934 novel *Such Is My Beloved*. Shields was interested in the fact that Callaghan's novels were published in both Canadian and American versions. She refused a publisher's suggestion that she revise a novel to portray an American setting.

185 Donna Scott (1928–2020) was a Canadian businesswoman who founded the fashion magazine *Flare*, chaired the Canada Council for the Arts from 1994 to 1998, and worked as the executive director of the Ontario Arts Council (*Canadian Encyclopedia*).

186 Shields's "Address to Graduands" includes the name "Carol Shields" and the date "Spring Convocation June 2, 1996," handwritten at the top of the first page, with the subtitle "University of Winnipeg Remarks." This six-page typescript, in the Carol Shields Fonds, Accession LMS-0212, 1994-13, [volume and file unavailable], has no emendations, but it has the name "Carol Shields" typed at the end.

187 Shields was the chancellor of the University of Winnipeg from 1996 to 2000.

188 Sven Birkerts, born in 1951, is an American essayist and literary critic best known for his 1994 book *The Gutenberg Elegies*, in which he suggests that the current decline in reading has resulted from the advance of electronic technologies (*Encyclopaedia Britannica*).

189 Laurence graduated from the University of Winnipeg, then United College, with an honours degree in English.

190 Martha Nussbaum (1947–), an American philosopher and professor of law and ethics at the University of Chicago, has published numerous books on ethics, animal rights, and feminism, including *Women and Human Development* (1999) (*Encyclopaedia Britannica*). Her 1988 book *The Fragility of Goodness* might have influenced Shields's 2002 novel *Unless*, which addresses goodness.

191 Carol Shields presented this talk to the administrators of the University of Winnipeg on her investiture as chancellor on 20 October 1996. The manuscript comes from Ottawa Archives.

192 "University Leadership and Social Change" has the subtitle "Change and Preservation—Culture, Values, and Society" typed at the top of the first page and the date "16 July 1998," written by hand, although the date included at the end of the speech is 17 August 1998. This six-page typescript of a convocation address delivered at the University of Ottawa, from the Carol Shields Fonds, Accession LMS-0212, 1997-04, volume 40, file 25, has no emendations but has the term "DRAFT" written across the first page. The University of Ottawa, as Shields mentions, was her alma mater, where she completed her master's degree in English in 1975.

193 Shields graduated from Hanover College in Indiana in 1957.

194 Adam Smith (d. 1790) was a Scottish economist and philosopher of importance during the Scottish Enlightenment.

195 In mentioning "the recent slaughter in Bosnia," Shields is referring to the Srebrenica massacre when units of the Bosnian Serb Army murdered over seven thousand Bosnian Muslim men and boys in July 1995.

196 Hutterites, also called the Hutterian Brethren, founded by Jacob Hutter in Germany in 1528, are an Anabaptist Christian sect who, like the Amish and Mennonites, live communally, reject personal ownership, refuse to hold public office, and are strict pacifists. This type of bookkeeping is attributed to the Amish on page 234.

197 Canadian author Sara Jeannette Duncan (1861–1922) was best known for her 1904 novel *The Imperialist* and her 1908 novel *Cousin Cinderella*. The typescript is located in the Carol Shields Fonds, Accession LMS-0212, 1994-13, volume 60, file 5.

198 In her citations, Shields is referring to these editions of Duncan's books: *Cousin Cinderella* (Macmillan, 1908), and *The Imperialist*, edited by Claude Bissell (McClelland and Stewart, 1971).

199 Canadian academic and literary critic Clara Thomas (1919–2013) was a long-time professor of English at York University and one of the first academics to focus on Canadian literature, especially the writing of Margaret Laurence.

200 In this essay, in addition to Clara Thomas's "*Cousin Cinderella* and the Empire Game," *Studies in Canadian Literature* 1, no. 2 (1976): 183–93, Shields uses two other notes to refer to Claude Bissell's "Introduction" in the 1971 McClelland and Stewart edition of *The Imperialist* and Thomas Tausky's article "The American Girls of William Dean Howells and Sara Jeannette Duncan," *Journal of Canadian Fiction* 4, no. 1 (1975): 146–58. Other sources listed in Shields's references, along with those mentioned above, are Alfred B. Bailey, "The Historical Setting of Sara Duncan's *The Imperialist*," *Journal of Canadian Fiction* 2, no. 3, 205–10; Pierre Cloutier, "The First Exile," *Canadian Literature* 59 (1974): 30–37; Daniel Francis, "Focus," *Chatelaine*, May 1976, p. 30; Carole Gerson, "Duncan's Web," *Canadian Literature* 63 (1975): 73–80; and Leon Slonim, "Character, Action, and Theme in *The Imperialist*," *Essays on Canadian Writing* 3 (1975): 15–20.

201 Claude Bissell (1916–2000) was a Canadian educator who served as the eighth president of the University of Toronto, 1958–71; the president of the Canada Council, 1960–62; and the first Mackenzie King Professor of Canadian Studies at Harvard University, 1967–68.

202 *Ébéniste* is the French word for a cabinet maker, especially one who works in ebony.

203 By "the First Empire," Duncan might be referring to the first empire of Japan.

204 Charles the First, or King Charles I, son of James I, acceded to the throne of England as its second Stuart monarch in 1625 and was executed on 30 January 1649 (*Encyclopaedia Britannica*).

205 "Knight Hospitaller" refers to the Order of Knights of the Hospital of Saint John of Jerusalem, a medieval and early modern Catholic military organization based in Malta, founded in 1099 by Blessed Gerard to offer hospitality to Crusaders (*Encyclopaedia Britannica*).

206 A brougham was an early form of electric car, designed like a horse-drawn carriage, in which the driver, often a chauffeur, sat outside and the passengers inside (*Encyclopaedia Britannica*).

207 Thomas Tausky, born in 1942, is a Canadian academic and literary critic who taught at the University of Western Ontario and edited works by Sara Jeannette Duncan.

208 The typescript is located in the Carol Shields Fonds, Accession LMS-0212, 1994-13, volume 60, file 3. "The Two Susanna Moodies" refers to the actual Susanna Moodie and the fictional character portrayed in Margaret Atwood's *The Journals of Susanna Moodie*, which, Shields claims, "bears little resemblance to Atwood's dour, introspective Susanna." *The Journals of Susanna Moodie*, a three-part text in poetic form, in which Atwood adopts Moodie's voice, was first published in 1970 and republished in 1997.

209 Shields documents Moodie and Atwood sometimes but not consistently. In her discussion of Margaret Atwood's work, Shields is referring to these editions: *The Journals of Susanna Moodie* (Oxford UP, 1970) and *Survival: A Thematic Guide to Canadian Literature* (Anansi Press, 1972). In this essay, she is also referencing Susanna Moodie's *Life in the Clearings* (Richard Bentley, 1853) and *Roughing It in the Bush* (Putnam, 1852).

210 William Carlos Williams (1883–1963) published *Paterson*, considered his epic masterpiece, set in Paterson, New Jersey, in five books from 1946 to 1968.

211 John Berryman (1914–72) was an American poet and scholar best known for *The Dream Songs* (1969); he published his *Homage to Mistress Bradstreet*, a tribute to the colonial poet Anne Bradstreet, in 1956.

212 The Plymouth Colony was settled by passengers from the *Mayflower*, all English Puritans, or Pilgrims, in Plymouth, Massachusetts, in 1620.

213 Don Gutteridge (1937–) is a Canadian author and professor emeritus of the University of Western Ontario who published widely in poetry, fiction, and non-fiction, including *Riel: A Poem for Voices* in 1972.

214 Louis Riel (1844–85) was a Canadian politician, founder of the province of Manitoba, and leader of the Métis people who led an Indigenous resistance against the government of Canada and Prime Minister John A. Macdonald in 1885 that was overcome in the Battle of Batoche by General Middleton. Riel was punished by execution.

215 *Billy the Kid* is Ondaatje's 1970 poem sequence.

216 Peter Stevens (1927–) is a Canadian author and professor emeritus of the University of Windsor.

217 Dr. Norman Bethune (1890–1939) was a Canadian thoracic surgeon, an advocate of socialized medicine, and a member of the Communist Party.

218 Belleville, Ontario, situated on the northeast shore of Lake Ontario between Toronto and Ottawa, figures significantly in Moodie's non-fiction texts.

219 Al Purdy (1918–2000) was a Canadian free-verse poet who composed thirty-nine works of poetry over a fifty-six-year career and won the Governor General's Literary Award for English-language poetry.

220 In addition to the Atwood and Moodie sources, Shields's short list of references for this essay includes Al Purdy, "Review," *Canadian Literature* 47 (1971): 80–84; and Douglas Barbour, "Reviews," *Canadian Forum* 50 (1970): 225.

221 "The Healing Journey" is an undated, thirteen-page typescript in the Carol Shields Fonds, Accession LMS-0212, 1994-13, volume 95, file 21. The first paragraph is crossed out, and there are several excisions and handwritten insertions. Her phrase "we are gathered today" indicates that this essay was delivered as a talk, the phrase recalling a minister addressing a congregation. Shields pencilled in the following statement before the opening paragraph: "I read so I know how people think." She inserted by hand the first four sentences at the beginning of the second paragraph, all included in this text. The reference to her thirty-fifth high school class reunion dates the talk to around 1998. She expresses her belief "that our most private thoughts and needs are, in fact, universally shared" as the aim of her writing.

222 In Genesis, Adam is given the privilege of naming the animals. Shields's statement suggests that novelists have the power of Adam and that their novels are like their children.

223 In *The Republic of Love* (1992), Shields renames certain streets in Winnipeg, where the novel is set, disturbing some residents of the city.

224 In her essay "Boxcars, Coat Hangers and Other Devices" (*SI* 23–30), Shields explains how she conjured up a visual image or metaphor to provide the structure for her early novels. Brenda Bowman, the heroine of Shields's novel *A Fairly Conventional Woman* (1982), sometimes awakens with the pattern for her new quilt embedded in her retinas.

225 Shields frequently viewed her life as falling into chapters, like a novel—her cancer, diagnosed in December 1998, being the last.

226 In *Jane Austen: A Life* (2001), Shields claims that "A home of one's own" is the aim of all Austen's heroines. She argues that Austen's "novels are about the search of an individual for his or her real home" (85).

227 Stephen Dedalus is the semi-autobiographical protagonist of James Joyce's 1916 novel.

228 Emma Woodhouse is the eponymous heroine of Jane Austen's novel *Emma* (1815).

229 Fanny Price is the heroine of Jane Austen's novel *Mansfield Park* (1814), to which Shields wrote the introduction for the Modern Library edition (2001).

230 "Times of Sickness and Health" is a short story from Shields's collection *The Orange Fish* (1989), reprinted in *The Collected Stories* in 2004 (340–54).

231 "They also serve who only stand and wait" is the final line of John Milton's sonnet "On His Blindness." Brenda Bowman in *A Fairly Conventional Woman* thinks of other women demonstrating for change while she sews quilts in her upstairs studio.

232 The labyrinth is the main symbol and structural device of Shields's 1997 novel, *Larry's Party*.

233 Mention of this reunion probably dates this talk to 1998, shortly after Shields published *Larry's Party*.

Notes to Part 2: Carol Shields's Previously Published but Uncollected Essays

1   Several awards were established in her name, including the Carol Shields student award at Red River Community College by the Manitoba Writers' Guild, the Carol Shields Writer-in-Residence award at the University of Winnipeg, and the Carol Shields Winnipeg Book Award.

2   Shields comments parenthetically, "(Lord, I hate that title!)" ("A Little Like Flying" 45).

3   "I've Always Meant to Tell You: A Letter to My Mother" is a nine-page typescript in the Carol Shields Fonds, Accession LMS-0212, 1997-04, volume 40, with a post-it fax note addressed to "C. Wardloe" from "Shields" on "6/9/96," with the signature "Carol Shields" and the note "(editing suggestions welcome)" handwritten at the end. It was published in *I've Always Meant to Tell You: Letters to Our Mothers* (1997), edited by Constance Warlow.

4   In "Getting Born," the opening poem in her third collection of poetry, *Coming to Canada*, Shields quotes her mother as saying, "You slipped out like a lump of butter" (*CP* 149).

5   Franklin Delano Roosevelt (1882–1945), known as "FDR," was the thirty-second president of the United States, serving from 1933 to his death in 1945.

6   The Warner family lived on Kenilworth Avenue in Oak Park, a suburb of Chicago.

7   *The Waltons* refers to a popular television series that ran for nine seasons, beginning in 1972, featuring a Depression-era family in Virginia's Blue Ridge Mountains, as seen from the point of view of the eldest son, John Boy, who goes on to college, serves in the Second World War, and becomes a novelist (*Wikipedia*).

8   Shields's poem "Our Mother's Friends" in *Intersect* (1974), ends with these words: Lovingly L – i – ly. (*CP* 119)

9   Mary Organ and Grace are also named in "Our Mother's Friends."

10   Ernest Hemingway published *The Sun Also Rises*, which is set in Paris and Spain and focuses on bullfighting, in 1926.

11   Mrs. McNinn, mother of the sister heroines of Shields's first two novels, *Small Ceremonies* and *The Box Garden*, expresses her innate artistic temperament by obsessively redecorating her house. Atwood explains in her foreword the comic and tragic aspects of this obsession.

12   International Women's Day was inaugurated in Austria, Germany, Switzerland, and Denmark on 19 March 1911, when over a million women and men celebrated. The movement spread to other countries, and it is now a global event celebrated annually on 8 March.

13   In *The Box Garden*, the protagonist-narrator, Charleen Forrest, presents her mother, Mrs. McNinn, who is remarrying in her seventies, with her first four books of poetry as a wedding gift because her mother has never read any of her daughter's poetry.

14   "At Home in Winnipeg" was first published in *Canadian Living*, Aug. 1992, p. 62, with photographs of Shields and the deli at De Luca's, where she shopped. A photocopy of the clipping is in the Carol Shields Fonds, Accession 1994-13, box 62, file 33.

15   This paragraph, which opens Shields's typescript and was sent by fax to Kathleen Harkins at *Canadian Living*, plus the next sentence, were not included in the published version. The typescript is in the Carol Shields Fonds, Accession 1994-13, box 62, file 33.

16   *Rien d'autre* means "nothing else" in French. Shields, who owned a house in France, often employed French terms, especially in her final novel, *Unless* (see, in this regard, Stovel, "Women's Ink").

17   The Red River Settlement, founded by the Earl of Selkirk at the confluence of the Red and Assiniboine Rivers in Manitoba, began in 1812 with Scottish and Irish settlers.

18   During the Winnipeg Strike, from 15 May to 26 June 1919, over thirty thousand strikers brought economic activity to a standstill in Winnipeg, then Canada's third largest city.

19   During the Winnipeg Flood of 1950, the Red River flooded the Dakotas and Manitoba from 15 April to 12 June 1950, inundating Winnipeg and its environs on 5 May, known as "Black Friday" to residents, in the worst flooding since 1861.

20   The typescript has her name and the date "11/4/92" at the bottom.

21   "Living at Home" was first published in *enRoute* magazine, Air Canada's magazine for passengers, in English and French, Dec. 1997, pp. 19–21. The clipping is in the Carol Shields Fonds, Accession 2-1997-04, box 45, file 35. It contains the following note: "Kathleen—I'm not at all sure this is what you want. (Also, it is a little over your specified 800 words—what to do? Also, I don't know your policy on italics, quotation marks, etc.) You can fax me today at the arts faculty or phone me at my office. Tomorrow I'll be running around doing errands, but you can leave a message at my home number, and I'll call you back. There may be elements here that won't work with your readership—please let me know." Shields added by hand, "I'll be out of Canada April 21–May 11."

22   In *The Stone Diaries*, Daisy's granddaughter Joan patches the crack in her bedroom ceiling.

23   Shields's poem "The Radio—1940" portrays her early fascination with the radio (*CP* 153).

24   W.H. Auden (1907–73), a controversial and influential British-born poet, playwright, essayist, and reviewer, was a member of the Communist Party who emigrated to the United States at the outset of the Second World War and taught in American universities.

25   *Various Miracles*, published in 1985, was Shields's first of three collections of short stories.

26   Jane Zednick (1953–) is a Canadian artist and independent bookseller in Ontario.

27   Shields frequently recalls observing strangers at home and conveys her curiosity about them or envy of them. This epiphanic vision reflects her belief in the magical experience of reading.

28   Shields is referring here to Winnipeg. The last sentence of this essay echoes Shields's poem "Coming to Canada—Age Twenty-Two" (*CP* 150).

29   "Sunday Dinner, Sunday Supper" was first published in *Ladies' Home Journal*, Sept. 1996, p.198, with a drawing of a family dinner and the caption "One enchanted me, the other bored me to tears. Both left their mark—on my memory and in me." The clipping is in the Carol Shields Fonds, Accession 2-1997-04, box 46, file 1.

30   "My Favourite Place: At Home in Deepest France" was first published in *Travel and Leisure*, Nov. 1994, pp. 87–88, with drawings of vacationers in France and the caption *"After years of rentals, we needed a place of our own."* Several of Shields's stories build to an epiphanic realization, often catalyzed by travel, frequently to France, including "Hinterland" in *The Orange Fish* collection (68–89). The

typescript is located in the Carol Shields Fonds, Accession LMS-0212, 1994-13, volume 62, file 46.

31   The "Marseillaise," the national anthem of France, also known as "Chant de guerre pour l'armée," was composed by Claude Joseph Rouget de Lisle in 1792 and adopted on 14 July 1795.

32   Shields captures the haunting sense of a deserted church in Brittany in her short story "Sailors Lost at Sea" in *Various Miracles* (28–42).

33   They communicate the suggestion that "The sun is shining. It's not so bad."

34   "Travelwarp" was first published in *Writing Away: The PEN Travel Anthology*, edited by Constance Rooke, McClelland and Stewart, 1994, pp. 276–80. A photocopy of the clipping is in the Carol Shields Fonds, Accession 2-1997-04, box 45, file 29.

35   Bonnie Prince Charlie (1720–88), the nickname of Charles Edward Stuart, was the Stuart claimant to the throne of England, Scotland, and Ireland from 1776 as King Charles III. Also known as "The Young Pretender" and "The Young Chevalier," he inspired the Jacobite Rebellion of 1745 (*Encyclopaedia Britannica*).

36   *The Spectator*, a prestigious weekly British magazine focusing on politics, culture, and current affairs, was founded in 1828, making it the oldest surviving weekly magazine in the world (*Encyclopaedia Britannica*).

37   American novelist and short-story writer John Steinbeck (1902–68) was awarded the Nobel Prize for Literature in 1962. His 1939 novel *The Grapes of Wrath* was awarded the Pulitzer Prize in 1940.

38   English novelist Paul Scott (1920–78) was best known for his tetralogy *The Raj Quartet*, written from 1965 to 1975, about the final years of British rule in India.

39   Trinidadian British author of fiction and non-fiction V.S. Naipaul (1932–2018) was best known for his 1979 novel *A Bend in the River*.

40   "A Legacy of Stone" was first published in *Islands* magazine, Sept. 1997, pp. 2–3. The clipping is in the Carol Shields Fonds, Accession 2-1997-04, box 45, file 49. It records Shields's visit to the Orkney Islands to research *The Stone Diaries*.

41   The Orkney Islands are located about thirty kilometres north of the Scottish mainland. Kirkwall Hoy is the second largest of the islands and is characterized by its red sandstone cliffs. Thurso, Scotland, is the most northerly town of mainland Great Britain.

42   The ellipses here and below represent lines at the top of the column cut off by photocopying at Library and Archives Canada.

43   The Iron Age occurred in Europe circa 1200 BCE and concluded circa 550 BCE. The Norse were Scandinavian, often called Vikings, who colonized wide areas of Europe, including Britain, throughout the ninth to eleventh centuries.

44   Several words have been omitted at this point in the essay because the photocopied text was illegible.

45   The Hudson's Bay Company, established in 1670, is a commercial enterprise originating from the Canadian fur trade that was integrally involved with the colonization of Canada.

46   The Ring of Brodgar, a Neolithic henge and stone circle six miles from Stromness on Mainland, the ironic name of the largest island in Orkney, is part of the UNESCO World Heritage Site known as the Heart of Neolithic Orkney (*World History Encyclopedia*).

47   "Others" was first published in *The Guardian*, 25 Aug. 1997, with drawings of women and the caption "In the third of our Guardian Woman summer series, Carol

Shields explains her obsession with other people's lives." The clipping is in the Carol Shields Fonds, Accession 2-1997-04, box 45, file 37. *Others* is the title of Shields's first collection of poetry, published in 1972.

48   In her husband-and-wife novels, *Happenstance* and *A Fairly Conventional Woman*, republished as *Happenstance: The Husband's Story and The Wife's Story*, Shields portrays Jack and Brenda Bowman as a relatively happily married couple who, nevertheless, "remained, ultimately, strangers, one to the other."

49   This attitude might underlie Shields's desire never to be the subject of a biography, even though Shields composed a biography of Jane Austen and portrays her first heroine, Judith Gill of *Small Ceremonies*, as composing a biography of Susanna Moodie.

50   Here Shields conveys the attitude that underlies her well-known essay "Narrative Hunger and the Overflowing Cupboard," a curiosity about other people shared by Judith Gill.

51   "What's in a Picture" was first published in *Civilization* magazine, Oct.–Nov. 1996, p. 112, with a photograph of an elderly woman, who appears just as Shields describes her in the piece. The clipping is in the Carol Shields Fonds, Accession 2-1997-04, box 45, file 54. Although Shields cannot identify the woman, her interpretation of her appearance reveals the perceptive reader and critic.

52   Shields includes photographs of her own children (with their permission), as well as "photos of unknown women," in *The Stone Diaries*.

53   Shields often expresses the "desire to redeem these forgotten women" through her work.

54   "Rare Petals" was first published in *Gardens Illustrated*, May 1998, p. 130. The clipping is in the Carol Shields Fonds, Accession 1997-04, box 45, file 130.

55   The joke here is based on the historical fact that fashionable women's skirts in the court of Versailles were so voluminous that ladies had to turn sideways to pass through doorways.

56   "A Purse of One's Own" was first published in *Allure*, Nov. 1995, p. 152, with a photograph of Shields captioned "The author at home in Canada with her handbag." The clipping is in the Carol Shields Fonds, Accession 2-1997-04, box 45, file 53.

57   The Wisconsin Dells are a scenic resort area located along the Wisconsin River in south-central Wisconsin characterized by unique rock formations.

58   Montparnasse is a popular area of Paris known for its bistros and cemetery and as the home to twentieth-century artists, such as Pablo Picasso.

59   Viewing pencil cases as "handbags in their embryonic form: training purses" suggests that girls of Shields's era were allowed an academic version of the purse in their youth.

60   "Heidi's Conundrum" was first published in *Sightlines*, 1990, pp. 4–5, with a photograph of Shields and the caption "*Author Carol Shields is a Governor General award winner, and her first play,* Arrivals and Departures [*sic*], *was recently published by Blizzard Publishing of Winnipeg.*" A book titled *Heidi's Conundrum* was published by Kevin Read in 2022.

61   American feminist playwright Wendy Wasserstein (1950–2006) was best known for her play *The Heidi Chronicles* (1988), which was awarded the Pulitzer Prize for Drama and portrays Heidi's experience with the women's liberation movement in the 1970s and 1980s. This might have been one of the plays that Carol and Don Shields viewed in Winnipeg.

62 Sofonisba Anguisciola was an Italian Renaissance painter born in Cremona who achieved international fame before she died in Palermo in 1625; Clara Peeters, born in Antwerp in 1594, was a Renaissance Dutch still-life painter; and Lily Martin Spencer, born in Exeter in 1852, became a popular American genre painter before her death in New York City in 1902 (*Encyclopaedia Britannica*).

63 Susan Frances Harrison, née Riley (1859–1935), was a Canadian poet and novelist, as well as a music composer and critic, who lived and worked in Ottawa and Toronto; Ethelwyn Wetherald (1857–1940) was a Canadian poet and journalist; and May Agnes Fleming (1840–80) was a successful Canadian popular novelist (*Canadian Encyclopedia*).

64 Carol and Don Shields subscribed to Winnipeg's Prairie Theatre Exchange and the University of Manitoba's Black Hole Theatre Company. Carol Shields had plays produced in Winnipeg.

65 The *Dinner Party* (created 1974–79) by American artist Judy Chicago (1939–) was first installed in the Brooklyn Museum and then toured broadly. Featuring thirty-nine place settings on a triangular table, representing thirty-nine mythical and historically famous women, it is considered the first significant feminist artwork. Like Betty Friedan's *The Feminine Mystique* (1963), it influenced Shields's burgeoning feminism.

66 "Parties Real and Otherwise" was first published in *Victoria*, pp. 44–46, with illustrations by Aude Kamlet and the caption "*One of the unlooked-for pleasures of writing fiction, muses this prize-winning novelist, is throwing all kinds of parties without ever leaving home. There are no last-minute jitters, no worry that the celebration won't go exactly as planned. After all, you get to make up everything, including the faux pas.*" A photocopy of the clipping is in the Carol Shields Fonds, Accession 2-1997-04, box 45, file 33.

67 In *Small Ceremonies* (158), Judith Gill's friend Nancy Kranz makes an observation to Judith about parties that Shields echoes here in one of many connections between her essays and novels.

68 "The Best Teacher I Ever Had ..." is addressed to "Alex C. Michalos" with his fax number at the top and Shields's signature at the end. The photocopy is housed in the Carol Shields Fonds, Accession 2-1997-04, box 45, file 46, with a note saying that the file was sent to Michalos at the University of Northern British Columbia.

69 *Mary Poppins*, a 1934 novel by P.L. Travers, was adapted as a musical film produced by Disney in 1964. *Alice's Adventures in Wonderland*, an 1865 novel by English writer Charles Lutwidge Dodgson (1832–98), a professor of mathematics at Oxford University, who published under the pseudonym Lewis Carroll, is a fantastical narrative intended for children that also intrigues adults. *Winnie-the-Pooh* is a 1926 children's book by English author A.A. Milne and English illustrator E.H. Shepard.

70 The Chicago El is the elevated train track. The Chicago Loop is a central area of the city.

71 "The Visual Arts" was first published in *The Royal Academy of the Arts* bulletin, fall 1997, with a photograph of Shields and the caption "Carol Shields on the Visual Arts" and the note "*Carol Shields is Chancellor of and English Professor at the University of Winnipeg. Among other honours, she has received the Governor General's Award and the Pulitzer Prize for Literature for her novel* The Stone Diaries. *Her keynote address at the Academy's Annual Dinner in Winnipeg was so inspiring that we thought we would include it here.*" The following note concludes the article: "*A*

translation of this article will appear in an upcoming issue of the Journal." A photocopy of the clipping is in the Carol Shields Fonds, Accession 2-1997-04, box 46, file 3.

72 The Royal Canadian Academy of Arts, founded in 1880, is the oldest national organization of professional Canadian artists.

73 Morley Blankstein (1924–2015) was a notable Canadian architect in Winnipeg.

74 The Winnipeg Art Gallery was established in Manitoba in 1912.

75 St-Germain-en-Laye is a town in north-central France now considered to be a suburb of Paris.

76 French painter Édouard Manet (1832–83) was known for his traditional style, impressionism, and realism.

77 *Tromp d'oeil* (commonly written as *tromp l'oeil*) translates to "optical illusion," and in painting it refers to works whose objects appear to be real.

78 Whereas Shields previously employed the universal "he," now she employs the more inclusive "he/she" formulation, her implicit feminism becoming more explicit.

79 Shields discusses the practice of painting windows in her introduction to *Mansfield Park* for the 2001 Modern Library edition and recreates it in her short story "Windows" in *Dressing Up for the Carnival* (109–20). She repeats her description in this essay—"Not a real light, of course, but the idea of light, which is infinitely more powerful than light itself"—in the clause "infinitely more alluring than light itself" in her story (120).

80 "A Delicate Balancing Act" focuses on the tension Shields experiences between honesty and courtesy in reviewing novels. Sensitive to disparaging reviews of her own work that she calls "cruelies," she hesitates to reveal "a glint of the fang," in her words (Howard and Howard 4), in her reviews of other writers' books (see Ramon).

81 Anatole Broyard (1920–90) was a writer, essayist, and literary critic who wrote for the *New York Times*.

82 Shields's terms "delight and instruction" might allude to Sir Philip Sidney's well-known dictum in his *Defense of Poesy*, published in 1595, that the aim of literature is to "teach and delight."

83 French existentialist philosopher Jean-Paul Sartre (1905–80) was best known for his 1944 wartime drama *No Exit*.

84 Noel Perrin (1927–2004) was a writer and professor known for his non-fiction essays on rural life.

85 English philosopher Thomas Hobbes (1588–1679) defined life without government as "nasty, brutish, and short" in his 1651 book *Leviathan*.

86 Shields often rails against the enforcement of the unities, especially the critical term "unity of vision." In her essay "Myths that Keep You from Writing," she objects that literary critics prescribe "something called unity of vision, as though anyone has ever possessed unity of vision or even wanted to" (*SI* 20).

87 Shields sometimes employs the term "miniature," perhaps ironically, about her own poetry, as in her phrase "my miniature art" in her short story "Segue." See Stovel, "Fragments." Shields's draft novel, titled "Moment's Moment," was revised posthumously by her daughter Sara Cassidy as the short story "Segue," which opens her *Collected Stories* (1–20).

88 The term "Austenesque" has been applied to Shields. Although she admired Austen greatly, as her biography of Austen demonstrates, she might have resented having that term applied to her own writing.

89 American author Grace Metalious (1924–64) was best known for her 1956 novel *Peyton Place*, adapted for the screen.

90 American writer Hortense Calisher (1911–2009) was known for her semi-autobiographical style and often published in *The New Yorker*.

91 Cynthia Ozick (1928–) is an American writer and essayist whose work, engaged with contemporary Jewish life, includes *The Din in the Head* (2006).

92 Shields assured me in 2003 that "My story 'Dolls, Dolls, Dolls' was the only autobiographical writing I've ever done" (*CS* 148–64).

93 How gender affects writers' fiction, especially women writers' fiction, is also a topic that Shields addressed in numerous essays, especially "The Short Story (and Women Writers)."

94 English poet John Milton (1608–74) composed *Paradise Lost*, published in 1667, which purports to "justify God's ways to Man" (Book 1, ll. 25–26).

95 "Divorce" is addressed to "Peggy Kaganoff of Harcourt Brace Trade Division." A photocopy, headed "DRAFT," is in the Carol Shields Fonds, Accession 2-1997-04, box 45, file 43.

96 Magnavox was an American electronics company that originated in 1917.

97 *Happenstance*, published in 1980, was followed by *A Fairly Conventional Woman*, written from the point of view of Brenda Bowman, published two years later. The pair of novels was republished as *Happenstance: The Husband's Story and The Wife's Story* in 1991.

98 *Small Ceremonies* and *The Box Garden* were reissued in England in 2003 as *Duet* by Fourth Estate, with "Judith" followed by "Charleen" on pages 201 to 406 and with the dedication "For Inez 1902–1971," Shields's mother.

99 "Carol Shields's Booker Prize Report" is extracted from a 2 December 1993 letter from Shields to Wachtel included in the chapter titled "Letters, 1990–1994" (*RI* 61–63). I would like to thank Eleanor Wachtel for giving me permission to reprint excerpts from her edition of conversations with Shields.

100 Victoria Barnsley (1954–) is an English entrepreneur who founded the Fourth Estate publishing company, which first published Shields's novels in Britain, in 1984.

101 Irish novelist Roddy Doyle, born in 1958, and best known for his 1987 novel *The Commitments*, adapted as a film with that title in 1991, won the Booker Prize in 1993 for his novel *Paddy Clarke Ha Ha Ha*.

102 Salman Rushdie (1947–) is a British author known for his controversial novel *The Satanic Verses*, for which he received significant backlash. "On 12 August 2022, while about to start a lecture at the Chautauqua Institution in Chautauqua, New York, Rushdie was attacked by Hadi Matar, a 24-year-old Lebanese American who rushed onto the stage and stabbed him repeatedly, including in the neck and abdomen" (Wikipedia). Rushdie lost one eye as a result of this attack and is hesitant about public speaking as a result.

103 Stephen Spender (1909–95) was an English poet best known for his literary criticism and reviews.

104 Renaissance painter Doménikos Theotokópoulos (1541–1614), known as El Greco, was a Greek-Spanish painter, sculptor, and architect known for his mannerist style, as in his painting *The Burial of the Count de Orgaz* (c.1587).

105 Caryl Phillips (1958–) is an English writer and Yale University professor known for his work *Crossing the River* (1993), among others.

106 Shields's December 2001 foreword to *The Stone Diaries* clarifies her aims and methods in this important text.

107 Shields was always interested in biography, beginning with her first novel, *Small Ceremonies*, in which her protagonist-narrator, Judith Gill, is composing a biography of Susanna Moodie, and finishing with her study *Jane Austen: A Life* in 2001.

108 Shields explains in her essay "Boxcars, Coat Hangers and Other Devices" (*SI* 23–30) how she conjured up a visual image or metaphor to provide the structure for each of her early novels, the "series of nesting boxes" for *The Stone Diaries* being her most elaborate structure at the time.

109 Christopher Potter was Shields's Fourth Estate editor in London. Shields remarked to me in May 2003 that she and Potter, who had established a firm friendship, had said goodbye to each other so many times that it had become, in her words, "a running gag."

110 Shields's afterword to Moodie's book *Life in the Clearings* was first published in McClelland and Stewart's 1989 edition (335–40).

111 Bentley invited Moodie to compose a second book, since *Roughing It in the Bush* had been very successful.

112 The [*sic*] in this quotation appears in the original.

113 Shields is referring here to the title character of the 1719 novel *Robinson Crusoe* by English writer Daniel Defoe, who died in 1731.

114 Shields's introduction is to the Modern Library edition (2001) of *Mansfield Park* by Jane Austen (ix–xii). Shields wrote to Howard on 5 November 1997, "I reread *Mansfield Park* this summer to see if I could figure out why Jane loved Fanny when no one else could. I found a few clues, not many, and have done a short essay for the salon.com on it" (Howard and Howard 375). Shields published *Jane Austen: A Life* in 2001. Her short story "Windows" in *Dressing Up for the Carnival* (109–20) echoes the practice of painting windows that she discusses in this introduction.

115 Shields refers to Austen's admission that "The work is rather too light & bright & sparkling;—it wants shade;—it wants to be stretched out here and there with a long Chapter . . . about something unconnected with the story . . . —or anything that would form a contrast & bring the reader with increased delight to the playfulness & Epigrammatism of the general stile [sic]" (quoted in *JA* 149).

116 Austen's "mockery of clergymen" is most apparent in the character of the Reverend William Collins in *Pride and Prejudice*.

117 "Goodness" is the topic of Shields's last novel, *Unless* (2002).

118 Shields's afterword is on pages 343–47.

119 The novel referred to here is her 1987 novel *Swann*, which marked a startling change in her fiction in the direction of innovative, experimental postmodernism.

120 This afterword to *Dropped Threads 2* (365–67) was published posthumously in 2003.

Notes to Conclusion

1   In "Benign Neglect," in *Maclean's Magazine*'s special issue on "The Vanishing Border" of 20 December 1999, 25, Andrew Philips recalled Margaret Atwood's definition of the 49th parallel.

2   Giardini remarks in "Reading My Mother," "my mother takes one foot off the ground, rarely both" (11).

3   While Jane Austen won three of the top ten spots, including the first spot for *Pride and Prejudice*, Shields's last novel *Unless* edged out Atwood's *Handmaid's Tale* for the tenth spot, while Atwood's *Blind Assassin*, winner of the Booker Prize in 2000, was ranked number twenty-five.

4   Please see my interview with Shields, "'Excursions into the Sublime': A Personal Reminiscence of Carol Shields."

5   Please see my "'Fragments on My Apple': Carol Shields's Unfinished Novel."

Notes to Afterword

1   Lorna Crozier, born in Swift Current in 1948, a Professor Emerita at the University of Victoria and Officer of the Order of Canada, is a Canadian poet, author of twenty-five books, including eighteen books of poetry. She is a recipient of the Governor-General's Award for Poetry and three lifetime achievement awards.

2   Patrick Lane (1939–2019), was a Canadian poet who also published essays, short stories, novels, and memoirs. An Officer of the Order of Canada, he received three lifetime achievement awards and the Governor General's Award for poetry.

WORKS CITED

Amiel, Barbara. "Look Back in Stupor." Review of *The Box Garden*, by Carol Shields, *Maclean's*, 5 September 1977, 54–56.

Anderson, Marjorie May. "Foreword." *Dropped Threads 2: More of What We Aren't Told*, edited by Marjorie May Anderson and Catherine Shields, 1–4. Toronto: Vintage Canada, 2003.

Atwood, Margaret. "'A Soap Bubble Hovering over the Void': A Tribute to Carol Shields." *Virginia Quarterly Review* 81, no. 1 (2005): 139–42, www.jstor.org/stable/26441736.

Colville, Georgiana M.M. "Carol's Party and Larry's Shields: On Carol Shields' Novel *Larry's Party* (1997)." *Études Canadiennes /Canadian Studies* 49 (2000): 85–96.

Crozier, Lorna. *Through the Garden: A Love Story (with Cats)*. Toronto: Random House Canada, 2020.

Dvořák, Marta. "'Controlled Chaos' and Carol Shields's 'A View from the Edge of the Edge.'" In *Relating Carol Shields's Essays and Fiction: Crossing Borders*, edited by Nora Foster Stovel, 95–111. Cham, Switzerland: Palgrave Macmillan, 2023.

Giardini, Anne. "Foreword." In *Relating Carol Shields's Essays and Fiction: Crossing Borders*, edited by Nora Foster Stovel, xix–xxiv. Cham, Switzerland: Palgrave Macmillan, 2023.

———. "Reading My Mother." *Carol Shields*, edited by Neil Besner and G.N.L. Jonasson, special issue of *Prairie Fire* 16, no. 1 (1995): 6–11.

Hay, Elizabeth. "Readers are an Unruly Lot." In *Carol Shields: Evocation and Echo*, edited by Aritha van Hark and Conny Steenman-Marcusse, 51–52. Groningen, Netherlands: Barkhuis, 2009.

Howard, Blanche. "Collaborating with Carol." In *The Arts of a Writing Life*, edited by Neil K. Besner, 47–56. Winnipeg: Prairie Fire Press, 2003.

———. "Foreword." In *A Celibate Season*, by Carol Shields and Blanche Howard, 1–9. Regina: Coteau Books, 1991.

Howard, Blanche, and Allison Howard, editors. *A Memoir of Friendship: The Letters between Carol Shields and Blanche Howard*. Toronto: Viking Canada, 2007.

Huggan, Isabel. "Remembering Carol." In *Carol Shields: Evocation and Echo*, edited by Aritha van Herk and Conny Steenman-Marcusse, 53–58. Groningen, Netherlands: Barkhuis, 2009.

Lecker, Robert. "All Plot, Little Thought: Review of *Small Ceremonies*." *Essays on Canadian Writing* 5 (1976): 80–82.

Levin, Martin. "Carol's Kindness." *Carol Shields: Evocation and Echo*, edited by Aritha van Herk and Conny Steenman-Marcusse, 131–34. Eelde, Drenthe, Netherlands: Barkhuis, 2009.

McMullen, Lorraine. "Carol Shields and the University of Ottawa: Some Reminiscences." *Carol Shields: The Arts of a Writing Life*, edited by Neil K. Besner, 39–46. Winnipeg: Prairie Fire Press, 2003.

Motyer, Arthur, with Elma Gerwin, and Carol Shields. *The Staircase Letters: An Extraordinary Friendship at the End of Life*. Toronto: Vintage Canada, 2007.

Neville, William. "Carol Shields and Winnipeg: Finding Home." *Carol Shields: The Arts of a Writing Life*, edited by Neil K. Besner, 27–37. Winnipeg: Prairie Fire Press, 2003.

Philips, Andrew. "Benign Neglect." *The Vanishing Border*, special issue of *Maclean's*, 20 December 1999, 24–25.

Ramon, Alex. "'Little Shocks of Recognition': Carol Shields's Book Reviews." In *Relating Carol Shields's Essays and Fiction: Crossing Borders*, edited by Nora Foster Stovel, 219–35. Cham, Switzerland: Palgrave Macmillan, 2023.

Roy, Wendy. "Misreading the Literary Evidence in Carol Shields's Mystery Plots." *English Studies in Canada* 34, nos. 2–3 (2008): 113–29.

Shields, Carol. "Afterword." *Dropped Threads: What We Aren't Told*, edited by Carol Shields and Marjorie May Anderson, vii–x. Toronto: Vintage Canada, 2001.

———. "Afterword." *Dropped Threads 2: More of What We Aren't Told*, edited by Carol Shields and Marjorie May Anderson, 365–67. Toronto: Vintage Canada, 2003.

———. "Afterword." *Life in the Clearings versus the Bush*, by Susanna Moodie, 335–40. Toronto: McClelland and Stewart, 1989.

———. "Booker [Prize] Report" in "Letters, 1990–1994." *Random Illuminations: Conversations with Carol Shields*, edited by Eleanor Wachtel, 62–63. Fredericton: Goose Lane Editions, 2007.

———. *The Collected Poetry of Carol Shields*. Edited by Nora Foster Stovel. Montreal: McGill-Queen's University Press, 2021.

———. *The Collected Stories of Carol Shields*. Toronto: Random House Canada, 2004.

———. "Coming to Canada—Age Twenty-Two." In *Coming to Canada: Poems*, by Carol Shields, 27. Ottawa: Carleton University Press, 1992.

———. *Dressing Up for the Carnival*. Toronto: Vintage Canada, 2001.

———. "Foreword." In *The Stone Diaries*, by Carol Shields, xvii–xix. New York: Viking, 1994.

———. "Interview with Carol Shields." With Eleanor Wachtel, *Room of One's Own: A Feminist Journal of Literature and Criticism* 13, nos. 1–2 (1989): 5–45.

———. "Introduction." In *Mansfield Park*, by Jane Austen, ix–xii. New York: Modern Library, 2001.

———. *Jane Austen: A Life*. New York: Viking, 2001.

———. *Larry's Party*. New York: Viking, 1997.

———. "Leaving the Brick House Behind: Margaret Laurence and the Loop of Memory." *RANAM: Recherches anglaises et nord americaines* 34 (1991): 75–77.

———. "A Little Like Flying: An Interview with Carol Shields." With Harvey De Roo, *West Coast Review* 23, no. 3 (1988): 21–56.

———. *The Orange Fish*. 1989. New York: Viking, 1990.

————. *Small Ceremonies: A Novel.* Toronto: McGraw-Hill Ryerson, 1976.

————. *Startle and Illuminate: Carol Shields on Writing*, edited by Anne Giardini and Nicholas Giardini. Toronto: Random House Canada, 2016.

————. *Susanna Moodie: Voice and Vision.* Ottawa: Borealis Press, 1977.

————. *Swann.* 1989. Toronto: Penguin Books, 1990.

————. "'Thinking Back through Our Mothers': Tradition in Canadian Women's Writing." In *Re(dis)covering Our Foremothers: Nineteenth-century Canadian Women Writers*, edited by Lorraine McMullen, 9–13. Ottawa: University of Ottawa Press, 1990.

————. "Three Canadian Women: Fiction or Autobiography." *Atlantis: A Women's Studies Journal* 4, no.1 (1978): 49–54.

————. *Unless.* Notting Hill, UK: Fourth Estate, 2002.

————. *Various Miracles.* 1985. New York: Penguin Books, 1989.

————. "A View from the Edge of the Edge." *Carol Shields and the Extra-Ordinary*, edited by Marta Dvořák and Manina Jones, 17–29. Montreal: McGill-Queen's University Press, 2007.

————. "The Writing Life." In *Carol Shields: Evocation and Echo*, edited by Aritha van Herk and Conny Marcusse, 139–144. Groningen, Netherlands: Barkhuis, 2009.

Staines, David, ed. "Introduction." In *The Worlds of Carol Shields*, edited by David Staines, 1–4. Ottawa: University of Ottawa Press, 2014.

Stovel, Nora Foster. "'American or Canadian': Carol Shields's Border Crossings." *A Review of Canadian Studies in the United States* 40, no. 4 (2010): 517–29.

————. "'Be a Little Crazy; Astonish Me': Carol Shields's Improvisational Flair in *Dressing Up for the Carnival*." In *Relating Carol Shields's Essays and Fiction: Crossing Borders*, 73–93. Cham, Switzerland: Palgrave Macmillan, 2023.

————. "'Excursions into the Sublime': A Personal Reminiscence of Carol Shields." *Studies in Canadian Literature* 38, no. 1 (2013): 267–80.

————. "'Fragments on My Apple': Carol Shields's Unfinished Novel." *Canadian Literature* 217 (Summer 2013): 186–96.

————. "Moral Seriousness with Comic Drama: Austen's Legacy of Life, Love, and Laughter to Carol Shields." *Persuasions* [The Jane Austen Society of North America Journal] 30, (2009): 88–100.

————, ed. *Relating Carol Shields's Essays and Fiction: Crossing Borders.* Cham, Switzerland: Palgrave Macmillan, 2023.

————. "'Women's Ink': French Translation and Female Power in Carol Shields's *Unless.*" *Canada and Beyond*, edited by Marie Carrière and Libe García Zarranz, special issue of *A Journal of Canadian Literary and Cultural Studies* 3, nos. 1–2 (2013).

Thomas, Joan. "An Epistolary Interview with Carol Shields." In *The Arts of a Writing Life*, edited by Neil K. Besner, 73–85. Winnipeg: Prairie Fire Press, 2003.

Turbide, Diane. "The Masculine Maze." *Maclean's*, 29 September 1997, 82.

Urquhart, Jane. "A Generous Spirit." In *Carol Shields: Evocation and Echo*, edited by Aritha van Herk and Conny Steenman-Marcusse, 135–38. Groningen, Netherlands: Barkhuis, 2009.

Van Herk, Aritha. "Debris." In *Carol Shields: Evocation and Echo*, edited by Aritha van Herk and Conny Steenman-Marcusse, 113–29. Groningen, Netherlands: Barkhuis, 2009.

Verduyn, Christl. *Her Own Thinker: Canadian Women Writers as Essayists*. Toronto: Guernica Editions, 2023.

Wachtel, Eleanor. *Random Illuminations: Conversations with Carol Shields*. Fredericton: Goose Lane Editions, 2007.

Waterston, Elizabeth. "Guilt, Guile, and Ginger in *Small Ceremonies*." In *The Worlds of Carol Shields*, edited by David Staines, 53–61. Ottawa: University of Ottawa Press, 2014.

York, Lorraine. "Large Ceremonies: The Literary Celebrity of Carol Shields." In *Carol Shields and the Extra-Ordinary*, edited by Marta Dvořák and Manina Jones, 238–55. Montreal: McGill-Queen's University Press, 2007.